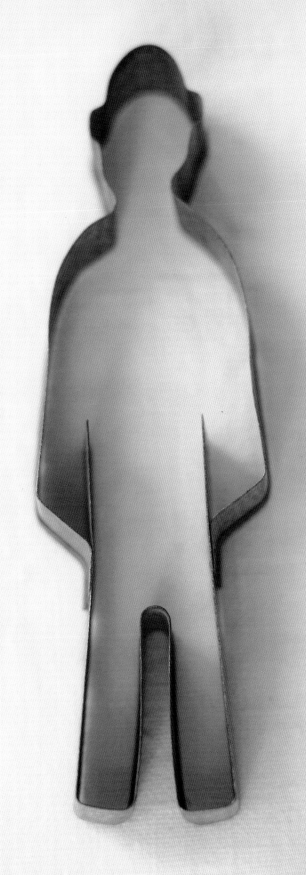

The
Really
Useful
Cookbook

The Really Useful Cookbook

David Herbert

MICHAEL JOSEPH
an imprint of
PENGUIN BOOKS

This book is dedicated to my parents,
who always support my crazy schemes.

Contents

1 Introduction

2 Biscuits

6 Breads

12 Breads – quick

16 Cakes

22 Casseroles & braises

28 Chocolate

34 Crumbles

40 Curries

46 Custards & creams

58 Deep-frying

64 Dips & dippers

70 Fish & fish cakes

80 Gratins

86 Ice-cream

94 Jams & preserves

98 Meatballs

104 Meringues

110 Muffins & small cakes

116 Omelettes & frittatas

120 Pancakes

126 Pasta

136 Pastry

142 Pies

154 Pizza

162 Pot-roasts

166 Puddings

170 Rice & risotto

178 Roast dinners

188 Roast vegetables

194 Salads & dressings

202 Sauces & gravy

208 Skewers

214 Soufflés

218 Soups

228 Stocks

232 Stuffed vegetables

238 Index

247 Conversions

247 Acknowledgements

247 Bibliography

Introduction

Some cooks have a fear of making pastry; others say they can't bake a cake. When I was learning to cook, my secret food fear was cooking rice. Not your fancy risotto or paella (they always made sense to me) – no, it was basic steamed rice that I went out of my way to avoid. Such a simple thing, but to me, the potential for error was huge. Eventually, I overcame the fear and taught myself to cook fluffy, ungluggy rice. It was so incredibly rewarding to master a new technique that I looked back and wondered what all the fuss had been about. The point is, sometimes it is great to be taken out of your comfort zone.

I have always had an avid interest in food, and because of this passion I taught myself to cook from books and magazines. I started by finding a good, simple recipe by a trusted writer (Anna del Conte for risotto or Margaret Fulton for baking) and followed their instructions to the letter. After practising it a few times and trying it out on friends (always good for the confidence), I began to vary the recipe and play with the flavours. Essentially, I started to cook more instinctively, often to the point of not following a recipe at all.

With *The Really Useful Cookbook*, I have attempted to write a cookbook that follows my own experience. It is full of great basic recipes that work every time (I have tested them all at least twice), with lots of really useful tips and tricks that I have learned along the way. My aim is to hold your hand and help take the guesswork out of cooking, giving you a new confidence in the kitchen. But this is more than a book for beginners; this is a book for anyone interested in cooking delicious food. The basic recipes are followed by lots of variations and new ideas to encourage you to branch out and experiment. All you need is here: from my granny's golden syrup pudding to perfect steamed rice, from pistachio and white chocolate friands to prawn fattouche. Face those cooking fears, try some new recipes and have fun!

Biscuits

If the idea of making a big batch of biscuit dough and freezing some for later appeals to you, these are the perfect recipes. Good results are spectacularly easy to achieve – in true domestic-goddess style, you can be pulling a tray of biscuits out of the oven in almost the time it takes to make a proper pot of tea (or mix that round of drinks to accompany the cheese biscuits).

Hints & Tips

✱ Soften the butter at room temperature for an hour or two before starting.

✱ Mix the ingredients using an electric mixer on a low speed and stop when all the ingredients are combined.

✱ Make sure the dough is well chilled, so that it is nice and firm before attempting to slice it. If it is too soft it won't slice thinly enough and the biscuits may spread too much when baking.

✱ The whole idea of these recipes is to have some biscuit dough available when you need it. I usually keep one log of dough in the fridge and some in the freezer. The dough will keep in the fridge for up to 2 weeks and may be frozen for up to 3 months. Allow any frozen dough to thaw in the fridge for 1–2 hours before slicing.

✱ Cut the chilled dough with a large, thin, sharp knife, wiping the knife occasionally with kitchen paper.

✱ Turn the dough every so often as you slice it – this prevents flattening and gives you nice round slices.

✱ Once the biscuits are sliced and on the baking sheet, I sometimes return them to the fridge or freezer to chill, if I have the time. This helps them to keep their shape while baking.

✱ Depending on your oven, rotate the baking sheet occasionally so the biscuits cook evenly. If you are cooking two trays of biscuits, swap them from top to bottom of the oven about halfway through the cooking time.

✱ Always let the biscuits cool for a few minutes on the baking tray (to firm) before transferring them to a wire rack to cool.

✱ Once cool, the biscuits can be stored in an airtight container for up to 5 days, however they may soften a little – really, it's best to bake these biscuits as you need them.

Orange & pecan thins

This is my original and favourite 'refrigerator' biscuit – the one that gave me that 'wow' moment and has changed my biscuit-making method forever. Now my freezer is always well stocked with biscuit dough and I bake a few at a time whenever the need arises (which is surprisingly often).

Preparation time: 15 minutes, plus refrigeration time
Cooking time: 10 minutes
Makes about 120

450 g butter, softened at room temperature
300 g caster sugar
250 g plain flour, sifted
250 g self-raising flour, sifted
2 large eggs, lightly beaten
175 g pecans, roughly chopped
finely grated zest of 1 orange

1   Mix all the ingredients in an electric mixer on a low speed until combined.

2   Divide the mixture into two or three portions, and roll each into a log about 5 cm in diameter. Wrap in baking paper, twisting the ends to seal, and chill until just firm. Remove from the fridge and roll the log on the bench top a couple of times to refine the log shape. Return to the refrigerator for at least 2 hours, or until very firm.

3   Preheat the oven to 180°C (Gas Mark 4) and line a baking sheet with baking paper.

4   Ensure the dough is well chilled, then unwrap the log and cut into thin (3–4 mm) slices. Place on the prepared baking sheet and bake for 10 minutes, or until golden. Cool on the baking sheet for 5 minutes before transferring to a wire rack to cool completely.

Really Useful Stuff
Adapt this basic mixture to suit you: the pecans can be changed to almonds, hazelnuts or walnuts if desired, or alternatively you can leave out the nuts altogether. Two teaspoons of vanilla extract make a nice addition, and you could use lemon or lime zest in place of the orange zest.

Once the dough is sliced and on the baking tray, you can sprinkle (and lightly press) a few chopped nuts or slivered or flaked almonds onto each biscuit before baking.

Make coconut thins by replacing the nuts with 100 g desiccated coconut and 1 teaspoon vanilla extract.

Chocolate spiral cookies

These look rather impressive with their two-tone spiral patterns, but are not at all difficult to make. The trick is to keep the dough chilled and avoid making these biscuits on a humid day.

Preparation time: 20 minutes, plus refrigeration time
Cooking time: 10 minutes
Makes about 60

350 g butter, softened at room temperature
250 g caster sugar
1 large egg, lightly beaten
1 teaspoon vanilla extract
400 g plain flour, sifted
1 teaspoon baking powder, sifted
4 tablespoons cocoa, sifted

1 Mix the butter, sugar, egg and vanilla in an electric mixer. Add the flour and baking powder and mix on a low speed until combined.

2 Divide the mixture into two portions. Beat the sifted cocoa into one portion and the leave the other portion plain. Refrigerate both mixtures for 1 hour.

3 Roll the plain dough (between two large sheets of baking paper) into a large rectangle about 3 mm thick. Roll the chocolate dough to the same size and thickness and then sit the chocolate layer on top of the plain layer. Place on a large sheet of baking paper and trim the edges so that both layers are the same size.

4 Roll up the dough from the long side (Swiss-roll style) into a tight log, using the baking paper to help. Twist the ends of the paper and chill the dough until just firm. Remove from the fridge and roll the log on the bench top a couple of times to refine the cylinder shape. Return to the refrigerator for at least 2 hours, or until very firm.

5 Preheat the oven to 180°C (Gas Mark 4) and line a baking sheet with baking paper.

6 Ensure the dough is well chilled, then unwrap the log and cut into thin (3–4 mm) slices. Place on the prepared baking sheet and bake for 10 minutes, or until golden. Cool on the baking sheet for 5 minutes before transferring to a wire rack to cool completely.

Really Useful Stuff
To make fruit mince spirals, divide the dough into two portions and roll out each portion between two sheets of baking paper into a rectangle about 4 mm thick. Spread each portion with about 100 g fruit mince (or enough to give a thin covering). Using the baking paper to help, roll up the dough from the long side (Swiss-roll style) into a tight log. Chill the dough until just firm, and then continue as above.

Very easy cheddar biscuits›

Forget fiddly canapés, these are always the star of my drinks parties – really easy to make and extremely more-ish.

Preparation time: 10 minutes, plus refrigeration time
Cooking time: 15 minutes
Makes about 50

200 g plain flour, sifted
175 g butter, chilled and diced
2 teaspoons chopped chives
150 g tasty cheddar, grated
50 g freshly grated parmesan
1 tablespoon lemon juice
pinch of salt

1 Place flour, butter, chives, cheddar, parmesan, lemon juice and salt in a food processor and process until the mixture comes together in a ball.

2 Place the mixture on a large sheet of baking paper, then roll into a log about 30 cm long with a 5 cm diameter, twisting the ends to seal. Chill for about 30 minutes, then remove from the fridge and roll the log on the bench top a couple of times to refine the cylinder shape. Return to the refrigerator for at least 2 hours, or until very firm.

3 Preheat the oven to 190°C (Gas Mark 5) and line a baking sheet with baking paper.

4 Ensure the dough is well chilled, then unwrap the log and cut into thin (3–4 mm) slices. Place on the prepared baking sheet and bake for 10–15 minutes, or until firm and just starting to turn golden around the edges. Cool on the baking sheet for 2–3 minutes before transferring to a wire rack to cool completely.

Really Useful Stuff
For a touch of spice , add a pinch of cayenne pepper to the mixture.

Once the dough is sliced and on the baking tray, sprinkle with a few sesame seeds and lightly press onto each biscuit before baking.

Breads

The smell of baking bread is one of my all-time favourite things. The process of making bread is extremely satisfying, and I love watching each loaf as it takes on a personality of its own. Rarely in cooking do the raw ingredients (flour, water and yeast) so little resemble the finished product: a delicious, nutritious miracle.

Yeast: these recipes all use dried yeast as it is readily available. If you are lucky enough to have a supply of fresh yeast, use double the weight given for the dried yeast. Fresh yeast should be crumbled into some of the warm water from the recipe and left to foam before use.

Hints & Tips

Flour: the better the flour, the better the bread. Only use bread-making or strong flour, which is available in larger supermarkets, health-food shops or delicatessens, and sometimes from growers' markets or local mills. Plain flour does not contain enough gluten, which is what gives the dough its elasticity.

Liquid: the quantity of liquid needed to produce a good dough varies, depending on the flour and the humidity or heat of the kitchen. You may need a little more to achieve the desired consistency, but make sure you add any extra liquid a little at a time. The temperature of the liquid is important – too hot and it may kill the yeast, too cold and it will inhibit the growth. Use lukewarm or tepid water.

Kneading: I usually use a combination of machine and hand kneading. Nothing beats kneading by hand (and many bakers say it is crucial to get your hands on the dough), but a combination of kneading in an electric mixer with a dough hook (for 5 minutes) and then by hand (also for 5 minutes) works well if you're short of time. The important thing is to work the dough by giving it a good pummelling, which in turn works the gluten (this is what makes the dough flexible and strong and allows the bread to rise). Regular bread dough cannot be harmed by too much kneading, so if you are unsure, knead for a few more minutes; the dough should feel elastic and smooth. If the dough is extremely soft or sticky (or if the day is very humid) knead in a little more flour, but only a little at a time.

Rising: bread develops flavour as it rises, and dough can be left to rise in a warm place, at room temperature or in the fridge, depending on your schedule. The cooler the position, the longer it will take to double in size, so by raising the dough overnight in the fridge you are actually increasing the flavour (if you plan to do this, use cold water in the dough rather than warm). When risen, punch down the dough and allow it to come to room temperature before shaping. The second rising will probably take less time than the first. If at any time you are interrupted during the rising stage and have to put off finishing the bread, slip the dough into the fridge or a cold place, then return it to room temperature before continuing.

Baking: make sure the oven is preheated before adding the bread. If you want a good crust, place a baking tray filled with water in the bottom of the oven to preheat – the steam helps to give a better crust. Alternatively, after adding the loaf to the oven you can spray it a few times with a water sprayer.

To test if cooked: when cooked, the bread should be well risen with a golden crust – and the kitchen should be filled with a lovely aroma. The loaf should sound hollow when tapped on the base.

Simple white loaf

This is the place to start if you have never made bread before – it can be this simple! If you are daunted at the thought of kneading by hand, you can still achieve great results by mixing the dough for a good 10 minutes on a medium speed in an electric mixer with a dough hook.

Preparation time: 25 minutes, plus standing time
Cooking time: 50 minutes
Makes 1 loaf

1 × 7 g sachet (2 teaspoons) dried yeast
1 teaspoon sugar
600 g white bread flour
1½ teaspoons salt
1 tablespoon olive oil

1   Dissolve the yeast and sugar in a small jug with 125 ml of tepid water. Stir well and leave for 10 minutes, or until it froths.

2   Place the flour and salt in the bowl of an electric mixer. Add the yeast mixture, olive oil and 250 ml of tepid water. Mix using a dough hook on a low speed until the mixture comes together and forms a dough. Increase the speed to medium and work for about 5 minutes, or until smooth and elastic. Add a little extra water if the dough seems too dry.

3   Knead the dough on a lightly floured surface for 5 minutes. Place in a clean, lightly oiled bowl, cover with a cloth or plastic wrap and leave in a warm place for 1–1½ hours, or until the dough has doubled in size.

4   Punch down the dough with your fist to expel the air. Knead on a lightly floured surface for 2 minutes, or until smooth. Shape the loaf and either place in a large greased loaf tin or on a baking tray. Cover and leave for another 45–60 minutes, or until the dough has doubled in size.

5   Preheat the oven to 200°C (Gas Mark 6).

6   Bake for about 40–50 minutes, or until the loaf has risen and is golden brown. If baking in a tin, turn out the loaf, place on a baking tray and return it to the oven for 5 minutes. When cooked, the loaf should be golden and sound hollow when tapped on the bottom. Allow to cool on a wire rack.

Really Useful Stuff
Make bread rolls by dividing the dough into golf-ball-size pieces and kneading lightly into shape. Or roll the dough into thin sausage shapes and tie into knots or spirals. Allow these to rise as in the basic recipe, then bake in a preheated 180°C (Gas Mark 4) oven for 15–20 minutes, or until golden. For a golden crust, brush the dough with a little milk or beaten egg before baking. If you like, sprinkle with poppy or sesame seeds or flakes of sea salt.

Vary the flavour and texture by replacing some of the white flour with a little wholemeal or rye flour.

Linseed & sunflower bread

This is an interesting variation on regular wholegrain bread. The linseeds and sunflower seeds give a delicious nutty texture here, while the wholemeal flour adds a good colour and depth of flavour.

Preparation time: 25 minutes, plus standing time
Cooking time: 45 minutes
Makes 1 loaf

1 × 7 g sachet (2 teaspoons) dried yeast
1 teaspoon sugar
250 g wholemeal bread flour
350 g white bread flour
1½ teaspoons salt
2 tablespoons linseeds
2 tablespoons sunflower oil
2 tablespoons sunflower seeds

1   Dissolve the yeast and sugar in a small jug with 125 ml of tepid water. Stir well and leave for 10 minutes, or until it froths.

2   Place both the flours, salt and linseeds in the bowl of an electric mixer. Add the yeast mixture, oil and 250 ml of tepid water. Mix using a dough hook on a low speed until the mixtures comes together and forms a dough, adding a little extra water if the dough is too dry.

3   Knead the dough on a lightly floured surface for 7–8 minutes or until smooth and elastic. Place in a lightly oiled bowl, cover with a cloth or plastic wrap and leave in a warm place for 1–1½ hours, or until the dough has doubled in size.

4   Punch down the dough with your fist to expel the air, then knead on a lightly floured surface for 2 minutes, or until smooth. Shape the loaf and either place in a large greased loaf tin or on a baking tray. Cover and leave for another 45–60 minutes, or until the dough has doubled in size.

5   Preheat the oven to 200°C (Gas Mark 6).

6   Brush the top of the loaf with a little water and sprinkle with the sunflower seeds. Bake for 30–40 minutes, or until the loaf has risen and is golden brown. If baking in a tin, turn out the loaf, place on a baking tray and return it to the oven for 5 minutes. When cooked, the loaf should be golden and sound hollow when tapped on the bottom. Allow to cool on a wire rack.

Really Useful Stuff
If you leave out the seeds and oil, this makes a delicious classic brown loaf.

Form the mixture into little rolls, sprinkle with poppy seeds and bake for about 15–20 minutes.

This is also good with the addition of some chopped dried fruit – add apricots, sultanas or raisins to the basic loaf and bake as above.

To add a nice topping to the loaf, shape it as directed, then brush with a little water and sprinkle with rolled oats (porridge oats).

Bread sticks (grissini) >

These are good to have with drinks, soups or instead of the bread basket with dinner. You can roll them as thick or as thin as you like – the thicker you make them the more bread-like they become.

Preparation time: 25 minutes, plus standing time
Cooking time: 15 minutes
Makes about 20

1 × 7 g sachet (2 teaspoons) dried yeast
1 teaspoon sugar
300 g white bread flour
1½ teaspoons salt
1 tablespoon freshly grated parmesan
2 tablespoons olive oil, plus extra for brushing
cornmeal or polenta, for sprinkling
sea salt, for sprinkling

1   Dissolve the yeast and sugar in a small jug with 185 ml of tepid water. Stir well and leave for 10 minutes, or until it froths.

2   Place the flour, salt and parmesan in the bowl of an electric mixer. Add the yeast mixture and olive oil. Mix using a dough hook on a medium speed until it forms a firm dough, adding a little extra water if the dough is too dry. Mix for about 5 minutes until smooth and elastic.

3   Knead the dough on a lightly floured surface for 2 minutes. Place in a lightly oiled bowl, cover with a cloth or plastic wrap and leave in a warm place for 1 hour, or until the dough has doubled in size.

4   Lightly grease a baking sheet and scatter with cornmeal. Preheat the oven to 200°C (Gas Mark 6).

5   Punch down the dough with your fist to expel the air, then knead on a lightly floured surface for 1 minute. Pinch off large walnut-size pieces of dough and roll each by hand into long thin sticks – there should be about 20 sticks. Place on the prepared baking sheet, brush with a little extra oil, then sprinkle with sea salt and a little cornmeal. Set aside in a warm place for 15 minutes.

6   Bake for 10–15 minutes, or until crisp and golden brown.

Really Useful Stuff
You can add all sorts of flavours to the basic mixture – try a sprinkling of sea salt, a little dried chilli, chopped olives or dried Italian herbs.

Brush the shaped grissini with a little water and sprinkle with sesame or poppy seeds before baking, if desired.

Fig, sultana & rosemary bread

This is my favourite fruit bread. The rosemary adds a delicious flavour and a slight savoury note – perfect with cheese or toasted as a snack.

Preparation time: 25 minutes, plus standing time
Cooking time: 35 minutes
Makes 2 loaves

1 × 7 g sachet (2 teaspoons) dried yeast
1 teaspoon sugar
400 g wholemeal bread flour
200 g white bread flour, plus extra for dusting
1½ teaspoons salt
50 g butter, softened
2 tablespoons golden syrup
100 g dried figs, chopped
100 g sultanas
3 tablespoons chopped rosemary

1 Dissolve the yeast and sugar in a small jug with 125 ml of tepid water. Stir well and leave for 10 minutes, or until it froths.

2 Place the flours, salt, butter and golden syrup in the bowl of an electric mixer. Add the yeast mixture and 250 ml of tepid water. Mix using a dough hook on a low speed until the mixture comes together and forms a dough. Increase the speed to medium and mix for about 5 minutes, or until smooth and elastic. Add a little extra water if the dough is too dry.

3 Knead the dough on a lightly floured surface for 1–2 minutes. Place in a clean, lightly oiled bowl, cover with a cloth or plastic wrap and leave in a warm place for 1–1½ hours, or until the dough has doubled in size.

4 Punch down the dough with your fist to expel the air, then knead on a lightly floured surface for 2–3 minutes. Sprinkle the dough with the dried fruit and rosemary, incorporating it into the mixture as you knead. Divide the mixture into two portions and shape each into a ball. Line a baking tray with baking paper, then place the balls of dough on the tray. Cover and leave for another 45–60 minutes, or until the dough has doubled in size.

5 Preheat the oven to 200°C (Gas Mark 6).

6 Slash the top of each loaf a couple of times with a sharp knife and dust each with a little flour. Bake for 40 minutes, or until the loaves have risen and are golden brown. When cooked, they should sound hollow when tapped on the bottom. Allow to cool on a wire rack.

Really Useful Stuff
Increase the sultanas to 150 g and leave out the figs to make a delicious sweet, herby loaf.

A handful of coarsely chopped hazelnuts makes a nice addition.

Form the dough into whatever shape you like.

Turkish-style pide

This makes a good flat, chewy bread, typical of those found in Turkish restaurants or pide bars. The dough is quite soft, which gives the bread its texture.

Preparation time: 30 minutes, plus standing time
Cooking time: 20 minutes
Makes 4 loaves

1 × 7 g sachet (2 teaspoons) dried yeast
1 teaspoon sugar
750 g white bread flour
2 teaspoons salt
2 tablespoons olive oil
sesame seeds or nigella seeds, for sprinkling

1 Dissolve the yeast and sugar in a small jug with 125 ml of tepid water. Stir well and leave for 10 minutes, or until it froths.

2 Place the flour and salt in the bowl of an electric mixer. Add the yeast mixture, olive oil and 300 ml of tepid water. Mix using a dough hook on a low speed until the mixtures comes together and forms a dough. Increase the speed to medium and mix for about 5 minutes, or until you have a really soft dough. Add a little more warm water if the dough is too dry.

3 Knead the dough on a lightly floured surface for 5–10 minutes, then shape into a large ball. Place in a clean, lightly oiled bowl, cover with a cloth or plastic wrap and leave in a warm place for 1–1½ hours, or until the dough has doubled in size.

4 Punch down the dough with your fist to expel the air. Knead on a lightly floured surface for 1 minute and then shape into four balls. Line two baking sheets with baking paper.

5 Use a rolling pin to shape each dough ball into ovals about 1 cm thick, then transfer two ovals to each baking sheet. Make a few indentations in the dough with your fingertips. Sprinkle a little warm water over the dough, cover, and leave in a warm spot for about 25 minutes.

6 Preheat the oven to 240°C (Gas Mark 9). Place a small baking dish filled with boiling water in the bottom of the oven.

7 Sprinkle the loaves with sesame or nigella seeds and bake for 10–15 minutes or until golden and risen. Slide the flat bread off the trays onto the oven shelves and cook for a further 5 minutes, or until crusty, golden and risen. Allow to cool on a wire rack.

Really Useful Stuff
You can use this dough to make Turkish-style pizza bases. Once the dough is shaped, sprinkle with some chopped garlic, blanched, squeezed and chopped spinach leaves and crumbled feta. Fold over the edges of the loaf slightly to partly enclose the topping and sprinkle with sesame seeds. Bake for 20 minutes, or until golden.

Breads – quick

Sweet and savoury quick breads are so easy to make that they really are a busy person's 'rabbit from the hat'. They are raised using baking powder (and sometimes bicarbonate of soda) rather than yeast, and can be assembled in the time it takes to preheat the oven.

Hints & Tips
The only rule here is that you mustn't overmix the batter – for once, a few lumps are OK. Combine the dry and wet ingredients as quickly as you can, and don't beat or even stir any more than necessary. When you see no more dry bits of flour, the job is done. I prefer to use buttermilk in quick breads – it seems to give them extra lightness and flavour. If you don't have any, simply use the same quantity of soured milk (made by adding a squeeze of lemon juice to fresh milk); regular milk and a dollop of plain yoghurt also works well.

Cheese & walnut damper

Here a classic damper (or soda bread) is given a flavour boost by adding wholemeal flour, walnuts and cheese. Great with cheese, soup, or simply spread with butter. It is also delicious toasted.

Preparation time: 20 minutes
Cooking time: 55 minutes
Makes 1 large loaf

280 g self-raising flour
140 g wholemeal flour
1 teaspoon baking powder
1 teaspoon salt
50 g butter, chilled and chopped
100 g walnuts, coarsely chopped
125 g grated cheese
300 ml milk
1 teaspoon lemon juice

1   Preheat the oven to 200°C (Gas Mark 6). Lightly grease a baking tray.

2   Sift the flours, baking powder and salt into a large mixing bowl. Rub the butter into the flour mixture with your fingertips until it resembles breadcrumbs. Stir in the walnuts and three-quarters of the grated cheese, then make a well in the centre.

3   Mix together the milk and lemon juice – the mixture will curdle slightly – and pour into the flour mixture. Mix gently, just until a soft dough forms. If the dough is too dry, add extra milk, a tablespoon at a time, and mix.

4   Gather the dough into a rough ball shape, turn out onto a lightly floured surface and knead gently. The dough should feel slightly damp. With floured hands, pat it into a round loaf shape and place on the prepared baking tray. Sprinkle the loaf with the remaining cheese and slash a cross in the top with a sharp knife, if desired.

5   Bake for 45–55 minutes, or until risen and golden and the loaf sounds hollow when tapped on the base. Remove from the tray and wrap in a clean cloth. Serve warm or cold.

Really Useful Stuff

Try making damper in a cast-iron frying pan if you have one lurking about, as cast iron is a wonderful conductor of heat and also serves to shape the dough as it cooks. Wrap the damper in a cloth as it cools if you want it soft, or not if you like it crusty.

Wholemeal flour adds a little texture to this loaf, but it also makes it slightly heavier than a regular damper. If you would prefer it to be less dense, omit the wholemeal and use all white flour.

The flavour of bacon goes really well with this loaf. Add a few rashers of cooked and chopped bacon or pancetta to the mixture and bake as for basic recipe.

Sun-dried tomatoes and bacon are a good flavour combination to add to a classic damper or soda bread. I prefer to use the softer, not completely dried tomatoes, sometimes called semi-dried or sun-blush. Leave out the walnuts and cheese and add 100 g roughly chopped semi-dried tomatoes and 1–2 tablespoons chopped basil to the basic recipe.

Banana bread

One day recently when in a rush, I simply placed all the ingredients in a food processor and pulsed until combined. It worked a treat! You can also mix the ingredients in a bowl with a wooden spoon, if preferred.

Preparation time: 10 minutes
Cooking time: 1 hour
Makes 1 medium loaf

210 g plain flour
1 teaspoon baking powder
1 teaspoon bicarbonate of soda
pinch of salt
125 g unsalted butter, softened at room temperature
250 g sugar
2 eggs, lightly beaten
3 very ripe bananas, chopped
125 ml buttermilk or regular milk soured with
    a squeeze of lemon juice
icing sugar, for dusting

1 Preheat the oven to 170°C (Gas Mark 3). Grease a medium loaf tin and line the base and sides with baking paper (leave a little overhanging the sides to help remove the bread from the tin).

2 Place all the ingredients except the icing sugar in a food processor and process, using quick bursts of the pulse action, until smooth. Don't overprocess the mixture. Transfer the mixture to the prepared tin and smooth the top.

3 Bake for 55–60 minutes, or until the top of the bread is firm and golden brown. Cool in the tin for 10 minutes before turning out onto a wire rack to cool completely.

4 Dust with icing sugar, or serve it toasted and buttered. The flavour improves on keeping.

Really Useful Stuff
Chocolate chips are a delicious addition to the basic recipe – stir 100 g dark chocolate chips into the mixture and bake as above.

Coconut bread ›

This is great either eaten the day it is baked or stored for a day or two (the flavour improves with keeping) and toasted and buttered.

Preparation time: 20 minutes
Cooking time: 1 hour
Makes 1 large loaf

350 g plain flour
2 teaspoons baking powder
1 teaspoon ground cinnamon
250 g caster sugar
150 g desiccated or shredded coconut
300 ml buttermilk or regular milk soured with
    a squeeze of lemon juice
2 eggs
1 teaspoon vanilla extract
75 g unsalted butter, melted
icing sugar, for dusting

1 Preheat the oven to 180°C (Gas Mark 4). Grease a large loaf tin and line the base and sides with baking paper (leave a little overhanging the sides to help remove the bread from the tin).

2 Sift the flour, baking powder, cinnamon and sugar into a large bowl and stir in the coconut. Make a well in the centre.

3 Whisk together the buttermilk, eggs, vanilla and melted butter. Pour the wet mixture into the well in the flour and stir with a wooden spoon until the ingredients are just combined. Do not overmix; the batter is fine a bit lumpy. Transfer the mixture to the prepared tin and smooth the top.

4 Bake for 60–65 minutes, or until the top of the bread is firm to the touch and golden brown. A skewer inserted in the centre should come out clean. Cool in the tin for 10 minutes before turning out onto a wire rack to cool completely.

5 Dust with icing sugar, or serve it toasted and buttered.

Really Useful Stuff
For extra coconut flavour, try replacing 100 ml of the buttermilk with 100 ml of coconut milk.

Cover the top of this bread with some foil or baking paper if it is colouring too quickly.

Cakes

In the 1830s when Anna, 7th Duchess of Bedford, single-handedly invented a new meal opportunity, cunningly designed to bridge the gap between an early lunch and a late dinner, the institution of afternoon tea was happily born. These days a little gossip over a cuppa with a slice of home-baked cake is one of the simplest ways to entertain friends. There is something distinctly hip about baking a cake at the moment, and tea time is enjoying a huge revival – a fittingly leisurely backlash against all those takeaway cappuccinos we gulp on the run.

Hints & Tips

✱ Take the butter out of the fridge at least 2 hours before you start; don't use heat to soften the butter as the butter tends to beat better (absorbing more air) when softened naturally.

✱ The eggs should also be at room temperature. If cold, place them in your mixing bowl, cover with warm (not hot) water and leave for 15 minutes. The eggs will be at room temperature and the bowl warmed, ready for mixing the cake.

✱ For best results, use the cake tin recommended in the recipe. If you don't have the correct tin, make sure that the mixture only fills whatever tin you are using to a maximum of three-quarters full.

✱ Creaming the butter and sugar until light and fluffy is essential. If you don't have electric beaters, a clean hand is more efficient than a wooden spoon – the warmth of your fingers speeds up the creaming process.

✱ Folding is a gentle method of combining ingredients. Use a large metal spoon to incorporate the ingredients (usually flour or egg whites) with slow and gentle movements. Each time you fold in the ingredients, use the metal spoon to go right through the mixture, using long strokes and turning the bowl slightly as you go, making sure the ingredients are evenly blended. It is better to do it slowly and surely without rushing.

✱ If the cake is colouring too quickly, cover with a sheet of foil about three-quarters of the way through cooking. Don't be tempted to open the oven door until at least two-thirds of the way through cooking or your cake may flop.

The 'all-in-one' method: as the name suggests, this method combines all the cake ingredients in one go. Rather than creaming the butter and sugar to add air, it uses extra raising agents to help with the rising of the cake (ie, a teaspoon of baking powder sifted with self-raising flour).

Use soft margarine or very soft butter, and ensure all the ingredients are at room temperature. Simply combine all the ingredients in a bowl and beat with a wooden spoon until the mixture just comes together (don't overbeat). Using the ingredients for the basic Victoria sponge cake, the all-in-one recipe can be used for cakes made in a round 19 cm cake tin.

Basic butter icing: sift 200 g icing sugar into a bowl and add 50 g chopped soft butter. Add 1–2 tablespoons of boiling water and beat with a wooden spoon until thick and smooth. Tint with food colouring if desired. You can add vanilla extract or replace the water with lemon juice, if desired.

Katie Stewart's Victoria sponge

I am the son of a woman who won prizes for her sponges. Something must have rubbed off on me as this is the cake I bake most often; in fact, a Victoria sponge was the first cake I ever made. I followed Katie Stewart's recipe in *The Times Cookery Book* in the late 1970s, and still use the recipe to this day.

Preparation time: 30 minutes
Cooking time: 25 minutes
Serves 8

175 g self-raising flour
175 g butter, softened at room temperature
175 g caster sugar
3 large eggs, at room temperature
½ teaspoon vanilla extract
3–4 tablespoons fruit jam
 (such as raspberry, apricot or plum)
caster or icing sugar, to serve

You will also need
two 19 cm sandwich cake tins (4 cm deep)

1 Preheat the oven to 180°C (Gas Mark 4). Lightly grease the tins and line the bases with baking paper. Sift the flour onto a plate.

2 In a large bowl, cream the butter and sugar with hand-held electric beaters for about 5–7 minutes until pale and fluffy.

3 Mix the eggs and vanilla together with a fork, then gradually beat into the creamed butter (in about five batches). Beat well after each addition. Add a little of the sifted flour with the last of the egg if the mixture looks as if it might separate.

4 When all the egg has been beaten in, lightly fold in the remaining flour with a metal spoon until combined. The mixture should drop from the spoon if given a slight shake.

5 Divide the mixture between the cake tins and spread level, then bake in the centre of the oven for 20–25 minutes. Touch the centre of each cake with your fingertips – if they feel springy and no imprint remains, they are done. Remove from the oven and leave to cool in the tins for 5 minutes, then turn out onto a wire rack to cool completely.

6 When cool, sandwich the layers together with the jam and dust the top of the cake with sugar.

Really Useful Stuff

Lemon sandwich
Follow the basic cake recipe, but replace the vanilla with the finely grated zest of one lemon, creaming it with the butter and sugar. Sandwich the cakes together with 4–5 tablespoons lemon curd and dust with icing sugar. You could also make this with the zest of an orange or two limes.

Coffee almond cake
Follow the basic cake recipe, but replace the vanilla with 1 tablespoon of instant coffee powder dissolved in 2 tablespoons of boiling water. Add 2 tablespoons of ground almonds to the sifted flour. Fold the cooled coffee into the mixture with the flour. Sandwich the cakes together with 3–4 tablespoons of coffee fudge frosting (see page 18) and swirl the remainder on top.

Marble loaf cake
Follow the basic cake recipe, but instead of using sandwich cake tins, grease a medium loaf tin and line the base with baking paper, letting it overhang on both long sides. In a small bowl, blend 1 heaped tablespoon of cocoa with 2 tablespoons of boiling water. Spoon half of the cake mixture into a separate bowl, add the chocolate paste and mix well. Now place alternate spoonfuls of the two cake mixes into the loaf tin. With a flat knife, cut through the mixture twice in opposite directions to swirl the contents, then tap the tin sharply so the mixture falls level. Bake for 40–45 minutes, or until firm to the touch. Cool in the tin for 5 minutes, then remove from the tin using the overhanging paper and cool on a wire rack. When cold, dust with icing sugar.

Pecan & coffee cake

This is my version of that classic iced coffee cake that you will find at most fetes or charity cake stalls. Sometimes I split the cake horizontally and make a little extra icing to sandwich the cakes together. You can also decorate the icing by pressing some pecans on top.

Preparation time: 20 minutes, plus cooling time
Cooking time: 50 minutes
Serves 8

---

60 g self-raising flour
200 g pecans
finely grated zest of 1 orange
175 g unsalted butter, softened at room temperature
175 g caster sugar
1 teaspoon vanilla extract
3 large eggs
2½ tablespoons strong black coffee
icing sugar, to serve (optional)

Coffee fudge frosting
200 g icing sugar
40 g unsalted butter
1 teaspoon instant coffee granules

You will also need
a 20 cm springform cake tin

1   Preheat the oven to 180°C (Gas Mark 4). Lightly grease the tin and line the base with baking paper.

2   Place the flour, pecans and orange zest in a food processor and whiz until coarsely ground.

3   With an electric mixer, beat the butter, sugar and vanilla for about 5 minutes, or until pale and fluffy.

4   Break the eggs into a jug and lightly beat. With the mixer on a medium speed, gradually pour the egg into the butter and sugar mixture. Add a tablespoon of the flour mixture between each addition of egg. Gently stir in the coffee and then the remaining flour mixture using a large metal spoon.

5   Spoon the batter into the prepared tin and bake for about 45–50 minutes, or until golden and risen. Remove from the oven and cool in the tin. Dust with icing sugar or spread with coffee fudge frosting.

6   To make the frosting, sift the icing sugar into a bowl. Place the butter, coffee granules and 2 tablespoons of water in a saucepan and stir over low heat until the butter has melted and the coffee has dissolved. Pour the coffee mixture over the icing sugar and beat with a wooden spoon until smooth. Stir until the frosting has cooled a little and is thick enough to leave a trail, then spread over the cake at once.

Really Useful Stuff
You can make the strong black coffee needed for the cake mixture using instant coffee granules.

Rich chocolate cake

For the best flavour use a good-quality dark chocolate (50 per cent cocoa solids). Even though this is a rich cake, the texture is lightened by the addition of whisked egg whites.

Preparation time: 25 minutes, plus cooling time
Cooking time: 50 minutes
Serves 8

---

175 g rich dark chocolate, broken into squares
125 g unsalted butter, chopped
125 g caster sugar
4 eggs, separated
1 teaspoon vanilla extract
50 g plain flour
1 teaspoon baking powder
cocoa, to serve

You will also need
a 20 cm springform cake tin

1   Preheat the oven to 180°C (Gas Mark 4). Lightly grease the tin and line the base with baking paper.

2   Melt the chocolate, butter and half the sugar in a large heatproof bowl set over a saucepan of hot water, stirring occasionally until the mixture is smooth. Stir in the remaining sugar.

3   Remove from the heat and whisk in the egg yolks and vanilla. Sift in the flour and baking powder and gently fold in with a large metal spoon.

4   Beat the egg whites in a clean bowl with clean beaters until soft peaks form. Carefully fold the whites into the chocolate mixture (being careful not to lose the air).

5   Pour the mixture into the prepared tin and bake for about 50 minutes, until risen and firm to the touch. Remove from the oven and cool in the tin for 15 minutes before turning out onto a wire rack to cool completely. Dust with a little cocoa before serving.

Really Useful Stuff
You can make this cake gluten free by replacing the flour with gluten-free flour or with ground almonds.

Claudia Roden's Middle Eastern orange & almond cake

This iconic cake, which graced the menu of most cafés in the 1990s, comes from Claudia Roden's *A New Book of Middle Eastern Food*. The book is worth looking for and the cake is definitely worth making, with its full-on orange flavour and moist almondy texture. A great cake for anyone avoiding flour.

Preparation time: 20 minutes, plus cooling time
Cooking time: 2 hours
Serves 8–10

2 oranges
5 eggs
250 g ground almonds
225 g sugar
1 teaspoon baking powder
icing sugar, to serve

You will also need
a 22 cm springform cake tin

1 Scrub the oranges under warm water to remove any wax from the skins. Put the oranges in a large, deep saucepan, cover with water and bring to the boil. Simmer for about 1 hour, or until very soft. Remove the oranges from the water and set aside to cool. Discard the water.

2 Preheat the oven to 180°C (Gas Mark 4). Lightly grease the tin and line the base with baking paper.

3 Using a plate to catch the juices, cut the cooled oranges into quarters and remove any pips. Purée the quarters in a food processor or blender.

4 Beat the eggs in a large bowl until frothy, then beat in the orange puree. Fold in the almonds, sugar and baking powder and mix until combined. Pour the batter into the prepared tin and bake for 50–60 minutes, or until firm to the touch and golden. Cook a little longer if needed.

5 Remove from the oven and cool in the tin for about 20 minutes before turning out onto a wire rack to cool completely. Dust with icing sugar to serve.

Really Useful Stuff
This recipe also works well with other citrus fruit – blood oranges are great, or try a mixture of oranges and limes.

Caramel upside-down pear cake

I just love a cake that doesn't need any icing. The caramel and pears give this cake a lovely topping, which keeps it nice and moist.

Preparation time: 20 minutes
Cooking time: 1 hour
Serves 8

4 large ripe pears, peeled
150 g unrefined golden caster sugar
125 g butter, softened at room temperature
120 g brown sugar
2 large eggs
125 g self-raising flour
pinch of ground ginger

You will also need
a 23 cm round cake tin

1 Preheat oven to 180°C (Gas Mark 4). Grease the tin with a little butter and line the base with baking paper.

2 Cut two of the pears into quarters and then into eighths, giving you 16 slices. Cut the remaining pears into 1 cm dice.

3 Place the caster sugar and 3 tablespoons of water in a small saucepan and bring to the boil over medium heat, stirring to dissolve the sugar. Boil gently without stirring until it forms a golden caramel. Carefully pour the caramel into the base of the prepared tin, swirling it to cover the paper. Arrange the pear slices in a decorative pattern on the caramel.

4 Beat the butter and brown sugar until pale and fluffy. Whisk the eggs in a jug, then gradually pour into the butter and sugar mixture, beating constantly until combined. Sift the flour and ginger onto the mixture, and gently fold them in with a large metal spoon. Stir in the diced pear.

5 Spoon the batter into the tin and smooth the top. Bake for 45–50 minutes, or until risen and firm to the touch. A skewer inserted into the centre of the cake should come out clean.

6 Cool in the tin for 5 minutes before turning out the cake onto a serving plate. Serve warm with ice-cream or custard or at room temperature with tea or coffee.

Really Useful Stuff
It is a good idea to let the cake cool in the tin for 5 minutes before turning it out as this allows the pear topping to set.

Nigel Slater's plum cake

This delicious nutty and fruity cake comes from food writer Nigel Slater. It's a real winner – the plums sink into the cake as it cooks, giving a lovely soft centre.

Preparation time: 20 minutes, plus cooling time
Cooking time: 45 minutes
Serves 8–10

150 g butter, softened at room temperature
150 g unrefined golden caster sugar
3 large eggs
75 g plain flour
1½ teaspoons baking powder
100 g ground almonds
50 g walnuts, finely chopped
16 plums, stones removed and cut into quarters

You will also need
a 20 cm square cake tin (about 6 cm deep)

1 Preheat the oven to 180°C (Gas Mark 4). Line the base of the tin with baking paper.

2 With an electric mixer, beat the butter and sugar for about 5–7 minutes, or until pale and fluffy.

3 Break the eggs into a jug and lightly beat. With the mixer on a medium speed, gradually pour the egg into the butter and sugar mixture. Add a tablespoon of flour between each addition of egg.

4 Sift the remaining flour and baking powder over the bowl and carefully fold into the batter with a large metal spoon. Fold in the ground almonds and walnuts.

5 Scrape the mixture into the prepared tin and arrange the quartered plums on top. There is no point in doing this with any real precision as they will sink into the cake as they cook.

6 Bake for about 45 minutes, then test with a skewer. If it comes out clean, without any wet cake mixture sticking to it, the cake is ready. Remove the cake from the oven and leave to cool in the tin for 15 minutes before turning out onto a wire rack to cool completely.

Really Useful Stuff
You can try lots of combinations with this recipe. Use other stone fruit, such as peaches or nectarines, or replace the walnuts with pecans or hazelnuts. A spoonful of vanilla extract beaten with the butter and sugar is also delicious.

Lemon syrup cake ›

Everyone needs a good recipe for lemon syrup cake. I have been making different versions for years and have finally settled on this as my favourite. Lots of lemon flavour and lots of syrup . . . yum.

Preparation time: 30 minutes, plus cooling time
Cooking time: 50 minutes
Serves 8–10

250 g unsalted butter, softened at room temperature
1 tablespoon finely grated lemon zest
250 g unrefined golden caster sugar
4 large eggs
275 g self-raising flour
1 teaspoon baking powder
100 ml buttermilk
juice of 1 lemon

Syrup
150 g unrefined golden caster sugar
juice of 1 lemon

Icing
300 g icing sugar, sifted
4 tablespoons lemon juice

You will also need
a 23 cm round cake tin

1 Heat the oven to 180°C (Gas Mark 4). Lightly grease the tin and line the base with baking paper.

2 With an electric mixer, beat the butter, lemon zest and sugar for about 5–7 minutes, or until pale and fluffy.

3 Break the eggs into a jug and lightly beat. With the mixer on a medium speed, gradually pour the egg into the butter and sugar mixture. Add a tablespoon of flour between each addition of egg.

4 Sift the remaining flour and baking powder over the bowl and carefully fold into the batter with a large metal spoon. Add the buttermilk and lemon juice and gently combine. Spoon into the prepared tin and bake for about 50 minutes, or until the cake is golden brown on top and firm to the touch.

5 Meanwhile, to make the syrup combine the sugar, lemon juice and 100 ml water in a saucepan. Stir occasionally over moderate heat until the sugar has dissolved, then boil for 2 minutes.

6 Remove the cake from the oven and poke holes all over the top with a skewer or toothpick. Carefully spoon the warm syrup over the cake and set aside to cool.

7 To make the icing, sift the icing sugar into a bowl and mix in enough lemon juice to give a thick, spreadable consistency. Spread over the cooled cake, allowing some of the icing to run down the sides. Any leftovers will keep in an airtight tin for up to 5 days.

Really Useful Stuff
If you want to make this ahead of time, the cooled cake (with the syrup) can be frozen for up to 1 month. Thaw to room temperature before icing.

Casseroles & braises

What's not to like about making a casserole or braised dish? The slow, steady cooking results in meat of melting tenderness and a richly flavoured sauce. It's inexpensive because the best results come from long, slow cooking of cheaper cuts of meat, it behaves itself in the oven until you are ready to serve it and, best of all, you can cook it a day or two ahead and the flavour actually improves when reheated.

Hints & Tips

Choosing cuts of beef: one of the great advantages of a casserole, stew or braised dish is that they are best made using cheaper cuts of meat. The long, slow cooking turns these normally tougher cuts into tender morsels, breaking down any muscle tissue to give extra flavour. If you are looking for suitable cuts of meat in the supermarket, look for packs labelled casserole, braising or skirt. At the butcher's look for cuts such as topside, silverside, chuck, blade, skirt, brisket, neck, thick flank, shin and leg. Save cuts such as fillet, rib eye (or even rump) for roasting. Names of cuts can vary from region to region, so ask your butcher for advice if you are unsure.

The pot: one of the best pots for a casserole or stew is an enamelled cast-iron dutch oven or lidded casserole dish. These have the advantage of being able to be used on the hob as well as in the oven. Cast iron is ideal as it absorbs heat slowly and conducts it steadily.

Cheating a little – no browning: sometimes I break a few rules when cooking and most people aren't any the wiser for it (as long as it doesn't compromise the flavour). If pushed for time, I sometimes leave out the step of browning the meat before adding it to the casserole (especially with lamb shanks or other meat on the bone). The difference with most dishes is slight enough that, to my mind, the browning isn't always worth the extra work. I usually remove the lid of the casserole about 20 minutes before the end of cooking time and this colours the meat nicely.

Finishing the dish: the Italians have it right when they add gremolata at the end of a braised dish (see Lamb shanks – Italian style, page 24). The simple mixture of garlic, herbs and lemon zest gives the dish a real boost before serving. Try different combinations of chopped fresh herbs, orange, lemon or lime zest or garlic, ginger and chilli to liven things up – look to add flavours that are already in the dish.

Quick fix: if your sauce lacks body or colour, stir in 2–3 tablespoons tomato paste or a little gremolata (see above).

To reheat: the best way to reheat a casserole is to place the pot on the hob, cover and bring it slowly to the boil. Simmer gently for 10–15 minutes, stirring occasionally. Sometimes you may need to add a little extra liquid (water, stock or wine) if the sauce thickens too much. You can also add a pastry or cobbler topping at this stage and cook as described on page 24.

To freeze: a casserole or braised dish can be successfully frozen for up to 2 months. Before freezing, make sure it is at room temperature and that the meat is covered with the sauce (otherwise it may dry out). A handy tip: freezing single-serve amounts will reduce the thawing time.

Simple beef casserole

If you have never made a casserole before, this is the place to start. This dish has a lovely flavour and plenty of juice, and couldn't be simpler as most of the cooking is done slowly in the oven. Don't leave out the orange zest as it really lifts the flavour of the meat.

Preparation time: 35 minutes
Cooking time: 3 hours
Serves 6–8

2 tablespoons olive oil
4 rashers streaky bacon, roughly chopped
6 small brown onions or golden shallots, peeled and quartered
3 cloves garlic, crushed
3 carrots, sliced
1.75 kg rump or chuck steak, cut into 2 cm cubes
1 tablespoon plain flour
500 ml beef stock
250 ml red wine
1 teaspoon grated orange zest
4 sprigs thyme
1 bay leaf
2 tablespoons chopped flat-leaf parsley
salt and freshly ground black pepper

1   Preheat the oven to 160°C (Gas Mark 2–3).

2   Heat the oil in a large frying pan over medium heat and cook the bacon for 2 minutes. Add the onion, garlic and carrot and cook, stirring occasionally, for 6–7 minutes, or until the onion is tender. Transfer to a casserole dish, add the beef and sprinkle with the flour. Mix well.

3   Stir the stock, wine, orange zest, thyme and bay leaf into the casserole and bring to the boil over medium heat. Cover, transfer to the oven and cook for 3 hours. Stir the meat occasionally as it cooks.

4   Remove from the oven and check the sauce – add a little extra water if it appears dry. Alternatively, if the sauce is a little watery, uncover and return to the oven to allow it to reduce. Stir in the parsley and season to taste. Serve with mashed potatoes or buttered noodles and plenty of crusty bread.

Really Useful Stuff
The beef casserole makes a great pie filling. Divide some of the mixture among individual soufflé dishes or deep ramekins and top with a circle of ready-rolled puff pastry. Brush the pastry with a little beaten egg and bake in a 180°C (Gas Mark 4) oven for 25–30 minutes. Or if you prefer, make one large pie. Spoon the filling into a pie dish, top with ready-rolled puff pastry and bake for 45–55 minutes or until the pastry is golden and risen.

Cobbler topping

A cobbler topping is a great addition to a simple beef casserole. Follow the recipe on page 23, then increase the oven temperature to 200°C (Gas Mark 6), add the cobbler topping and bake until golden.

Preparation time: 10 minutes
Cooking time: 15 minutes
Makes enough to cover one large casserole

500 g self-raising flour
½ teaspoon salt
200 g chilled butter, chopped
2 tablespoons chopped parsley or chives
50 g grated cheddar (optional)
250 ml milk, plus extra for brushing
2 teaspoons lemon juice

1 Preheat the oven to 200°C (Gas Mark 6).

2 Sift the flour and salt into a large bowl and add the chopped butter. Using your fingertips, rub the butter into the flour until it resembles coarse breadcrumbs. Stir in the herbs and cheese (if using).

3 Combine the milk and lemon juice and pour into the flour. Mix it gently with a large flat knife or a metal spoon. It should form a soft dough – don't knead or overwork it. Gather into a ball and flatten slightly. Flatten to a thickness of 3 cm on a floured surface and then cut out rounds with a pastry cutter. Arrange the rounds on the top of the casserole and brush them with a little milk. Bake uncovered for 12–15 minutes, or until risen and golden.

Really Useful Stuff
Don't handle the cobbler mixture too much. It needs a light hand – a little like making scones.

Lamb shanks – Italian style

Adding whole chillies to the casserole is an easy and subtle way to add a little spice; remove them before serving. If the shanks are large, serve one per person.

Preparation time: 25 minutes
Cooking time: 2 hours 20 minutes
Serves 4–6

3 tablespoons olive oil
6 large lamb shanks
2 cloves garlic, crushed
1 onion, sliced
3 sticks celery, sliced
400 g tin chopped Italian tomatoes
500 ml dry white wine
finely grated zest and juice of 1 lemon
2 large red chillies, whole
2 sprigs rosemary
salt and freshly ground black pepper

Gremolata
1 clove garlic, finely chopped
3 tablespoons finely chopped flat-leaf parsley
  finely grated zest of 1 lemon

1 Preheat the oven to 160°C (Gas Mark 2–3).

2 Heat half the oil in a large frying pan over medium heat. Cook the shanks, two or three at a time, until browned, being careful not to overcrowd the pan, as the meat will then steam rather than sear. Add a little extra oil if needed. Transfer to a large casserole dish.

3 Heat the remaining oil in the frying pan over medium heat. Add the garlic, onion and celery and cook, stirring occasionally, for 6–7 minutes, or until the vegetables are tender but not coloured. Transfer to the casserole dish.

4 Stir the tomatoes, wine, lemon zest and juice into the casserole and bring to the boil over medium heat. Tuck in the whole chillies and rosemary. Cover, transfer to the oven and cook for 2 hours, turning the shanks occasionally as they cook. Add a little water if the sauce is too thick. If the sauce needs thickening, remove the shanks and keep warm, then reduce the liquid over high heat until it reaches a sauce consistency. Season to taste. Remove the chillies and skim off any fat before serving.

5 To make the gremolata, mix the garlic, parsley and lemon zest together. Sprinkle over each lamb shank. Serve with mashed potatoes and cannellini or borlotti beans.

Really Useful Stuff
You can also make this dish with a boned and rolled shoulder of lamb using the same ingredients for the sauce. Cook for about 2½ hours, or until meltingly tender. Serve with gremolata.

Guinea fowl with peas & pancetta

Guinea fowl are worth looking for – they are a delicious tasty bird, slightly smaller than a chicken. If you can't find them, use two medium-sized chickens instead.

Preparation time: 35 minutes
Cooking time: 1½ hours
Serves 4

2 guinea fowl
4 tablespoons plain flour
4 tablespoons olive oil
salt and freshly ground black pepper
150 g thickly sliced pancetta, diced
12 very small onions, peeled
2 leeks, washed and sliced in 5 mm thick rings
2 cloves garlic, crushed
500 ml white wine
500 ml chicken stock
1 bay leaf
250 g frozen peas, thawed
2 tablespoons chopped flat-leaf parsley

1 Preheat the oven to 180°C (Gas Mark 4).

2 Joint the birds by removing the drumsticks and thighs in one piece and by slicing off the breasts. Dust lightly with flour.

3 Heat half the oil in a large frying pan over medium heat. Season the guinea fowl and cook in batches until browned, adding a little extra oil if needed. Be careful not to overcrowd the frying pan, as the meat will then steam rather than sear. Transfer to a large casserole dish.

4 Heat the remaining oil in the frying pan over medium heat. Add the pancetta, onions, leeks and garlic and cook, stirring occasionally, for 7–10 minutes, or until the vegetables are tender and the onions are lightly coloured. Transfer to the casserole dish.

5 Stir the wine, stock and bay leaf into the casserole and bring to the boil over medium heat. Cover, transfer to the oven and cook for 1 hour, stirring occasionally. Stir in the peas, return to the oven and cook for a further 15 minutes. If the sauce needs thickening, remove the pieces of guinea fowl and keep warm, then reduce the liquid over high heat until it reaches a sauce consistency. Remove the bay leaf and season to taste. Stir in the chopped parsley and serve the guinea fowl with the cooking juices and vegetables from the pan.

Really Useful Stuff
Guinea fowl are worth looking for to use in this dish as they give it a gamier flavour. If you can't find any, chicken works just as well – use breast fillets and legs (with thighs attached).

Using red wine instead of white makes a nice variation.

You can also add some sautéed button or small mushrooms to the pot about 25 minutes before the end of cooking time.

Braised pork chops with cider & fennel

For this recipe, ask your butcher to cut you some good thick pork chops, with some fat left on. I love this dish – the combination of pork, fennel and cider gives a terrific flavour.

Preparation time: 25 minutes
Cooking time: 1¼ hours
Serves 4

4 pork loin chops
4 tablespoons plain flour
4 tablespoons olive oil
4 rashers streaky bacon, diced
2 golden shallots, sliced
2 leeks, washed and sliced in 5 mm thick rings
1 small fennel bulb, thinly sliced
2 cloves garlic, crushed
250 ml dry cider
1 brambly or granny smith apple, peeled, cored and coarsely grated
4 sprigs thyme
1 bay leaf
500 ml chicken stock
salt and freshly ground pepper

1 Preheat the oven to 200°C (Gas Mark 6).

2 Lightly dust the chops in the flour. Heat 2 tablespoons of the oil in a large frying pan over medium heat and cook two chops at a time, browning both sides. Add a little extra oil if needed. Transfer to a large casserole dish – the chops need to sit in a single layer.

3 Heat the remaining oil in the frying pan over medium heat and cook the bacon for 2 minutes. Add the shallots, leeks, fennel and garlic and cook, stirring occasionally, for 6–7 minutes, or until the vegetables are tender but not coloured. Transfer to the casserole dish.

4 Pour the cider into the pan, return it to the heat and use a wooden spoon to help lift any bits of meat or vegetables that are stuck to the base. Swirl the pan and pour the liquid over the pork.

5 Add the apples, thyme and bay leaf to the casserole and pour in enough stock to just cover the chops. Bring to the boil over medium heat, then cover, transfer to the oven and cook for 30 minutes. Reduce the heat to 170°C (Gas Mark 3) and cook for a further 45 minutes, or until tender, turning the chops occasionally. Remove the lid about 15 minutes before the end of the cooking time – this helps the chops colour nicely. Season well and remove the bay leaf. Serve with the juice, apple and leeks from the pan, and some mashed potato if desired.

Really Useful Stuff
You can use apple juice in place of the cider if desired, or white wine.

Fennel adds a nice subtle flavour to the braised chops, but you can leave it out if you like.

Beef goulash

It is the unique flavour of paprika that defines a proper goulash. Paprika is made by drying and grinding the sweet and hot capsicums (peppers) grown in Hungary. It's much milder than cayenne pepper and has a characteristic sweetness – its main purpose is to add flavour and colour, rather than heat. Look for paprika labelled 'noble sweet'.

Preparation time: 25 minutes
Cooking time: 1¼ hours
Serves 4

3 tablespoons plain flour
1 kg rump or chuck steak or lean beef,
    cut into 2 cm cubes
2–3 tablespoons vegetable oil
2 onions, thinly sliced
1 tablespoon sweet paprika
1 bay leaf
5 allspice berries, crushed
500 ml beef or chicken stock
    (or 500 ml water and 1 stock cube)
2 tablespoons cornflour
2 tablespoons tomato paste
Tabasco sauce
chopped flat-leaf parsley, to serve
sour cream, to serve

1   Place the flour in a clean plastic bag. Shake a few pieces of meat in the bag until lightly dusted. Repeat until all the pieces of meat are coated.

2   Heat 2 tablespoons of the oil in a large frying pan over medium heat. Cook the beef in batches until browned, adding a little extra oil if needed. Be careful not to overcrowd the frying pan, as the meat will then steam rather than sear. Transfer to a large casserole dish or lidded saucepan.

3   Add a little more oil to the frying pan if necessary and cook the onion over low heat until tender. Add the onion, paprika, bay leaf and allspice to the casserole and cook, stirring, for 2–3 minutes. Pour in the stock and bring to the boil. Cover the pan and simmer gently for 1 hour, stirring occasionally, until the meat is tender.

4   Mix the cornflour with 50 ml cold water and add to the casserole with the tomato paste and a dash or two of Tabasco sauce. Bring back to the boil and simmer gently for about 5 minutes or until thickened slightly. Garnish with chopped parsley and serve with sour cream.

Really Useful Stuff
Boiled egg noodles dressed with a little butter, chopped parsley and freshly ground black pepper make a tasty accompaniment to goulash.

Chinese-style red pork ›

Braising in soy sauce is a popular Chinese cooking method. It gives the meat a distinctive colour and flavour, and the braising liquid also makes a delicious sauce. You'll need to start this recipe a day in advance.

Preparation time: 25 minutes
Cooking time: 3 hours
Serves 6

1.5 kg pork belly, with bones and rind
200 ml light soy sauce
4 tablespoons Chinese rice wine or dry sherry
2 whole star anise
2 cloves garlic, peeled
3 spring onions, roughly chopped
4 x 4 mm thick slices ginger
1 tablespoon raw, demerara or light brown sugar
1 long red chilli, roughly chopped
about 600–700 ml chicken stock or water

1   The day before, put the piece of pork belly in a large ovenproof saucepan or flameproof casserole and add the soy sauce, rice wine or sherry, star anise, garlic, spring onions, ginger, sugar and chilli, along with enough stock or water to just cover the meat. Bring slowly to the boil over a low heat, cover and simmer very gently for about 2½ hours. Leave to cool and then chill overnight.

2   Preheat the oven to 190°C (Gas Mark 5). Skim any fat off the top of the cooking liquid. Remove the meat from the liquid, cut away the bones and cartilage from the underside of the pork belly and discard them (this makes it easier to carve later). Return the meat to the pan and then transfer to the preheated oven and cook, uncovered, for about 20–25 minutes, or until the skin is dark and crisp and the liquid has reduced a little.

3   To serve, remove the piece of pork from the cooking liquid and cut into 4 mm slices. Strain the liquid into a jug or bowl, to use as a dipping sauce. Serve the pork belly with noodles and sliced spring onions or steamed Chinese vegetables, if desired, and the dipping sauce on the side.

Really Useful Stuff
Pork belly is perfect for slow cooking. The method varies from cook to cook, but I always braise the pork in one piece and prepare it at least a few hours (up to 24) before I want to reheat and serve it.

You can follow the recipe using chicken, duck, beef or even fish, adjusting the cooking time accordingly. For red chicken, use leg pieces (with the thigh attached) and braise for about 45 minutes, or until tender.

Chocolate

Just quietly, my favourite indulgence is a 4 o'clock chocolate fix – I keep a secret stash both at home and in the office. In addition to this, of course there are many occasions when I eat chocolate in public, and I absolutely love to cook with it. This most versatile ingredient instantly becomes the star of any dish, whether it's a rich creamy mousse, dense chocolate cake or simply a mug of good-quality hot chocolate. Attention-seeking, sure, but I don't hear anybody complaining.

Hints & Tips

In its purest form (the raw cacao bean), chocolate has amazing health-giving properties. It is the number one dietary source of magnesium, and is exceptionally high in sulphur, the 'beauty mineral'. Plus it is rich in antioxidants, is a natural anti-depressant and, to top it off, an aphrodisiac! In fact, it contains over 300 identifiable chemical compounds, making it one of the most complex foods known to man.

Types of chocolate

Plain or dark chocolate: used for cooking, this may have anywhere between 30 per cent and 75 per cent cocoa solids (check the label). The higher the cocoa solids, the richer the depth of flavour. For most baking recipes I use a dark chocolate with about 50 per cent cocoa solids; for truffles or ganache, I prefer a higher percentage.

Couverture chocolate: used mainly for chocolate and confectionery, this has a high cocoa-butter content, which gives it a glossy appearance. Mostly used by professionals, it is quite expensive.

White chocolate: technically not chocolate as it doesn't contain any cocoa solids – just cocoa butter, milk and sugar.

Milk chocolate: contains similar ingredients to dark chocolate but with added milk (and usually sugar) – it has a mild, creamy, sweet flavour.

Cocoa powder: this is what is left when all the cocoa butter has been extracted from the roasted and ground cocoa beans. It is unsweetened and quite bitter, but has a good chocolate flavour when used in baking.

Chocolate chips: these are usually available in dark, milk or white chocolate. They are perfect for cookies, cupcakes and muffins as they tend to be lower in fat than eating chocolate, which means they don't melt as quickly and so magically stay whole during baking.

Drinking chocolate: a mixture of cocoa powder and sugar, which is added to hot milk to make hot chocolate.

How to melt chocolate

✱ Chocolate doesn't like to be overheated; it should never be melted over direct heat except when it is with other ingredients.

✱ Break the chocolate into small pieces or chop it using a sharp, clean knife (chocolate readily absorbs flavours so make sure the board or surface doesn't have any food odours). Transfer the chopped chocolate to a clean, heatproof bowl and set it over a saucepan of very hot (but not boiling) water, making sure that the base of the bowl doesn't touch the water. Stir the chocolate as it starts to melt. When melted and completely smooth, remove from the heat and set aside to cool slightly before using.

✱ Don't overheat the chocolate, or let any water or steam come into contact with it as it is melting – the chocolate may seize (become stiff). If this happens, you must start again with new chocolate.

Some basics

Hot chocolate sauce: put 150 g dark chocolate, 100 ml cream and 50 g unsalted butter (cubed) in a heatproof bowl set over a saucepan of very hot water and stir occasionally until smooth. If you like, add 1 tablespoon of brandy or liqueur at the end of the cooking time and remove from the heat. Drizzle over ice-cream or hot puddings. Any excess sauce may be stored in the fridge for up to 1 week (reheat over low heat before serving).

Chocolate ganache: bring 125 ml cream to just under the boil in a small saucepan. Remove from the heat and add 250 g chopped dark chocolate. Stir until smooth, then set aside to cool. When cool and set, beat with a wooden spoon until fluffy. Great as a filling or icing for cakes.

Chocolate truffles

Chocolate truffles are the ultimate chocolate treat, and this rich, elegant confectionery is so easy to make. I never worry too much about creating perfect little balls – in fact, I think odd-shaped truffles have a much more chic appearance.

Preparation time: 25 minutes, plus refrigeration time
Cooking time: 5 minutes
Makes 20

125 ml cream
250 g good-quality dark chocolate, roughly chopped
40 g unsalted butter, cubed
1 tablespoon Cognac or brandy
cocoa, for dusting

1 Heat the cream in a small saucepan and gently bring to the boil. Remove from the heat and add the chocolate and butter. Mix until smooth. Add the Cognac or brandy and stir well until combined. Cover and refrigerate until firm.

2 Using two teaspoons, shape the mixture into balls 2 cm in diameter. Roll each ball between the palms of your hands to smooth them out. If the weather is humid, making this difficult to do, roll the mixture into rough shapes, then freeze for 10 minutes and re-roll.

3 Coat the truffles by tossing in cocoa. They are best eaten fresh, but will keep in an airtight container in the fridge for up to 2 weeks.

Really Useful Stuff

Try rolling the truffles in finely chopped hazelnuts, macadamias or almonds instead of cocoa.

Vary the flavour by replacing the Cognac with Cointreau, Grand Marnier or cherry-flavoured brandy.

Generally, the darker and richer the chocolate, the less sweet it will be. Not everyone appreciates dark, bitter chocolate so I sometimes add a commercial dark chocolate bar as part of the mixture.

Hot chocolate mousse

This is a great recipe – it's made like a chocolate mousse but is then baked in the oven, giving you a soufflé-like pudding that's lovely and moist in the centre.

Preparation time: 20 minutes
Cooking time: 10 minutes
Serves 4

150 g dark chocolate, chopped
3 eggs, separated
3 tablespoons caster sugar
1 tablespoon brandy

You will also need
4 ramekins or heatproof cups

1 Preheat the oven to 200°C (Gas Mark 6). Lightly grease the ramekins or cups.

2 Melt the chocolate in a heatproof bowl set over a saucepan of hot water, stirring occasionally until smooth.

3 Whisk the egg yolks and caster sugar until frothy. Mix the chocolate into the egg yolks, then beat in the brandy and 2 tablespoons of very hot water.

4 Whisk the egg whites in a clean, dry bowl with electric beaters until soft peaks form. Fold a little of the whites into the mousse to slacken it and then carefully fold in the remainder. Mix until there are no streaks or pockets of egg white.

5 Gently pour the mixture into the prepared ramekins. Place the ramekins on a baking tray and bake for 7–8 minutes, or until risen slightly but still soft in the centre.

Really Useful Stuff
The mousse can be made up to 24 hours before cooking. Cover with plastic wrap and keep in the fridge until needed.

For a real treat, make a hole in the top of the cooked pudding and drop a small scoop of vanilla ice-cream in the centre just before you're ready to serve.

Chocolate fudge cookies

These cookies are made with melted chocolate, which gives them a fudgy, chewy textures rather than a crisp one. The cookies will be soft when they first come out of the oven, so let them sit on the tray for 5 minutes before transferring to a wire rack.

Preparation time: 20 minutes, plus refrigeration time
Cooking time: 15 minutes
Makes about 15

125 g dark chocolate, chopped
1 teaspoon vanilla extract
125 g unsalted butter, softened at room temperature
175 g light brown sugar
1 large egg
150 g plain flour
1 teaspoon bicarbonate of soda
3 tablespoons cocoa
250 g dark chocolate, extra, cut into s
   mall pieces or chocolate chips

1 Preheat the oven to 170°C (Gas Mark 3). Line two baking sheets with baking paper.

2 Melt the chocolate and vanilla in a heatproof bowl set over a saucepan of hot water, stirring occasionally until smooth. Allow to cool.

3 In an electric mixer, beat the butter and sugar for about 4–5 minutes until pale and creamy. Beat in the egg and the cooled chocolate until smooth. Sift the flour, bicarbonate of soda and cocoa over the mixture and gently fold it in. Stir in the extra chocolate pieces, then cover and place in the fridge for 20 minutes.

4 Roll heaped tablespoons of the mixture into balls and place on the baking sheets – making sure you leave enough space for spreading. Flatten the balls slightly with a fork.

5 Bake for 10–15 minutes or until firm (the tops may look a bit cracked). Cool on the sheets for 5 minutes before transferring to wire racks to cool completely.

Really Useful Stuff
When cool, store these cookies in an airtight container. They may soften slightly after a day or two.

Chocolate & cherry strudel

This recipe came about one Christmas when I was trying to avoid the whole traditional thing and serve something to suit the hoard of chocolate addicts in my family. It is very rich, so serve small slices.

Preparation time: 25 minutes
Cooking time: 40 minutes
Serves 6–8

5 sheets filo pastry
50 g ground almonds
3 tablespoons caster sugar
100 g unsalted butter, melted
icing sugar, to serve

Filling
100 g whole blanched almonds
250 g good-quality dark chocolate, chopped
2 tablespoons caster sugar
400 g tin pitted black cherries in syrup, drained
    and coarsely chopped

1 Preheat the oven to 180°C (Gas Mark 4) and line a baking sheet with baking paper.

2 For the filling, place the almonds in a single layer on a baking sheet and toast for 3–4 minutes. Allow to cool.

3 Place the toasted almonds, chocolate and sugar in a food processor and coarsely chop, using the pulse action. Set aside.

4 Lay out the pastry and cover with a damp tea towel while you work (to stop it drying out too much). Combine the ground almonds and sugar in a small bowl.

5 Lay out a sheet of pastry and brush with some of the melted butter. Top with a second sheet. Brush the second sheet with butter and sprinkle evenly with about a third of the ground almond and sugar mixture. Top with a third and fourth sheet and repeat the butter and sprinkling. Top with the final sheet of pastry and brush with a little butter.

6 Spread the chocolate mixture over the pastry, leaving a 3 cm border. Spread the chopped cherries along the centre. Tuck in the edges then, starting from the long edge, gently but firmly roll the pastry into a log. Place seam-side down on the prepared baking sheet and brush with any remaining butter.

7 Bake for 30–35 minutes, or until golden, then transfer to a wire rack to cool slightly. Trim the ends with a sharp knife, dust with icing sugar and cut into 3 cm slices. Serve with cream or ice-cream, if desired.

No-cook chocolate & hazelnut torte

Whenever a friend tells me they can't cook, I give them this foolproof recipe. Needless to say, it works every time. Serve this deliciously rich torte in small slices.

Preparation time: 25 minutes, plus refrigeration time
Cooking time: nil
Serves 8–10

100 g plain sweet biscuits
150 g good-quality dark chocolate, broken into pieces
1 large egg
1 large egg yolk
1 teaspoon vanilla extract
3 tablespoons caster sugar
100 g unsalted butter
100 g shelled hazelnuts, toasted and coarsely chopped
cocoa, for dusting
whipped cream or ice-cream, to serve

You will also need
an 18 cm springform cake tin

1 Lightly grease the tin and line the base with baking paper.

2 Put the biscuits in a plastic bag and lightly crush with a rolling pin – they should be broken into coarse, uneven pieces.

3 Melt the chocolate in a heatproof bowl set over a saucepan of hot water, stirring occasionally until smooth.

4 Put the egg, egg yolk, vanilla and sugar in the bowl of an electric mixer, and beat vigorously for 4–5 minutes, or until the mixture is pale and thick. Melt the butter in a small heavy-based saucepan and pour the hot butter onto the mixture in a steady stream while still beating at a high speed. Beat in the melted chocolate.

5 Using a large metal spoon, gently fold in the chopped nuts and crushed biscuits until combined. Pour the mixture into the prepared tin, spreading it gently and evenly. Cover with plastic wrap, then chill for at least 3 hours or overnight, until firm.

6 Remove from the tin and dust with cocoa. Serve chilled with whipped cream or ice-cream.

Marbled chocolate pudding with hot chocolate sauce

This rich chocolate pudding is made in a classic ceramic pudding basin, like a traditional Christmas pudding. Instead of steaming it in a saucepan, it is best cooked with the basin sitting in a roasting tin of water – a combination of steaming and baking.

Preparation time: 25 minutes
Cooking time: 1½ hours
Serves 4–6

100 g dark chocolate, broken into pieces
100 g white chocolate, broken into pieces
150 g butter, softened at room temperature
150 g light brown sugar
3 eggs, beaten
150 g self-raising flour

You will also need
a 1 litre ceramic pudding basin and a deep roasting tin

1 Preheat the oven to 160°C (Gas Mark 2–3) and lightly grease the pudding basin.

2 Melt the white and the dark chocolate in separate bowls over saucepans of hot water, stirring occasionally until smooth.

3 Cream the butter and sugar with hand-held electric beaters for about 5 minutes, or until light and fluffy. Gradually add the beaten egg, a little at a time, continuing to beat until well mixed. Sift the flour over the mixture and fold it in with a large metal spoon. Spoon half of the mixture into a separate bowl and stir in the dark chocolate. Combine the white chocolate with the remaining cake batter.

4 Spoon alternate, large spoonfuls of each mixture into the pudding basin until three-quarters full. Using a flat knife, swirl the mixture to create a marbled effect.

5 Cover the top of the pudding basin with a circle of baking paper and then with a larger circle of pleated foil. Fold the foil over the rim of the basin and tie securely with string. Place the basin in a deep roasting tin and transfer to the oven. Pour enough boiling water into the tin to come about a third of the way up the sides of the basin. Steam for about 1½ hours, or until firm. Turn out of the basin and serve with hot chocolate sauce (see page 28).

Really Useful Stuff
The mixture can be made up to 2 hours before steaming, and kept in the fridge until ready to cook. Once cooked, it should be served immediately.

It is much safer to pour the boiling water into the roasting tin once it is positioned in the oven.

Sunken chocolate soufflé cake ›

This is one occasion when a sunken cake is the effect you are looking for. The cake rises a little while cooking but because of the small amount of flour used, it sinks when it cools, giving you a lovely, rich, fudgy centre. A little instant coffee added to the recipe seems to intensify the chocolate flavour.

Preparation time: 25 minutes
Cooking time: 50 minutes
Serves 8

275 g luxury Belgian plain chocolate
175 g unsalted butter,
1 tablespoon strong black coffee
150 g caster sugar
5 large eggs, separated
50 g plain flour
icing sugar, to serve (optional)

You will also need
23 cm springform cake tin

1 Combine the chocolate, butter, coffee and half the sugar in a heatproof bowl set over a saucepan of hot water, stirring occasionally until the mixture is smooth. Remove from the heat and set aside to cool.

2 Preheat the oven to 180°C (Gas Mark 4). Lightly grease the tin and line the base with baking paper.

3 Transfer the chocolate mixture to a large bowl and add the egg yolks, one a time, beating well after each addition. Sift the flour over the mixture and fold it in with a large metal spoon.

4 In a separate clean, dry bowl, whisk the egg whites with clean beaters until they form stiff peaks. Gradually whisk in the remaining sugar.

5 Stir a large spoonful of the beaten egg white into the chocolate mixture to help slacken it a little, then gently fold in the rest with a large metal spoon. Pour the mixture into the prepared tin and bake for 45–50 minutes, or until the cake has risen and is firm to the touch, but still a little soft in the centre (a skewer inserted into the centre of the cake should come out a little damp).

6 Allow the cake to cool completely in the tin – it will sink a little as it cools. Carefully remove it from the tin, dust with icing sugar (if using) and serve.

Really Useful Stuff
If you are making this ahead, wrap the cooled cake well and freeze until needed.

Crumbles

Everyone loves a crumble. Comforting and traditional, they're a doddle to make, and incredibly versatile. With the combination of sumptuously sticky, slightly tart fruit and golden, buttery, crunchy topping, who could resist?

Hints & Tips

✳ To make a quick crumble, simply sprinkle a good-quality muesli or granola over fruit before cooking.

✳ For a quick filling, use a 400 g tin of fruit, drained. Peaches, apricots, plums and pears are all good choices, and even better with a few frozen berries added to the mix. Sweeten the fruit, if needed, and sprinkle with the basic topping on page 35.

✳ Always bake your crumble on a baking tray – this catches any bubbling juices that may overflow and burn at the bottom of your oven.

✳ A crumble is a great dessert to make in advance. You can cook it up to 24 hours before you need it, then store in the fridge and reheat in a 180°C (Gas Mark 4) oven until heated through and bubbling.

✳ I often make a large batch of crumble mixture (four times the basic recipe) and keep it in small lots in the freezer – it's great to have on hand for a fast winter treat. And not just for crumbles – leftover topping is delicious sprinkled on top of cakes, tarts or muffins before baking.

Crumble variations

Spiced crumble topping: add ½ teaspoon ground ginger to the basic recipe.

Nutty crumble topping: add 4 tablespoons roughly chopped pecans, almonds, hazelnuts or walnuts in place of the almonds.

Coconut crumble topping: add 4 tablespoons desiccated or shredded coconut in place of the almonds.

Oatmeal crumble topping: add 50 g rolled oats (porridge oats) in place of the almonds.

Chocolate crumble topping: add 50 g chocolate chips or chopped dark chocolate in place of the almonds.

Brown sugar crumble topping: use 150 g brown sugar in place of the granulated sugar in the basic recipe.

Gluten-free crumble topping: replace the plain flour with 50 g ground almonds and 100 g gluten-free flour.

Savoury topping: rub 100 g butter into 125 g plain flour until the mixture resembles coarse breadcrumbs. Stir in 50 g coarsely grated parmesan and season well. This is a particularly good way of making roasted vegetables really special. Place a mixture of roasted sweet potato, pumpkin, parsnip, carrots or beetroot in an ovenproof dish, sprinkle with the savoury topping and bake at 180°C (Gas Mark 4) for about 30–35 minutes, or until golden. The savoury topping is also great baked on top of ratatouille.

Apple & blueberry crumble

The slightly exotic flavour of blueberries goes beautifully with apples. Try using a combination of apple varieties, if they're available.

Preparation time: 25 minutes
Cooking time: 45 minutes
Serves 6

800 g bramley, granny smith or golden
   delicious apples, peeled, cored and chopped
185 g caster sugar
juice of 1 lemon
300 g blueberries

Basic crumble topping
150 g plain flour
150 g granulated sugar
125 g chilled butter, diced
50 g flaked almonds

You will also need
1 litre ovenproof dish

1 Preheat the oven to 180°C (Gas Mark 4). Lightly grease the dish.

2 Place the apples in a large saucepan with the caster sugar and lemon juice and cook over low heat, stirring occasionally, for about 10 minutes until slightly softened.

3 Transfer the apples and most of the juice to a large bowl and cool slightly. Stir in the blueberries, then transfer the fruit to the prepared dish.

4 To make the crumble topping, rub together the flour, sugar and butter with your fingertips until the mixture resembles breadcrumbs and starts to clump together. Alternatively you can put the ingredients in a food processor and pulse until just combined. Stir in the flaked almonds.

5 Sprinkle the crumble mixture evenly over the fruit and press down lightly. Place the dish on a baking sheet (to catch any juices that may bubble over) and bake for about 35–45 minutes, or until golden and bubbling.

Really Useful Stuff
This crumble can also be prepared in six individual 200 ml ramekins or ovenproof teacups (as pictured above) – just reduce the cooking time to about 25 minutes.

Apple and blueberry is a great basic combination, and variations are only limited by your imagination. It is good to use two different fruits, one of which should give off lots of bubbly juices when cooked (like berries). Pear and blackberry works well, as does quince and blackberry or raspberry.

You can make these ahead of time and then reheat in a 180°C (Gas Mark 4) oven before serving.

Banana & caramel crumble

This recipe brings together two of my two favourite things: caramel sauce and bananas. The combination works well, but save it for a chilly night!

Preparation time: 25 minutes
Cooking time: 50 minutes
Serves 6

50 g pecans
4–5 ripe bananas

Caramel sauce
60 g butter, diced
100 g light brown sugar
125 ml double cream

Crumble topping
125 g plain flour
125 g brown sugar
110 g butter, chilled and diced
50 g rolled (porridge) oats
30 g desiccated coconut

You will also need
a 1 litre ovenproof dish

1 Preheat the oven to 180°C (Gas Mark 4). Lightly grease the dish.

2 To make the caramel sauce, place the butter, brown sugar and cream in a small saucepan. Bring to the boil, then reduce the heat and simmer for 5 minutes.

3 To make the crumble topping, rub together the flour, sugar and butter with your fingertips until the mixture resembles breadcrumbs and starts to clump together. Alternatively you can put the ingredients in a food processor and pulse until just combined. Stir in the oats and coconut.

4 Place the pecans on a baking tray and toast in the oven for 2–3 minutes.

5 Slice the bananas and place in the prepared dish. Stir in the pecans and enough of the caramel sauce to moisten the bananas. Sprinkle the crumble mixture evenly over the fruit and press down lightly.

6 Place the dish on a baking sheet and bake for 35–40 minutes, or until golden and bubbling. Serve with custard, cream or ice-cream.

Really Useful Stuff
A handful of chocolate chips makes a delicious addition to the crumble filling.

Pear & chocolate crumbles

The classic flavours of pear and chocolate work really well in this crumble. The chocolate chips add a nice surprise when guests take their first mouthful.

Preparation time: 25 minutes
Cooking time: 40 minutes
Serves 4

4–5 ripe pears, peeled, cored and chopped
100 g brown sugar
juice of 1 lemon
1 teaspoon finely grated lemon zest

Crumble topping
100 g plain flour
100 g granulated sugar
75 g butter, chilled and diced
100 g dark chocolate chips

You will also need
four 250 ml ramekins, soufflé dishes or ovenproof tea cups

1 Preheat the oven to 180°C (Gas Mark 4) and lightly grease the dishes.

2 Combine the pears, brown sugar, lemon juice and zest and divide among the prepared dishes.

3 To make the crumble topping, rub together the flour, sugar and butter with your fingertips until the mixture resembles breadcrumbs and starts to clump together. Alternatively you can put the ingredients in a food processor and pulse until just combined. Stir in the chocolate chips.

4 Divide the crumble mixture among the ramekins and press down lightly. Place the dishes on a baking sheet and bake for 35–40 minutes, or until golden and bubbling. Serve with cream or ice-cream.

Really Useful Stuff
Add a handful of blackberries to the filling mixture.

Roast pears with muesli topping

This recipe uses toasted muesli or granola as an instant crumble, giving a wonderfully crunchy topping.

Preparation time: 10 minutes
Cooking time: 50 minutes
Serves 4

6 ripe pears, peeled
2 tablespoons chopped crystallised ginger (in syrup)
2 tablespoons syrup from crystallised ginger
finely grated zest of 1 lime
95 g brown sugar
30 g butter
150 g toasted muesli or granola

1 Heat the oven to 180°C (Gas Mark 4).

2 Halve the pears lengthways and scoop out the cores. Place the pears cut-side up in a baking tin (just large enough to hold them in a single layer) and top with the crystallised ginger.

3 Combine the ginger syrup, lime zest, brown sugar and 125 ml water in a small saucepan, bring to the boil, then pour over the pears. Dot each of the pear halves with a little butter.

4 Bake for 35 minutes, turning and basting occasionally, then remove from the oven and sprinkle with the toasted muesli or granola.

5 Return to the oven and bake for a further 10–15 minutes, or until the pears are tender and the topping is nicely golden and crisp. If the syrup starts to dry up, carefully add a little hot water to the dish (without getting the topping wet).

6 Serve warm or at room temperature, drizzled with the pan juices and accompanied by a generous spoonful of ice-cream, thick cream or crème fraîche.

Plum crumble

Plums are in season in early autumn, just as we start to think about crumbles. The red wine, ginger and vanilla give them a lovely, gently spiced flavour.

Preparation time: 15 minutes
Cooking time: 55 minutes
Serves 4

20 g butter
15 ripe plums, halved, stones removed
100 ml light red wine
100 ml golden syrup
3 tablespoons caster sugar
½ teaspoon ground ginger
pinch of allspice
1 teaspon vanilla extract

Crumble topping
150 g plain flour
150 g granulated sugar
125 g chilled butter, diced
50 g chopped walnuts

You will also need
a 1 litre ovenproof dish

1 Preheat the oven to 200°C (Gas Mark 6) and lightly grease the dish.

2 Heat the butter in a large saucepan over low heat, add the plums and cook gently for 2–3 minutes. Add the wine, golden syrup, caster sugar, ginger, allspice, vanilla and 2½ tablespoons of water and bring to the boil, stirring to dissolve the sugar. Simmer gently for about 5 minutes or until the plums are soft. Transfer to the prepared dish.

3 To make the crumble topping, rub together the flour, sugar and butter with your fingertips until the mixture resembles breadcrumbs and starts to clump together. Stir in the chopped walnuts.

4 Sprinkle the crumble mixture evenly over the fruit and press down lightly. Place the dish on a baking sheet and bake for 35–45 minutes, or until golden and bubbling.

Peach & raspberry crumble cake

A crumble topping adds a delicious crunchy texture to this fruity cake. There is no need to be particular when placing the fruit on top of the cake since it sinks slightly as it cooks.

Preparation time: 30 minutes
Cooking time: 1 hour
Serves 10

250 g plain flour
2 teaspoons baking powder
pinch of salt
200 g butter, diced, softened at room temperature
250 g caster sugar
finely grated zest of 1 lemon
4 eggs
185 ml sour cream or crème fraîche
100 g raspberries
2 large ripe peaches, peeled, stones removed,
    and cut into thin wedges
icing sugar, to serve

Crumble topping
40 g butter
40 g plain flour
40 g demerara sugar
40 g flaked almonds

You will also need
a 23 cm springform cake tin

1 Preheat oven to 180°C (Gas Mark 4). Lightly grease the tin and line the base with baking paper.

2 Sift together the flour, baking powder and salt.

3 Using an electric mixer, beat the butter, sugar and zest on a medium speed for 3–4 minutes, or until pale and fluffy and really well mixed. Continue to beat, gradually adding the eggs, and following each egg with a tablespoon of flour.

4 With the machine on a low speed (or with a wooden spoon) mix in the remaining flour, alternating with the sour cream, mixing until smooth. Spoon the batter into the prepared cake tin. Arrange the raspberries and peach wedges on top, pushing them into the batter slightly.

5 To make the topping, rub the butter into the flour and sugar until crumbly and then stir in the almonds. Sprinkle the crumble mixture over the fruit and press down lightly.

6 Bake for about 1 hour, or until golden, risen and firm to the touch. A skewer inserted in the centre should come out clean. Allow the cake to cool in the tin for 10 minutes before transferring to a wire rack to cool completely. Sprinkle with icing sugar before serving.

Really Useful Stuff
I have made this cake with just blueberries on the top, and you can also use raspberries or blackberries. Ripe nectarines, apricots, pears or even mangoes also work well here.

Mushroom & goat's cheese crumble ›

Crumble toppings also work well for savoury dishes. For this recipe, use one large mushroom per person and serve as a lunch dish or as an accompaniment to a grilled steak.

Preparation time: 20 minutes
Cooking time: 25 minutes
Serves 4

4 large flat mushrooms
2 tablespoons olive oil
1 golden shallot or small brown onion, chopped
1 clove garlic, crushed
75 g fresh white breadcrumbs
4 tablespoons freshly grated parmesan
1 tablespoon chopped chives
1 tablespoon chopped flat-leaf parsley
finely grated zest of ½ lemon
30 g butter, melted
salt and freshly ground black pepper
100 g log goat's cheese

1 Preheat the oven to 190°C (Gas Mark 5). Remove the stems from the mushrooms and roughly chop. Leave the caps whole.

2 Heat 1 tablespoon oil in a frying pan over medium heat and cook the mushroom trimmings, onion and garlic for 4–5 minutes, or until the onion is soft. Transfer to a bowl. Add the breadcrumbs, parmesan, chives, parsley and lemon zest and combine. Stir in the melted butter, then season well with salt and pepper.

3 Brush the mushroom caps with the remaining oil. Slice the goat's cheese log into four 1 cm thick disks and place one on top of each mushroom. Divide the breadcrumb mixture among the mushrooms and press down lightly.

4 Place the mushrooms on a baking sheet and bake for about 20 minutes, or until golden and tender.

Really Useful Stuff
Goat's cheese is good here as it puffs up when cooked, but other cheeses are also suitable – chunks of feta work well, as does mozzarella. Small rounds of camembert make a divine variation as the cheese goes very runny, almost like a sauce inside the camembert skin.

Curries

Curries appear in various forms all over India and southeast Asia. The term describes a dish with lots of sauce or gravy, and in those regions most curries are served as an accompaniment to rice or bread (the main part of the meal). In the West, it is often the other way around. No two curries are alike and no two cooks following the same recipe will dish up the same result – which is all part of the fun of cooking with spices.

Hints & Tips

* Make sure you use an enamelled or stainless-steel saucepan – avoid reactive metals like copper or aluminium. Use a heavy-based saucepan if you are frying the spices first.

* Traditionally Indian curries are cooked using ghee (clarified butter), but I generally use vegetable oil instead.

* Store any leftover dried spices in labelled screw-top jars, but don't keep them for more than 6 months – dried spices lose their intensity and start to taste dusty if stored for too long.

* I always use rubber gloves when handling hot chillies. The heat of fresh chillies varies but is most pungent when raw. Remove the seeds if you want less heat. If the curry is too liquid, reduce by boiling uncovered for a few minutes.

* If the curry isn't spicy enough at the end of cooking, you can fry some of the spices from the recipe with chopped green chilli for a few minutes, until soft. Then add this to the curry and heat through.

* Most curries can be made ahead and frozen. If you want to freeze a curry made with fish or prawns, simply make the sauce (leaving out the fish) and then freeze. The fish only takes about 5 minutes to cook, so add it when reheating the curry sauce after thawing.

* Remember that these recipes are only guides, and you can vary the spices to suit your tastes. Taste as you go, making adjustments where desired.

Thai red curry paste

Making your own red curry paste is easy, and it fills the kitchen with glorious aromas. To ensure a smooth paste, roughly chop all the ingredients first and then use either a blender or mortar and pestle (the shrimp paste must be added last to smooth out the mixture). If you use a mortar and pestle, it's important to roughly pound the firmer ingredients, such as lemongrass, before you add the softer ones.

Preparation time: 15 minutes
Cooking time: 5 minutes
Makes about 200 ml

3 dried long red chillies
1 teaspoon black peppercorns
1 teaspoon coriander seeds
1 teaspoon cumin seeds
10 small red chillies, roughly chopped
2 stems lemongrass, white parts roughly
    chopped
3 cm piece galangal, chopped
3 tablespoons chopped red Asian shallots
3 cloves garlic, crushed
1 tablespoon finely grated kaffir lime zest
    (or regular lime zest)
5 cleaned coriander roots, chopped
2 teaspoons shrimp paste

1   Halve the dried chillies lengthways and discard the seeds. Soak the dried chillies in a bowl of boiling water for 5 minutes, then drain.

2   Heat a frying pan over medium heat, add the peppercorns, coriander seeds and cumin seeds and toast gently until they begin to smell fragrant. Remove from the heat and either crush in a mortar or place in a blender.

3   Pound or blend the drained and fresh chilli, lemongrass and galangal. Add the shallots, garlic, lime zest, coriander root and shrimp paste and pound or blend to a smooth paste. You may need to add a little oil or water (or a dash of Thai fish sauce) to the mixture if using the blender, to help the blades turn.

Really Useful Stuff
Use this curry paste to make a classic red duck curry, as pictured above (see recipe on page 44).

Any leftover paste can be stored in the fridge for 7 days, or try freezing it in an ice tray (1–2 large ice cubes is about the right amount for a curry to feed 4 people) for up to about 3 months.

Goan prawn curry

A typical Goan curry has quite a thin sauce and should be a lovely orange colour (from the turmeric). This has a moderate heat and is deliciously spiced with cardamom, ginger and tamarind pulp and enriched with coconut milk.

Preparation time: 20 minutes
Cooking time: 35 minutes
Serves 4

750 g large uncooked prawns
2 tablespoons vegetable oil
1 large onion, thinly sliced
1 clove garlic, crushed
½ teaspoon ground turmeric
1 teaspoon ground coriander
1 teaspoon ground cumin
1 teaspoon chilli powder
4 cardamom pods
2 tablespoons chopped ginger
2 green chillies, finely chopped
400 ml coconut milk
1–2 teaspoons tamarind pulp

1 Remove the heads from the prawns, then peel and remove the veins. Wash the prawns in cold water and drain thoroughly.

2 Heat the oil in a large saucepan and fry the onion and garlic over low–medium heat for about 5 minutes. Add the turmeric, coriander, cumin, chilli powder and cardamom pods and cook, stirring occasionally, for a further 5 minutes, or until the onion has softened and starts to colour. Add the ginger and chilli and cook for 1–2 minutes.

3 Stir in the coconut milk and tamarind and bring the sauce to the boil. Reduce the heat and simmer gently for 15 minutes or until reduced and slightly thickened. The sauce should be of pouring consistency.

4 Add the prawns and simmer gently for about 5 minutes, or until cooked. Serve with steamed rice.

Really Useful Stuff
This curry can also be made with firm-fleshed white fish or salmon fillets. Cut the fish into 3 cm pieces and simmer in the sauce for about 5 minutes.

Basic chicken curry

This gives you a lovely mild chicken curry. Like many curries, the sauce adapts well to other ingredients, such as lamb, fish or vegetables, so feel free to experiment.

Preparation time: 20 minutes
Cooking time: 1 hour
Serves 2

2 tablespoons vegetable oil
1 large onion, finely chopped
2 cloves garlic, chopped
1 cm piece ginger, grated
1–2 green chillies, chopped
1 teaspoon ground coriander
½ teaspoon ground turmeric
½ teaspoon ground cumin
½ teaspoon garam masala
1 teaspoon paprika
2 tomatoes, chopped or grated
500 g skinless chicken thighs
salt and freshly ground black pepper
chopped coriander leaves, to garnish

1 Heat the oil in a large heavy frying pan over low heat and fry the onion, stirring frequently, for about 15 minutes or until deep brown. Add the garlic, ginger, chilli and spices and fry for another 1–2 minutes. Add the tomato and 125 ml water, turn up the heat a little and simmer gently for 10–15 minutes. The curry sauce should have reduced and thickened.

2 Add the chicken and toss in the sauce over low heat for about 5 minutes. Pour in 200 ml water, bring to the boil, then reduce the heat and simmer very gently for about 25 minutes or until the chicken is cooked. Season to taste and adjust the spices if needed. Add a little boiling water if the sauce needs thinning – it should be the thickness of pouring cream.

3 Sprinkle with chopped coriander and serve with rice or Indian bread.

Really Useful Stuff
To make a lamb curry, use 300 g cubed stewing lamb instead of the chicken. For salmon curry, use two salmon steaks and reduce the cooking time after the salmon has been added to 10 minutes.

Chicken saag

Even though this curry looks all green and healthy-looking from the puréed spinach in the sauce, it still has a moderate kick, courtesy of the chilli powder and curry powder. Reduce the chilli if you prefer a milder curry.

Preparation time: 20 minutes
Cooking time: 45 minutes
Serves 4

2 tablespoons vegetable oil
250 g English spinach leaves, rinsed and dried
1 long green chilli, roughly chopped
2.5 cm piece ginger, roughly chopped
2 cloves garlic, peeled
1 onion, finely chopped
2 bay leaves
½ teaspoon black peppercorns
4 tomatoes, skins removed, flesh chopped (see note below)
2 teaspoons Indian-style curry powder (see right)
1 teaspoon chilli powder
3 tablespoons plain yoghurt, plus extra to serve
8 chicken thighs

1 Heat 1 tablespoon of the oil in a large frying pan over high heat and add the spinach. Cook, moving the spinach around in the pan until it wilts. Transfer the spinach to a food processor, along with the chilli, ginger, garlic and about 3 tablespoons of water and process until smooth.

2 Heat the remaining oil in a large saucepan, add the onion, bay leaves and peppercorns and sauté over medium heat for about 7 minutes, or until the onion has softened and starts to colour. Add the tomato, curry powder and chilli powder and cook for a further 5 minutes, or until the tomato has softened.

3 Add the spinach purée and 200 ml water. Bring to the boil, then reduce the heat and simmer over low heat for about 5 minutes. Stir in the yoghurt, a little at a time. Add the chicken pieces to the sauce, cover and cook, turning occasionally, for about 25 minutes, or until tender. Serve with a dollop of yoghurt and warm naan bread or rice.

Really Useful Stuff
To skin tomatoes, make a cross at the base of each tomato with a sharp knife. Place the tomatoes in a large heatproof bowl or pan and cover with boiling water. Let them sit in the water for about 50–60 seconds, then pour off the water. The skins should now peel off the tomatoes (starting at the cross).

Indian-style curry powder

Use this in any recipe that calls for an Indian-style curry powder. Not only will it taste far superior to any commercially prepared one, it also allows you to adjust the spice and heat to suit your individual taste.

Preparation time: 10 minutes, plus cooling time
Cooking time: 5 minutes
Makes about 6 tablespoons

3 tablespoons coriander seeds
1 tablespoon cumin seeds
1 tablespoon mustard seeds
1 teaspoon cardamom seeds (removed from pods)
8 whole cloves
5 cm cinnamon stick, broken
2–3 small dried red chillies or ½ teaspoon ground chilli powder
½ teaspoon freshly grated nutmeg
1 tablespoon ground turmeric

1 Put the coriander seeds, cumin seeds, mustard seeds, cardamom seeds, cloves and cinnamon stick in a small frying pan. Place over medium heat and toast, stirring frequently, for 1–2 minutes. The spices will colour slightly and give off a wonderful aroma. Remove from the heat and set aside to cool.

2 Add the dried red chillies, grated nutmeg and ground turmeric and mix well to combine. Grind to a powder in a mortar and pestle, spice mill or electric coffee grinder. Store in an airtight container in a cool dark place for up to 6 months.

Really Useful Stuff
This curry powder is best stored in a screw-top glass jar – it should keep for several months.

Red duck curry

I love the heady flavour of an authentic red curry – that wonderful combination of heat, colour, saltiness and sweetness. Even though good-quality prepared red curry pastes are available, you get a far better result if you make your own. Pictured on page 41, this curry is moderately hot.

Preparation time: 20 minutes
Cooking time: 1 hour
Serves 4

400 ml coconut milk
250 ml chicken stock
1 stem lemongrass, sliced
3 kaffir lime leaves, sliced
3 cm knob ginger, chopped
3 duck legs or 4 duck breasts
1 tablespoon vegetable oil
4 tablespoons red curry paste (see page 41)
2 tablespoons palm sugar or soft brown sugar
4 tablespoons fish sauce
4 kaffir lime leaves, extra
300 g green beans, trimmed
salt and freshly ground black pepper
coriander leaves, to serve

1 Pour the coconut milk and chicken stock into a large saucepan, add the lemongrass, lime leaves and ginger and bring to the boil. Add the duck, then cover and simmer over low heat for 45 minutes, or until tender.

2 Remove the duck pieces and strain the liquid, reserving about 500 ml. Skim off any fat that has risen to the surface. When the meat is cool, shred into bite-sized pieces. This can be done the day before, if desired.

3 Heat the oil and curry paste in a wok or large saucepan and cook for about 2 minutes. Stir in the palm sugar and cook for 1–2 minutes, or until it caramelises slightly. Add the fish sauce and the reserved liquid and bring to the boil.

4 Add the shredded meat to the wok and bring to a gentle simmer. Stir in the beans and simmer for 5–7 minutes, or until tender. Season to taste. Sprinkle with coriander leaves and serve with steamed jasmine rice.

Really Useful Stuff
You can easily use chicken instead of duck for this recipe. The chicken only needs to be simmered (in the first stage of cooking) for about 25 minutes.

Simple sweet potato & pea curry ›

This delicious mild curry is easy to make and works really well with sweet potato, pumpkin, potato or cauliflower.

Preparation time: 15 minutes
Cooking time: 30 minutes
Serves 4

2 tablespoons vegetable oil
2 onions, sliced
600 g sweet potato, cut into 2.5 cm chunks
1 teaspoon cumin seeds
1 teaspoon ground turmeric
½ teaspoon chilli powder
2 cloves garlic, crushed
1 teaspoon grated ginger
3 tablespoons tomato paste
500 ml vegetable stock (or water)
150 g frozen peas
salt and freshly ground black pepper
3 tablespoons roughly chopped coriander leaves

1 Heat the oil in a large frying pan over medium–low heat and saute the onion, sweet potato and cumin seeds for about 15 minutes, or until the onion has softened.

2 Stir in the turmeric, chilli powder, garlic and ginger and cook for 1 minute. Add the tomato paste and stock and bring to the boil. Reduce the heat and simmer gently for about 10 minutes, or until the sweet potato is tender.

3 Add the peas and simmer gently until just cooked. Season to taste and sprinkle with coriander. Serve with steamed rice.

Custards & creams

An enduring memory from my childhood was my mother's delicious baked custard – a sublime combination of eggs, cream, sugar and vanilla. Indeed, as a teenager I planned to make my fortune by growing vanilla beans, but, like many childhood schemes, practicalities got in the way and it didn't eventuate. If I had to choose my all-time favourite dish it would definitely come from the next few pages – but the decision would be extremely difficult. I love them all and make them with great regularity.

Hints & Tips

✳ The most important thing to remember when making custard is to beat the egg yolks and sugar together in a bowl and then pour the warm milk or cream over them rather than adding the egg mixture to the saucepan. This stops the egg from scrambling. Once the egg mixture has been blended into the milk, the custard can be returned to the pan.

✳ Cook the custard slowly over low heat and stir continuously, making sure the spoon goes right to the corners of the pan. The bottom of the pan is where you will first feel the custard starting to thicken. If you are unsure whether the custard is ready, and to avoid it overcooking, remove the pan from the heat occasionally as it starts to heat and give the custard a stir, then return to the heat if more cooking is needed.

✳ If you're making baked custard (where the custard is thickened by cooking in the oven), cook it in a water bath. Sit the custard dish (or ramekins for individual custards) in a deep baking tin and add enough hot (not boiling) water to come two-thirds of the way up the sides of the dish. I usually place the baking tin with the dish of custard in the oven first and then pour in the hot water – this is safer than trying to carry a tin full of hot water and custard to the oven.

✳ With individual custards, it's a good idea to place a tea towel in the bottom of the baking tin before adding the ramekins. This keeps them steady, stopping them from sliding about when you move them in and out of the oven. After cooking, leave to cool in the water.

How to whip cream

✳ The cream to use for whipping should have a minimum of 35 per cent fat content (check the label); the higher the fat content, the quicker it will thicken.

✳ Make sure the cream is well refrigerated before you start. If I think of it, I often put the bowl and whisk in the fridge as well. The cream will whip more easily and to a higher volume when very cold.

✳ I use a wire balloon whisk, but you can use hand-held electric beaters if preferred.

✳ Start slowly. If you set electric beaters on high straight away, you'll get cream all over the place. As you whip, the cream will become lighter and foamier – at this stage it will start to thicken. Continue to whip until the cream stands in soft peaks. The peak should bend over at the top when you remove the whisk. When you get close to this point, slow down – if you take the cream too far, it will clump and separate.

✳ If you do over-whip the cream, sometimes gradually folding in 2–3 tablespoons of unwhipped cream (or milk) can help, but be careful not to stir too vigorously.

Classic custard

This is a traditional English-style pouring custard that is thickened with a little cornflour. The cornflour also helps prevent the custard from curdling.

Preparation time: 10 minutes
Cooking time: 10 minutes
Makes 750 ml

300 ml full-cream milk
300 ml double cream
6 large egg yolks
1 heaped tablespoon cornflour
4 tablespoons caster sugar
1 teaspoon vanilla extract

1 Combine the milk and cream in a medium saucepan and bring to the boil.

2 Whisk the egg yolks, cornflour, sugar and vanilla together in a bowl. Gradually mix the hot milk and cream into the egg mixture.

3 Return the mixture to the pan and cook over low heat, stirring constantly, until the mixture thickens to a custard consistency. Watch carefully and bring it to just under the boil, then immediately remove from the heat. Transfer to a bowl and leave to cool.

Really Useful Stuff
When the custard thickens it is important to remove it from the heat before it curdles. Remember that the heat of the pan will continue to cook the custard. To avoid this, place the saucepan in a sink filled with cold water or immediately pour the hot custard into a chilled bowl.

To stop a skin forming on the custard when cold, keep a layer of plastic wrap in contact with the surface.

Crème Anglaise

This is a pouring custard (thinner than the classic custard on the previous page). Serve warm or at room temperature with puddings, fruit pies or poached or fresh fruit.

Preparation time: 10 minutes
Cooking time: 10 minutes
Makes about 750 ml

650 ml full-cream milk
1 vanilla bean
6 egg yolks
125 g caster sugar

1   Pour the milk into a small saucepan. Using a sharp knife, split the vanilla bean in half lengthways, then scrape out the seeds and add the pod and seeds to the milk. Bring the mixture to simmering point over low heat.

2   In a large mixing bowl, whisk together the egg yolks and sugar for 4–5 minutes, or until the sugar has dissolved and the mixture is thick and pale. Gently whisk the hot milk mixture, including the vanilla bean pod, into the egg mixture.

3   Return this mixture to the saucepan and cook over low heat, stirring constantly with a wooden spoon, until the mixture thickens to the consistency of cream and coats the back of the spoon when lifted from the pan (rather than just running off the spoon). Stir right into the corners of the pan, and do not allow the mixture to boil or it will curdle.

4   Remove the pan from the heat as soon as you feel the custard thickening and strain through a sieve into a bowl, discarding the vanilla pod. Crème anglais can be stored in an airtight container in the fridge for up to 5 days. Simply bring to room temperature before use.

Really Useful Stuff
Crème Anglaise is usually served cold or at room temperature. If you want to serve it warm, heat it very gently over low heat, making sure you don't bring it to the boil.

Chocolate custard
Add 55 g grated dark chocolate to the warmed milk before adding to the egg yolks.

Orange custard
Instead of using a vanilla pod, add the finely grated zest of 1 orange to the milk at step 2 above.

Liqueur custard
Once the custard has been prepared, add 2–3 tablespoons of kirsch, brandy or any other liqueur or flavoured brandy and stir well.

Classic trifle ›

I base my trifle on my grandmother's – she always added a little sweet wine to the cream before whipping, and jelly was completely banned. Plain, store-bought cake is fine here. For a touch of glamour, I like to decorate the trifle with lots of edible silver balls or dragees, which are available at cookware shops or large supermarkets.

Preparation time: 25 minutes, plus refrigeration and standing time
Serves 8

250 g plain cake
4 tablespoons good-quality raspberry jam
100 ml Oloroso (sweet) sherry
300 g raspberries
750 ml classic custard (see page 47)
toasted flaked almonds and silver dragees, to serve (optional)

Syllabub cream
finely grated zest of ½ lemon
2–3 tablespoons caster sugar
125 ml sweet white wine
350 ml double cream

1   Cut the cake into slices 1 cm thick and arrange a single layer over the base of a large glass trifle bowl. Spread the layer with half the raspberry jam, then sprinkle with half the sherry and half the raspberries. Repeat with another layer of cake (you may not need to use all of it) and the remaining jam, sherry and raspberries. Pour the custard over the cake, cover with plastic wrap and chill for at least 3 hours.

2   To make the syllabub cream, mix together the lemon zest, sugar and wine and leave to macerate for 30 minutes. Strain through a fine sieve into a large bowl, then add the cream and whip until the mixture just holds its shape. Be careful not to overwhip it.

3   Spoon the cream over the trifle and return it to the fridge until you are ready to serve. Just before serving, decorate with toasted almonds and silver dragees, if desired.

Really Useful Stuff
I usually soak the sponge and add the custard the day before serving, then whip the cream and decorate just before eating.

‹ Custard tarts

I have fond memories of eating custard tarts from the school tuckshop in the 1970s. These days, bought tarts never seem to taste as good (perhaps good memories and nostalgia play a part), but this recipe lives up to expectations of soft custard and freshly grated nutmeg.

Preparation time: 20 minutes, plus refrigeration and standing time
Cooking time: 1 hour
Makes 4

1 quantity chilled sweet shortcrust pastry (see page 137)
425 ml cream
2 large eggs
3 large egg yolks
100 g caster sugar
1 tablespoon brandy
1 teaspoon vanilla extract
freshly grated nutmeg, to serve
cream, to serve

You will also need
four 10 cm loose-based flan tins (3 cm deep)

1   Preheat the oven to 190°C (Gas Mark 5).

2   Divide the pastry into two portions. Place one portion in the fridge while rolling the other. Roll out the pastry between two sheets of baking paper or on a lightly floured work surface until about 3 mm thick. Cut two circles large enough to fit the base and sides of two of the tins. Repeat with the remaining pastry.

3   Prick the pastry bases thoroughly with a fork and bake blind for 10–15 minutes. Remove from the oven and reduce the temperature to 170°C (Gas Mark 3).

4   Meanwhile, place the cream in a saucepan and heat until small bubbles appear at the edge of the pan.

5   Beat the eggs, yolks and sugar until thick, then stir in the brandy and vanilla. Pour the warm milk into the egg mixture and mix well.

6   Place the flan tins on a baking sheet. Pour the custard mixture into the pastry cases. Sprinkle with grated nutmeg and bake for 25–30 minutes, or until the filling has just set (but still wobbles). Serve warm from the oven with cream. Also delicious cold.

Really Useful Stuff
The flavour of freshly grated whole nutmeg is important here, rather than using the ready-ground version. Use a fine grater for best results.

You can also make one large tart in a 25 cm loose-based flan tin. Increase the cream to 500 ml and cook for 30–40 minutes

Orange & cardamom custards

Orange and cardamom is a favourite combination of mine, and it works particularly well in these little custards. The Grand Marnier helps to boost the orange flavour.

Preparation time: 15 minutes, plus standing time
Cooking time: 40 minutes
Makes 6

300 ml milk
450 ml cream
zest of 2 oranges in long strips
3 cardamom pods
2 eggs
8 large egg yolks
185 g caster sugar
2 tablespoons Grand Marnier

You will also need
six 200 ml ramekins

1   Heat the milk, cream, orange zest and cardamom pods in a large saucepan over low heat until small bubbles appear at the edge of the pan. Remove from the heat and set aside for 30 minutes to allow the flavours to develop.

2   Preheat the oven to 140°C (Gas Mark 1). Place a tea towel in a large baking tin and sit the ramekins on the tea towel.

3   Beat the eggs, yolks and caster sugar until thick. Gently reheat the cream and milk until steaming and then pour into the bowl of beaten eggs. Mix well and stir in the Grand Marnier.

4   Strain the mixture into a large jug, discarding the orange zest and cardamom pods, and then pour into the ramekins. Transfer the baking tin to the oven, then pour very hot (not boiling) water into the tin until it comes two-thirds of the way up the side of the ramekins. Cover the whole tin with foil.

5   Bake for about 30 minutes – the custards should be set, but still have a wobble to them when moved (they continue to cook a little while cooling). Allow to cool in the water. Serve at room temperature.

Really Useful Stuff
Another way to check if the custards are cooked is to stick a flat-bladed knife in the centre of the custard – it should come out clean.

Crème brûlée

Crème brûlée is a delicious baked custard with a hard caramel topping. Until kitchen blowtorches became available this had been hard to achieve at home as an intense heat is needed to caramelise the sugar.

Preparation time: 20 minutes, plus standing and refrigeration time
Cooking time: 40 minutes
Makes 6

500 ml cream
250 ml full-fat milk
1 vanilla bean
8 egg yolks
150 g caster sugar, plus extra for the topping

You will also need
six 10–12 cm diameter ovenproof dishes, 3–4 cm deep,
  and a cook's blowtorch

1 Combine the cream and milk in a saucepan. Split the vanilla bean in half lengthways, then scrape out the seeds and add the pod and seeds to the pan. Gently heat the mixture until it just reaches boiling point, then set aside for 10–15 minutes to allow the vanilla to infuse.

2 Preheat the oven to 150°C (Gas Mark 2). Place a tea towel in a large baking tin and sit the six dishes on the tea towel.

3 Beat the egg yolks and sugar in a bowl until pale and fluffy. Pour the warm milk into the eggs, whisking well to combine.

4 Strain the custard into a large jug, discarding the vanilla pod, and pour into the dishes. Transfer to the oven, then pour very hot (not boiling) water into the tin until it comes two-thirds of the way up the side of the dishes. Bake for 25–30 minutes, or until set, but still slightly wobbly in the centre. Cool, then refrigerate for at least 4 hours, or until ready to serve. They can sit in the fridge, covered, for up to 2 days.

5 To serve, sprinkle the top of the custards with an even layer of caster sugar. Melt the sugar by holding the blowtorch 10 cm away, then move it closer to caramelise the tops. Serve within 30 minutes.

Really Useful Stuff

One of the most important things to remember when making crème brûlée is the depth of the custard. Avoid those deep little soufflé dishes and use shallower, wider ones – a little like a gratin dish. The maximum depth of custard should be about 3 cm.

Instead of a vanilla bean, you can use 1 teaspoon vanilla extract.

Passionfruit syllabub›

Syllabub is a fancy 19th-century British version of whipped cream, and definitely worth reviving. The addition of sweet wine or liqueur transforms the cream into something really special.

Preparation time: 15 minutes, plus cooling time
Cooking time: 5 minutes
Serves 6

8 passionfruit
100 ml freshly squeezed orange juice
75 g caster sugar
100 ml sweet white wine or flavoured liqueur
300 ml double cream

You will also need
6 small glasses

1 Cut seven of the passionfruit in half and scrape the pulp into a small saucepan. Add the orange juice and sugar, bring to the boil and simmer for 2–3 minutes. Remove from the heat and allow to cool.

2 Pass the mixture through a sieve into a large bowl and discard the seeds. Stir in the wine or liqueur.

3 Add the cream. Using a balloon whisk or hand-held electric beaters, whip until the mixture starts to form peaks, being careful not to overwhip. Taste and add a little extra sugar, if desired. Spoon into six small glasses.

4 To serve, cut the remaining passionfruit in half and spoon a little of the seeds and pulp onto each dessert. Best served immediately.

Really Useful Stuff

To make a ginger syllabub, use about 3 tablespoons crystallised ginger (in syrup). Place the ginger and syrup in a bowl (chopping the ginger into smaller pieces, if desired) along with 100 ml sweet white wine and 300 ml double cream. Whip until it forms soft peaks, adding sugar to taste, if needed.

For a classic lemon syllabub, add the juice of 1 lemon, 2 tablespoons lemon curd and 1–2 tablespoons sugar to the cream. Whip until it forms soft peaks, adding extra sugar if needed.

‹ Panna cotta

The orange zest and vanilla extract give these little desserts a subtle but interesting flavour.

Preparation time: 15 minutes, plus standing and cooling time
Setting time: 4 hours
Serves 6

125 ml cup milk
1 × 7 g sachet (2 teaspoons) powdered gelatine
600 ml cream
185 g caster sugar
zest of ½ orange in long strips
1 teaspoon vanilla extract
fresh fruit, to serve (optional)

You will also need
six 125 ml moulds

1 Pour the milk into a small bowl. Stir in the gelatine and set aside for 10 minutes.

2 Place the cream, sugar, orange zest and vanilla in a saucepan and slowly bring to the boil, stirring until the sugar dissolves. Remove from the heat, add the gelatine mixture and stir until the gelatine dissolves. Set aside to cool for 15 minutes.

3 Strain the mixture, discarding the zest, and pour into the moulds. Refrigerate for at least 4 hours or until set.

4 To serve, dip the outside of each mould in hot water for 10 seconds, run a sharp knife around the inside and invert the panna cotta onto serving plates. Serve as is or with fresh seasonal fruit.

Really Useful Stuff
Panna cotta can be made ahead and stored, covered, in the fridge for up to 3 days.

Boodles orange cream

Like many dishes in this chapter, this creamy dessert is an adaptation of a Victorian British favourite. It was originally created in the kitchen of Boodles, a gentlemen's club in London.

Preparation time: 30 minutes, plus refrigeration time
Cooking time: 50 minutes
Serves 8–10

1 lemon
3 oranges
85 g caster sugar
500 ml double cream
4 tablespoons Grand Marnier
toasted almonds, to serve

Cake
175 g butter, softened at room temperature
175 g caster sugar
3 large eggs
100 g self-raising flour, sifted
100 g ground almonds
1 teaspoon baking powder
2 teaspoons finely grated orange zest

You will also need
a 20 cm square cake tin and 8–10 small glasses

1 Preheat the oven to 180°C (Gas Mark 4). Lightly grease the cake tin and line the base with baking paper.

2 To make the cake, put all the ingredients in a large mixing bowl and lightly beat with a wooden spoon until just combined. It is important not to overbeat the batter – just enough to make a smooth mixture.

3 Pour or spoon the mixture into the prepared tin, smooth the top and bake on the middle shelf of the oven for about 45–50 minutes. The cake is cooked when it looks well risen and golden, and the top should spring back when lightly touched with a fingertip. Let the cake sit in the tin for 5 minutes, then turn out onto a wire rack to cool.

4 Finely grate the zest from the lemon and two of the oranges and squeeze the juice of all the fruit. Combine the zest, juice and sugar in a bowl and stir until the sugar has dissolved.

5 Add half the mixture to the cream and whip until just starting to thicken. Gradually whisk in the remaining mixture, making sure that the cream is only at soft-peak stage.

6 Cut the cake into 1.5 cm cubes and use to line the bases of the glasses (you may not need all the cake). Drizzle with Grand Marnier, then spoon on the cream mixture. Decorate with toasted almonds and serve.

Really Useful Stuff
If making ahead of time, don't add the whipped cream until you are ready to serve.

Strawberry fool

This is the easiest dessert I know, and it's perfect in early summer when strawberries are at their best.

Preparation time: 15 minutes, plus refrigeration time
Serves 4

250 g strawberries, hulled
2–3 tablespoons icing sugar
250 ml double cream

You will also need
4 decorative glasses

1   Mash the strawberries with the icing sugar until soft and pulpy. (I prefer the slightly lumpy effect obtained by mashing with a fork or potato masher; however, the fruit can just as easily be pulsed in a blender.)

2   Whip the cream until soft peaks form, then stir into the fruit mixture. Taste and add a little extra fruit, if desired.

3   Spoon the fool into decorative glasses and place in the fridge for at least 30 minutes. Serve chilled with thin shortbread or wafer biscuits, if desired.

Really Useful Stuff

Although it doesn't dissolve as easily in the fruit, caster sugar can be used in place of the icing sugar.

Most crushed or chopped fruit can make a delicious fool, but soft fruits such as strawberries or raspberries, or ripe stone fruit like peaches or nectarines work the best. Equal quantities of strawberries and raspberries make a great combination.

Make a mango fool by using the chopped flesh of two mangoes, or a passionfruit fool by using the pulp of six passionfruit and a squeeze of lime juice.

The addition of a tablespoon or two of yoghurt gives an interesting flavour, but you may need to add a little more sugar.

Eton mess ›

Creamy desserts don't get much better than this. Whipped cream, ripe strawberries and meringue – what a combination!

Preparation time: 20 minutes
Serves 6

500 g ripe strawberries, hulled
2–3 tablespoons icing sugar
½ lemon
500 ml double cream
6–8 individual meringues or meringue nests

1   Purée half the strawberries in a blender with the icing sugar and a squeeze of lemon juice. Taste and add extra sugar, if needed. Pass the mixture through a coarse sieve.

2   Halve the remaining strawberries, or roughly chop them if they are large.

3   Whip the cream until soft peaks form – be careful not to overwhip.

4   Break the meringues into chunky bite-sized pieces and place in a large mixing bowl. Add the strawberries, then gently fold in the whipped cream. Carefully fold in all but 2 tablespoons of the purée to give a sort of marbled effect. Pile the whole lot into serving dishes, spoon the rest of the purée over the top.

Really Useful Stuff

Although this is traditionally made with strawberries, it is also delicious with raspberries, blackberries or even passionfruit. Ready-made meringues are perfect for this.

Deep-frying

Nothing beats a golden ring of calamari, a crispy fried artichoke, a crunchy sesame-coated prawn toast or a generous serve of fish and chips. And the only way to obtain such delicious morsels is to deep-fry. The process can put some people off, but I assure you it is fast and easy and the equipment can be as simple as a deep saucepan of oil and a slotted spoon.

Hints & Tips

* Use a deep-fat fryer, deep heavy-based saucepan or large heavy wok. Fill your deep-fryer or pan no more than half full of oil (one third full, if using a wok). Make sure there is enough oil to surround the food completely and enough space in the pan to accommodate the bubbling that happens when the food is first added. Never leave the pan unattended.

* You need to use a variety of oil that can take high temperatures. Some oils reach smoke point and begin to break down at high temperature. I usually look for sunflower or safflower oil or a mixed, generic vegetable oil.

* If you are using a deep-fryer with a temperature gauge, set the temperature for 180°C (except for chips – see page 62). Test the temperature by dropping a cube of bread into the oil – it should brown in about 15 seconds. If the oil begins to smoke, immediately remove the pan from the heat. It is vital that the oil is at the correct temperature before you start to fry.

* Always cook the food in small batches to stop the oil cooling down too much, which can cause the food to absorb too much fat and not brown as well.

* If using a deep-fryer, dip the basket in the hot oil before using – this prevents the food sticking to the basket.

* After deep-frying, oil can be filtered through a sieve lined with kitchen paper and reused – it should be replaced after a few uses or when dark.

* Dispose of cooking oil sensibly. Never pour it down the drain, as this can cause problems when it solidifies. Small amounts can be thrown out with the rest of your household rubbish – allow it to cool and solidify first.

Batter

With the exception of chips, wedges and some fried vegetables, most food is coated before frying, either with breadcrumbs, seasoned flour or a batter. This protects delicate food from the hot fat, keeping it moist and succulent, and gives the delicious crisp coating that is part of the joy of fried food. The type of coating depends on the type of food being fried. For example, a delicate piece of fish can be simply dusted with flour, whereas a larger piece of fish needs a batter. Batters containing egg whites (like a Japanese-style tempura) will be light and crisp, while batters containing whole eggs or yolks will be richer and thicker.

Beer batter: sift 250 g self-raising flour and ¼ teaspoon salt into a bowl and season well with salt and freshly ground black pepper. Gradually whisk in about 300 ml chilled beer to form a smooth batter. It should be the consistency of double cream and coat the back of a wooden spoon. The batter can be diluted with a little water or chilled beer, if needed. Take care to add the beer gradually – if you add too much liquid at the beginning it is difficult to work out the lumps. If lumps do occur, strain the batter through a sieve. Perfect for fish.

Tempura batter: sift 50 g plain flour, 50 g cornflour, 1½ teaspoons baking powder and a pinch of salt into a mixing bowl. Whisk together 1 egg and 200 ml chilled water, then mix into the dry ingredients to form a smooth batter. A teaspoon of sesame seeds makes a nice addition to the batter. Delicious with vegetables or seafood.

Fried calamari

This classic dish is easy to create at home. Rather than using a batter, I just dust the calamari in seasoned flour.

Preparation time: 15 minutes
Cooking time: 10–20 minutes
Serves 4–6

1 kg cleaned squid or calamari
vegetable oil, for deep-frying
200 g plain flour
sea salt and freshly ground black pepper
lemon or lime wedges, to serve

1 Preheat the oven to 160°C (Gas Mark 2–3) and line a baking sheet with baking paper.

2 Cut along each side of the squid or calamari bodies so they open out flat. Dry well with kitchen paper. Score the skin with a sharp knife and cut into 6 cm diamonds or 4 cm wide strips.

3 Pour the oil into a large deep saucepan, frying pan or wok to a depth of 3–4 cm and heat to 180°C (a cube of bread should brown in 20 seconds).

4 In a shallow dish, combine the flour, 1 teaspoon sea salt and a little pepper. Dip the squid or calamari pieces in the flour mixture and toss to coat. Shake off any excess.

5 Add the calamari to the oil in batches and cook for 5–10 minutes (depending on the thickness of the calamari) or until golden. Remove with tongs or a slotted spoon and drain on crumpled kitchen paper. Transfer to the prepared baking sheet and keep warm in the oven while cooking the rest. Taste and season with a little extra salt and pepper if necessary. Serve with lemon or lime wedges.

Really Useful Stuff

The trick to achieving really crisp fried calamari is the temperature of the oil. If you are cooking in batches, make sure the oil has returned to the correct heat before adding the calamari.

You can also cut the calamari into rings before frying. Don't throw away the tentacles – they are delicious fried!

Add a little celery salt to the seasoned flour. Or a pinch or two of chilli powder makes a spicy variation. The calamari are delicious served with mayonnaise or tartare sauce (see page 205).

Prawn toasts

I have loved prawn toasts since the first time I had them in Chinatown about 15 years ago. The addition of sesame seeds gives them a delicious crunch.

Preparation time: 15 minutes
Cooking time: 10 minutes
Makes 24

250 g uncooked prawns, peeled, deveined and roughly chopped
1 egg white
2 spring onions, chopped
1 teaspoon grated ginger
1 tablespoon roughly chopped coriander leaves
1 tablespoon cornflour
6 slices white bread
50 g sesame seeds
vegetable oil, for deep-frying

1 Place the prawns, egg white, spring onion, ginger, coriander and cornflour in a food processor and process using the pulse action until just combined, but still a little chunky.

2 Spread each slice of bread evenly with the prawn mixture and sprinkle generously with sesame seeds. Trim the crusts and cut each slice into quarters.

3 Pour the oil into a large frying pan to a depth of 2.5 cm and heat to 180°C (a cube of bread should brown in 20 seconds).

4 Add the toasts to the pan in batches, starting with the prawn mixture face down. Cook for 1–2 minutes, or until golden and crisp, turning to cook both sides. Repeat with the remaining toasts. Serve immediately.

Really Useful Stuff
To get ahead you can make the prawn mixture a few hours before cooking. Simply spread on the bread and fry when you're ready to serve.

Cheese croquetas

These delicious Spanish cheese croquettes make great nibbles to have with drinks and are perfect as part of a tapas plate.

Preparation time: 15 minutes, plus refrigeration time
Cooking time: 10 minutes
Makes about 12

125 g manchego cheese, finely grated
50 g fresh breadcrumbs
2 tablespoons finely chopped chives
pinch of paprika
2 large egg whites
salt and freshly ground black pepper
vegetable oil, for deep-frying

1 Line a baking tray with baking paper.

2 Combine the cheese, breadcrumbs, chives and paprika in a bowl.

3 Using a balloon whisk or hand-held electric beaters, whisk the egg whites in a clean bowl until they form stiff peaks. Using a large metal spoon, gently fold the breadcrumb mixture through the egg whites, and season with salt and pepper.

4 Using the palms of your hands, roll the mixture into walnut-sized balls. Transfer to the prepared baking tray and refrigerate for 30 minutes (or up to 2 hours if you want to make them ahead of time).

5 Pour the oil into a large frying pan to a depth of 1 cm and heat to 180°C (a cube of bread should brown in 20 seconds). Add the croquetas in batches and fry over medium heat, turning frequently, for 2–3 minutes or until golden. Drain on kitchen paper and serve hot.

Really Useful Stuff
Manchego is a delicious hard cheese produced in Spain. If it's not available, I generally use a mixture of parmesan and gruyère.

Deep-fried artichokes

If you fry artichokes at a low temperature until tender and then deep-fry again quickly at a higher temperature, the leaves open like petals, giving you a wonderful crunchy texture.

Preparation time: 25 minutes
Cooking time: 25 minutes
Makes 6

6 small artichokes
2 lemons, quartered
approximately 1 litre combined olive oil and vegetable oil
sea salt
good-quality mayonnaise (see page 205),
    flavoured with a squeeze of lemon juice,
    or salsa verde (see page 206), to serve

1 Bend back and snap off all the lower outer petals of each artichoke from the middle down to the base. Continue until you reach the leaves that are thin and half light green. Using a vegetable peeler or paring knife, peel the stem and trim to about 5 cm.

2 Slice the top off each artichoke, cutting across the top of the 'flower' with a large knife. Using a paring knife tip or a pointed spoon, gently remove the fuzzy inner choke at the centre of the leaves. Rub the trimmed artichokes with lemon to stop them going brown.

3 Pour enough oil into a deep saucepan or sauté pan to easily cover the artichokes. Add the artichokes, place the pan over medium–low heat and heat to a temperature of about 150°C (a cube of bread will brown in 35 seconds). Cook for 10 minutes or until tender, turning occasionally. Remove the artichokes and drain on kitchen paper.

4 Increase the heat to medium–high and bring the oil to 180°C (a cube of bread will brown in 20 seconds). Add two artichokes at a time and fry for about 30 seconds, or until the leaves unfold and turn golden brown.

5 Drain on kitchen paper and sprinkle with sea salt. Serve immediately with lemon-flavoured mayonnaise or salsa verde.

Really Useful Stuff
If you can't find small artichokes, use the normal size but make sure you take off most of the outer leaves until you reach the pale green ones, and cut each into four wedges.

Stuffed zucchini flowers

Zucchini flowers are usually available in early summer. They have a subtle flavour and delicate texture, and are delicious filled with this fresh ricotta stuffing.

Preparation time: 30 minutes, plus standing time
Cooking time: 20 minutes
Serves 4

16 zucchini (courgette) flowers
250 g fresh ricotta
75 g freshly grated parmesan
finely grated zest of ½ lemon
salt and freshly ground black pepper
vegetable oil, for deep-frying

Batter
250 g plain flour
1 teaspoon salt
120 ml olive oil
385 ml warm water
2 egg whites

1 To make the batter, sift the flour and salt into a bowl and make a well in the centre. Mix the oil with the warm water, pour into the bowl and whisk until you have a smooth batter. Leave for at least an hour, then beat the egg whites until soft peaks form and gently fold into the batter.

2 To clean the zucchini flowers, gently brush off any dirt with a dry tea towel (don't rinse them with water). Check inside for any insects and shake them out. Open the flowers slightly and remove the stamens.

3 Combine the ricotta, parmesan and lemon zest in a large bowl and season to taste with salt and pepper. Carefully place 1–2 tablespoons of the cheese mixture into each flower, being careful not to overfill, and twist the ends to close.

4 Pour the oil into a large saucepan to a depth of 6 cm and heat to 180°C (a cube of bread should brown in 20 seconds). Line a plate with kitchen paper. When the oil is ready, dip four zucchini flowers into the batter (using tongs), then add to the oil and deep-fry over medium heat for 3–4 minutes or until golden brown. Remove with a slotted spoon and transfer to the plate to drain. Repeat with the remaining zucchini flowers, reheating the oil between batches. Serve immediately.

Really Useful Stuff
You can stuff the flowers up to 12 hours before you are ready to cook them. Place on a tray lined with baking paper, cover with plastic wrap and refrigerate until ready to fry.

Chopped mozzarella and anchovies make a great variation on the stuffing.

Beer-battered fish

Even though I love fish and chips by the seaside, I still think the best fish and chips are made freshly at home.

Preparation time: 10 minutes
Cooking time: 20 minutes
Serves 4

4 × 200 g white fish fillets (try flathead or haddock)
salt and freshly ground black pepper
flour, for dusting
1 quantity beer batter (see page 58)
lemon wedges, to serve

1   Preheat the oven to 160°C (Gas Mark 2–3) and line a baking sheet with baking paper.

2   Season the fish fillets with salt and lightly dust them with seasoned flour.

3   Heat a deep-fryer or large, deep saucepan filled with oil to a depth of 5 cm to 180°C (a cube of bread will brown in 20 seconds).

4   Cook two fillets at a time. Pick up each fillet with a pair of tongs and dip into the batter, then let it drain for a few seconds. Carefully lower each fillet into the hot fat and fry, turning once, for 8–10 minutes, or until golden and crispy. Remove from the pan, drain on kitchen paper and transfer to the prepared baking sheet. Place in the oven to keep warm while you fry the remaining fillets.

5   Serve the battered fish with chips, lemon wedges and salad.

Really Useful Stuff
You can replace the beer in the batter with water or soda water if desired.

If making the batter ahead of time, it may need thinning a little before use as it can thicken while standing.

Chips

The secret to good chips lies in using the correct potatoes and cooking the chips twice. Look for potatoes labelled as suitable for frying or chipping.

Preparation time: 15 minutes
Cooking time: 15 minutes
Serves 6

6–8 large floury potatoes, such as desiree, maris piper or King Edward
sunflower or vegetable oil, for deep-frying
sea salt

1   Peel the potatoes and cut into finger-length pieces or thin wedges. Rinse in cold water, drain and pat dry with kitchen paper (washing away the starch helps make crisper chips).

2   Heat a deep-fryer or large, deep saucepan filled with oil to a depth of 5–6 cm to 150°C (a cube of bread will brown in 35 seconds). Add the potatoes and fry gently over low heat for 8–10 minutes, or until they are tender but not coloured too much. Remove from the pan with a slotted spoon and drain on kitchen paper. You can do this up to 2 hours before the final frying.

3   When ready to serve, increase the temperature of the oil to 180°C (a cube of bread will brown in 20 seconds), return the chips to the pan and cook for 3–4 minutes, or until golden and crispy. Drain, then transfer to a metal bowl and toss with a little sea salt. Serve immediately.

Really Useful Stuff
If using potato varieties with smooth skin (such as desiree), there is no need to peel them – just scrub and dry, then cut into thin wedges.

Dips & dippers

I grew up in the days when French onion dip and crackers were served at most drinks parties. Dips are indeed a great idea for entertaining and a wonderfully social dish (lots of people gathered around a bowl of dip is a sure way to make new friends), but these days I prefer a more updated ritual, leaving the 'French onion' version to my memories.

A few easy dippers

Belgium endive leaves
The separated leaves from endive (witlof) make great dippers. Separate the leaves by cutting off the base and carefully prying the leaves apart. Look for other small firm leaves like little gem, radicchio or baby cos.

Cheese straws
Preheat the oven to 200°C (Gas Mark 6) and line a baking sheet with baking paper. Brush a sheet of ready-rolled puff pastry with a little melted butter and scatter with grated cheddar and parmesan. Cut into lengths about 1 cm wide and twist into loose spirals. Place on the baking sheet and bake for 10–15 minutes, or until golden.

Chilli pita triangles
Preheat the oven to 180°C (Gas Mark 4). Split a pita bread in half lengthways, giving you two thin rounds. Brush with olive oil and sprinkle with a little chilli powder or cayenne pepper. Transfer to a large baking sheet and bake until crisp. Remove from the oven and cut into triangles.

Olive oil toasts
Preheat the oven to 160°C (Gas Mark 2–3). Slice French bread or ciabatta into thin slices and brush on both sides with olive oil. Place in a single layer on a large baking sheet and bake for 10 minutes, or until dry and crisp, turning once.

Roast cob loaf
A hollowed-out and baked cob loaf makes a great vessel for serving dip. To do this, preheat the oven to 180°C (Gas Mark 4). Cut the top off a small cob or round loaf and empty out the shell by pulling out chunks of bread. Break the chunks of bread into pieces about 1 cm thick and as long as you can make them. Place the bread pieces and the cob shell on a baking sheet and bake for 10–15 minutes, or until dry and crisp (keep an eye on them – the bread pieces may cook more quickly than the cob). Remove and allow to cool. Fill the cob with dip and serve with the crusty bread pieces on the side.

See also grissini (page 8) and very easy cheddar biscuits (page 4).

Spiced hummus

Hummus is quick and easy to make using tinned chickpeas. It may be used as a dip or as an accompaniment to grilled meat and chicken – grilled lamb chops with hummus is an unbeatable combination.

Preparation time: 10 minutes
Cooking time: nil
Makes about 250 ml

425 g tin chickpeas, drained and rinsed
4 cloves garlic, crushed
3 tablespoons lemon juice
3 tablespoons tahini
½ teaspoon ground cumin
¾ teaspoon cayenne pepper
1 teaspoon sweet paprika
3 tablespoons olive oil
salt and freshly ground black pepper
extra virgin olive oil, to serve

1 Place the chickpeas, garlic, lemon juice, tahini, and spices in the bowl of a food processor. With the motor running, slowly add the olive oil and process until smooth. Add a little extra oil or lemon juice if the mixture is too thick, and season to taste with salt and pepper.

2 Transfer to a serving bowl. Drizzle with extra virgin olive oil and serve with pita bread. Any leftover hummus can be stored in an airtight container in the fridge for 2–3 days.

Really Useful Stuff
Make sure you drain and rinse the chickpeas before using.

Tzatziki

Tzatziki is a simple Greek dip made with cucumber and yoghurt. It is delicious as a classic dip served with vegetables and other dippers, but is also a great sauce to go with grilled lamb, chicken or fish, hamburgers or roast vegetables.

Preparation time: 10 minutes, plus standing time
Cooking time: nil
Makes about 500 ml

400 g Greek-style plain yoghurt
salt and freshly ground black pepper
2 small cucumbers, halved lengthways and seeds removed
1 clove garlic, crushed
3 tablespoons chopped mint, plus extra to serve
1 tablespoon chopped dill
1 tablespoon olive oil
lemon juice

1 Combine the yoghurt with 1 teaspoon salt. Line a sieve with muslin (or a clean Chux or J-cloth) and pour in the salted yogurt. Sit the sieve over a bowl and leave to drain for about 2 hours.

2 Grate the cucumber halves on a coarse grater and place in another lined sieve or colander. Lightly salt the cucumber and leave to drain over a bowl for about 30 minutes.

3 Combine the yoghurt, cucumber, garlic, mint, dill and olive oil. Add a squeeze of lemon juice, to taste. Season with salt and pepper if needed, then cover and place in the fridge to chill before serving.

Really Useful Stuff
Tzatziki can be made without draining the yoghurt but will be quite wet if not used immediately. Draining the yoghurt gives the dip a much better texture.

Spiced carrot purée with feta

Carrots work really well with spices and salt, and blend to make a delicious purée. Roasting the carrots brings out their sweetness, giving a great flavour contrast to the saltiness of the feta.

Preparation time: 20 minutes
Cooking time: 45 minutes
Makes about 250 ml

700 g organic carrots
1 head garlic, skin on
3 tablespoons olive oil
Tabasco sauce, to taste
2 tablespoons plain yoghurt
2 tablespoons chopped mint
salt and freshly ground black pepper
100 g feta
1 tablespoon black sesame seeds
extra virgin olive oil, to serve (optional)

1   Preheat the oven to 200°C (Gas Mark 6).

2   Scrub the carrots and cut into 2.5 cm pieces. Place in a roasting tin with the garlic and drizzle with the olive oil. Roast, shaking the tin every 15 minutes, for about 45 minutes, or until the carrots are soft. Transfer to a large bowl and allow to cool a little.

3   Slice the head of garlic in half horizontally and squeeze the soft garlic paste over the carrots in the bowl. Either mash with a fork or process in a food processor until just smooth (a little bit of texture is good). Add a few drops of Tabasco and stir in the yoghurt and half the mint. Season to taste with salt, pepper and extra Tabasco, if needed. Allow to cool slightly.

4   Spoon the mixture into a shallow bowl and top with crumbled feta, sesame seeds and the remaining mint. Drizzle with a little extra olive oil, if desired. This is good served with toasted pita bread cut into triangles.

Really Useful Stuff
You can make the carrot purée ahead of time, then crumble the feta over the top before serving.

This dip is also delicious made with sweet potatoes. Follow the recipe above, but reduce the roasting time to about 15 minutes or until just tender.

Quail eggs with dipping spice

Quail eggs are the perfect size for finger food and I often serve this unusual dish at drinks parties. The idea is to shell the eggs, dip them in the spiced salt, then pop them in your mouth.

Preparation time: 10 minutes
Cooking time: 5 minutes
Makes 12

12 quail eggs
2 teaspoons sea salt
½ teaspoon freshly ground black pepper
½ teaspoon ground coriander
¼ teaspoon paprika
pinch of chilli powder
2 teaspoons sesame seeds

1   Place the eggs in a saucepan full of cold water over medium heat and bring to the boil. Simmer for about 3 minutes, then pour off the water and refill the pan with cold water (this helps to stop the cooking). Set aside to cool.

2   Meanwhile, make a spiced salt mixture by combining the salt, pepper, coriander, paprika, chilli and sesame seeds. Transfer to a small serving bowl.

3   Shell the eggs and serve with the spiced salt.

Really Useful Stuff
Boiled quail eggs are also delicious served with za'atar, a Middle Eastern spice mix. To make za'atar, combine 2 teaspoons sea salt, 1 teaspoon sesame seeds, ¼ teaspoon ground cumin and ½ teaspoon chopped dried thyme.

For a variation on the spiced salt, replace some of the sea salt with celery salt. Alternatively, serve the eggs with a simple mixture of celery salt, ground black pepper and sesame seeds.

Chilli dipping sauce

This Vietnamese-style sauce is great for dipping fresh cooked prawns, spring rolls or Thai fish cakes. The flavour should be a balance of sweet, sour, salt, chilli and garlic.

Preparation time: 10 minutes
Cooking time: nil
Makes about 200 ml

3 tablespoons fish sauce
2 tablespoons rice vinegar
2 tablespoons lime juice
2 teaspoons palm sugar or soft brown sugar
2–3 red chillies, seeded and finely sliced
1 clove garlic, finely chopped
1 spring onion, green parts only, finely sliced

1   Combine the fish sauce, vinegar and lime juice in a small bowl, add the sugar and stir to dissolve.

2   Stir in the chilli, garlic and spring onion. Taste and adjust the flavours if necessary by adding more lime juice, sugar, or even a little water. Stir well and serve immediately (if you make it ahead of time, the chilli flavour can often dominate).

Really Useful Stuff
Try adding 1–2 teaspoons chopped coriander leaves or some coarsely grated carrot (to add some crunch). There are no fixed rules with this sauce – taste as you go and adjust the balance of flavours to suit you.

Spiced prawn dip ›

This lightly spiced prawn purée is best made on the day you want to eat it.

Preparation time: 15 minutes, plus refrigeration time
Cooking time: 10 minutes
Makes about 500 ml

50 g butter
2 cloves garlic, crushed
1 long red chilli, seeds removed and chopped
600 g uncooked prawns, peeled and deveined
2 tablespoons sour cream
1 tablespoon lemon juice
1 tablespoon roughly chopped flat-leaf parsley
freshly grated nutmeg or mace
Tabasco sauce (optional)
salt and freshly ground black pepper

1   Heat the butter in a large frying pan and cook the garlic and chilli, stirring occasionally, for 3–4 minutes, or until softened. Add the prawns and cook until they are pink and cooked through. Allow to cool a little.

2   Transfer the mixture to a food processor, add the sour cream and process using the pulse action until coarsely chopped. Don't overprocess – it should not be smooth.

3   Spoon the mixture into a bowl and stir in the lemon juice, parsley and nutmeg. Add a few drops of Tabasco, if desired, and season to taste with salt and pepper. Chill for 30 minutes before serving with toasted bread slices.

Really Useful Stuff
If you want to make this in advance, cook the garlic and prawn mixture up to 2 hours ahead, then continue from step 2 and chill before serving.

Fish & fish cakes

Although I never really appreciated it at the time, I was extremely lucky to have grown up by the sea – not only for the beauty of the place, but for the thrill of being able to catch my own supper most days after school. Sadly, these days I have to get in the queue at the fish markets like everyone else, but I've never lost my sense of excitement about cooking fish or of seeing the huge variety of seafood available. Remember to make friends with your fishmonger and to seek advice as to what is best and in season; availability and price vary according to time, tide, luck, risk and weather.

Hints & Tips

Choosing your fish

✱ Go to a fishmonger that you know or one that has a good turnover. Don't be afraid to ask your fishmonger to fillet, scale and remove any fins as required. I always ask for the bones, and either make fish stock with them straightaway or freeze them and use to make a large batch of stock when needed.

✱ In whole fish the eyes should look bright and the scales should be moist and shiny. Let your nose be your guide – the fish should have a pleasant smell and not smell too fishy or of ammonia.

✱ You will need about 400–500 g per person for a fish on the bone, and about 250–300 g per person for a fillet.

✱ Anyone who is a little nervous about cooking fish should start with salmon – it is incredibly versatile, works well with simple cooking methods such as baking or roasting, and is available as cutlets, fillets or as a whole fish.

✱ Try to cook your fish as soon as possible after purchasing. If storing overnight, rinse it, wrap it in foil and place in the coldest part of the fridge (usually at the bottom). Placing a freezer pack on top of the parcel is also a good idea.

When is it cooked?

✱ Remember that it is the thickness of the fish rather than the length that determines the cooking time. When fish is cooked, the flesh will change from translucent to opaque and will flake easily – use the tip of a knife and insert it into the thickest part of the fish. With a whole fish, the eye will turn white when the fish is cooked, and the fins should pull easily from the fish.

✱ Be aware that a large baked fish will continue to cook when removed from the oven, so it should be served immediately to avoid overcooking.

✱ Some fish, such as tuna or salmon, are best served a little undercooked. Salmon makes this particularly easy to gauge as it has an in-built cooking guide: it changes colour from dark pink to a pale opaque pink as it cooks.

Fish cakes

✱ Use cheaper varieties of white fish for your fish cake recipes, or two different types of fish or seafood. If you are using two types (for example, white fish and salmon), chop one a little coarser than the other, giving you a nice variety of tastes and textures.

✱ To make fresh breadcrumbs, remove the crusts from day-old bread and cut into chunks. Process in a food processor until breadcrumbs form. Store in the fridge for 1–2 days or freeze in a plastic freezer bag until ready to use.

✱ Check the seasoning before cooking the fish cakes. Fry a small amount of the mixture until cooked through and taste it, then adjust the seasoning as needed.

✱ It is best to chill the fish cakes well before cooking – this helps to firm them up and stops them falling apart when cooking. Rolling un-crumbed cakes in a little flour will also help them keep their shape.

✱ All of the fishcake recipes in this chapter can be assembled and refrigerated for up to 8 hours before cooking.

✱ Alternatively, you can pan-fry the fish cakes until golden-brown, allow to cool and then refrigerate for up to 12 hours. Reheat the cakes in a preheated 200°C (Gas Mark 6) oven for 10–14 minutes, or until cooked though.

✱ Fish cakes are best served with lemon or lime wedges and a simple sauce. I love them with good-quality bought or homemade mayonnaise (see page 205) but you can also use crème fraîche, sour cream or plain yoghurt mixed with fresh herbs such as basil, chives or chervil.

Fish baked with couscous

These parcels are a real visual surprise when opened. Allow your guests to open their own at the table so they enjoy the aromas that are released.

Preparation time: 15 minutes, plus standing time
Cooking time: 20 minutes
Serves 4

200 g couscous
6 spring onions, thinly sliced
finely grated zest of 1 lemon
1 teaspoon ground cumin
pinch of saffron threads
2 tablespoons roughly chopped flat-leaf parsley
2 tablespoons roughly chopped coriander leaves
18–20 cherry tomatoes, halved
salt and freshly ground black pepper
4 thick white fish fillets (cod, barramundi or snapper)
extra virgin olive oil, for brushing and drizzling
4 thin slices lemon
lemon wedges, to serve

1 Preheat the oven to 200°C (Gas Mark 6).

2 Place the couscous, spring onion, lemon zest and cumin in a large heatproof bowl. Add the saffron threads to 400 ml water and bring to the boil. Pour the water over the couscous, cover tightly with plastic wrap and set aside for 7–10 minutes. Stir in the parsley, coriander and cherry tomatoes and toss to fluff up the couscous. Season well with salt and pepper.

3 Tear off four sheets of foil about 45 cm in length. Brush the centre with a little olive oil and place one quarter of the couscous in the centre of each. Top with a fish fillet and a slice of lemon. Drizzle with a little extra virgin olive oil and season lightly. Bring the edges of the foil over to enclose the fish and seal well by folding the edges. Make sure you leave some air space in the parcels – they should be securely sealed but not wrapped tightly.

4 Place the fish parcels on a large baking sheet and bake for 15–20 minutes (the parcels should have puffed up a little).

5 Serve on warm plates with lemon wedges.

Really Useful Stuff
You can assemble the parcels up to 6 hours before cooking – just place in a preheated oven when you're ready to cook.

Italian-style stuffed sardines

Sardines are well worth eating as they contain high levels of omega fats. The herby stuffing balances the flavour of these lovely small fish. Ask your fishmonger to remove the heads and clean, gut and butterfly the sardines – this way they will lay nice and flat.

Preparation time: 20 minutes
Cooking time: 20 minutes
Serves 4–8, depending on the size of the sardines

16 sardines, butterflied
3 tablespoons olive oil
sea salt and freshly grated black pepper
400 g cherry tomatoes, halved (or quartered if large)
1 clove garlic, crushed
squeeze of lemon juice
1 tablespoon balsamic vinegar

Stuffing
300 g ricotta
50 g fresh breadcrumbs
3 tablespoons freshly grated parmesan
2 eggs, beaten
2 tablespoons chopped flat-leaf parsley
2 tablespoons chopped basil
1 clove garlic, chopped
2 teaspoon capers, rinsed (optional)

1 Preheat the oven to 190°C (Gas Mark 5). Lightly grease a large, flat baking tray.

2 Rinse the sardines well and dry with kitchen paper.

3 To make the stuffing, combine all the ingredients in a bowl. Mix well, then taste and adjust the seasoning.

4 Open out the sardines and lay half of them, skin-side down, on the prepared baking tray. Divide the stuffing mixture among the sardines and spread to cover. Top with the remaining sardine halves, skin-side up (like sandwiches). Drizzle with a little olive oil, season with pepper and roast for about 20 minutes, or until starting to colour.

5 Combine the remaining ingredients to make a fresh tomato salsa and season with a little sea salt. Serve two sardines per person with the salsa on the side.

Really Useful Stuff
You can prepare the fish ahead of time and chill for up to 8 hours before cooking. If the sardines are large, secure them by tying with kitchen string.

Malaysian-style baked snapper

The fish in this recipe are brushed with a delicious spiced chilli paste that also works well with other whole fish, such as bream or mackerel.

Preparation time: 15 minutes
Cooking time: 15 minutes
Serves 4

vegetable oil, for brushing
4 whole plate-size snapper or bream, cleaned and scaled
mint leaves, to serve
2 limes, quartered, to serve
steamed rice, to serve

Spice paste
3 golden shallots, roughly chopped
4 cloves garlic, crushed
2 teaspoons sambal oelek or chilli paste
1 teaspoon brown sugar
2–3 tablespoons coconut cream or lime juice

1 Preheat the oven to 200°C (Gas Mark 6). Brush a large baking tray with a little oil (you may need two trays, depending on the size of the fish).

2 Rinse and dry the fish and place them on the prepared tray. Make 2–3 diagonal slashes on each side of the fish.

3 To make the spice paste, blend the shallots, garlic, sambal oelek and brown sugar in a blender or small food processor. Add enough coconut cream or lime juice to form a thick, brushable paste.

4 Brush each side of the fish with the spice mixture and roast in the oven for 10 minutes. There is no need to turn the fish.

5 Heat the grill to high and cook the fish for 2–3 minutes, or until golden. Garnish with mint leaves and serve with lime wedges and steamed rice.

Really Useful Stuff
The paste can also be used on thick fish fillets – lightly brush one side with the paste and place under a hot grill until cooked.

Salt-baked fish

Roasting in a casing of salt is a delicious way to cook whole fish with a delicate texture. It allows the fish to cook slowly, retaining the moisture. The salt crust is easily broken away when serving.

Preparation time: 20 minutes
Cooking time: 35 minutes
Serves 4–6

about 3 kg salt
3 egg whites
1 tablespoon thyme leaves
1.5 kg whole barramundi, cleaned and scaled
2 lemons
2 fresh bay leaves
freshly ground black pepper

1　Preheat the oven to 220°C (Gas Mark 7).

2　Place the salt in a large bowl, mix in the egg whites and stir in the thyme leaves. Tip just under half the salt into the base of a large roasting tin. Rinse the fish and dry well with kitchen paper. Cut one of the lemons into slices and insert the slices and the bay leaves in the cavity. Season the cavity with pepper.

3　Lay the fish on the salt base and cover with the remaining salt, leaving the tail out (the salt crust should be about 1 cm thick). Cover the tail with foil. Sprinkle with a little water and bake for 30–35 minutes, depending on the size of the fish.

4　Remove from the oven and take to the table. Use a wooden spoon to tap the mound and break the crust, then scrape the salt off the fish and push it to the side of the tin. Gently slide away any remaining skin. Place a fish slice or cake slice under the front section of the top fillet and lift off the fillet. Transfer to a platter. Lift away the back bone, then slide the fish slice between the bottom fillet and the skin and transfer the fillet to the platter. Cut the reserved lemon into wedges and serve with the fish.

Really Useful Stuff
A 1.5 kg fish should take about 30–35 minutes to cook. Test by inserting a metal skewer into the middle of the fish for about 5 seconds to see if it is warm all the way through (check by placing the skewer just above your top lip – this is a really sensitive place to detect the heat).

Lyn Hall's fish baked with potatoes, olives, tomato & Mediterranean herbs

Lyn Hall is a talented English cookery teacher, writer and demonstrator who has a delicious touch with Mediterranean and French food. This recipe is a favourite of mine – a tasty all-in-one dish that can be served from oven to table.

Preparation time: 30 minutes
Cooking time: 1½ hours
Serves 4

4 bay leaves
2 large onions, finely sliced
2 large potatoes, cut into 3 mm thick rounds
about 150 ml olive oil
8–10 sprigs thyme
salt and freshly ground black pepper
900 g large vine-ripened tomatoes
1 kg whole snapper, bream, salmon or sea bass,
　　cleaned and scaled
4 slices lemon
4 cloves garlic, lightly crushed
2 tablespoons oregano leaves
70 g black olives, pitted
75 ml white wine
3 tablespoons shredded basil

1　Preheat the oven to 220°C (Gas Mark 7). Lay the bay leaves at the base of a large baking dish. Add the onion and potato in alternate layers, sprinkling as you go with the olive oil, and seasoning with thyme, salt and pepper. Bake, uncovered, for 45–50 minutes, basting with the oil twice during cooking.

2　Meanwhile, blanch the tomatoes and peel off the skins. Cut them into quarters and remove the seeds.

3　Rub the cavity of the fish with one of the lemon slices, and season with salt and pepper. Place the garlic, remaining lemon slices, some oregano leaves and 1 tablespoon of olive oil inside the cavity.

4　Set the fish on the hot potato and onion, season well and cover with layers of tomato, olives and the remaining oregano, seasoning again as you go. Baste with the pan juices, sprinkle with the white wine and remaining olive oil (about 3 tablespoons). Cover and return to the oven for 35 minutes.

5　When the fish is ready, scatter with the basil. Take to the table, and serve the fish from the dish, spooning the cooking juices over the top.

Really Useful Stuff
To blanch and skin the tomatoes, make a small cross in the base of each one with a sharp knife. Place the tomatoes in a large heatproof bowl and pour on enough boiling water to cover them. Let the tomatoes sit for 40–60 seconds, then pour off the boiling water. The skins should now slip off easily, starting at the cross.

When baking whole fish, use a dish that will go from the oven to the table. Not only does this look spectacular, it also makes it easier to serve as it can be tricky to transfer a cooked fish to a serving platter.

Oven-roasted salmon with lemon butter sauce

Whole salmon is the perfect fish to roast whole, and the lemon sauce makes a lovely accompaniment

Preparation time: 15 minutes
Cooking time: 30 minutes
Serves 4

2 tablespoons olive oil
1.5 kg whole salmon, cleaned and scaled
1 fennel bulb, thickly sliced
1 lemon, sliced
salt and freshly ground black pepper
20 g butter
juice of ½ lemon
4 tablespoons white wine

Lemon butter sauce
120 ml lemon juice
200 g chilled butter, diced

1 Preheat the oven to 220°C (Gas Mark 7). Brush a large sheet of foil with the olive oil and place on a large baking sheet.

2 Rinse the salmon and dry well with kitchen paper. Place the salmon in the centre of the foil and stuff the cavity with the fennel and lemon, then season well with salt and pepper. Dot the top of the salmon with butter, then bring the sides of the foil up and pour the lemon juice and wine over the fish. Pinch the foil together to enclose the fish, making sure you leave some air space – the parcel should be securely sealed but not wrapped tightly. Bake for 30 minutes.

3 Meanwhile, to make the lemon butter sauce, bring the lemon juice to the boil in a small saucepan over medium heat. Whisk in the diced butter, a little at a time, until melted and well combined. Remove from the heat and allow to cool slightly before serving.

4 When the salmon is cooked, transfer the parcel to a large platter and open it at the table (the aroma is great). Remove the skin if desired, then use a large spoon and knife to serve fillets of the fish. Serve with the lemon butter sauce, new potatoes and green beans.

Monkfish wrapped in prosciutto ›

This looks spectacular served whole, either in the roasting dish straight from the oven or on a platter. The prosciutto protects the fish and adds an unusual flavour, and the cooking juices provide all the sauce you need.

Preparation time: 15 minutes
Cooking time: 30 minutes
Serves 4

60 g butter, softened, plus extra for dotting
1 tablespoon chopped chives
1 tablespoon chopped flat-leaf parsley
1 teaspoon finely grated lemon zest
1 kg piece monkfish (ask your fishmonger to remove the skin and separate into 2 fillets)
8 slices prosciutto or parma ham
2 lemons, quartered

You will also need
six 15 cm lengths kitchen string

1 Preheat the oven to 200°C (Gas Mark 6).

2 Mix the butter, chives, parsley and lemon zest together. Use the butter mixture to sandwich together the two pieces of fish. If the pieces come from the tail section, join the thinner bit of one piece with the thicker piece of the other, giving you an even thickness throughout.

3 Wrap the fish in the prosciutto, holding the fillets together firmly as you go. Tie the fish securely with string – you will need to tie each piece about 2.5 cm apart. Dot the surface with a few small bits of butter. If not baking straight away, refrigerate until you're ready to cook.

4 Place the fish in a small roasting dish and squeeze the juice of two of the lemon quarters over the fish. Bake for about 25–30 minutes. Serve from the roasting dish at the table with the remaining lemon quarters. This is delicious with wilted spinach.

Really Useful Stuff
Monkfish is a firm-fleshed fish that is well suited to roasting. For a meat-free version, wrap the fish in blanched English spinach or silverbeet leaves and tie in place. If using tail fillets that are thicker at one end, lay the pieces together at opposite ends so combined they become the same thickness.

‹ Salmon fish cakes

Salmon fish cakes are so delicious it is worth poaching some fresh salmon to make them.

Preparation time: 20 minutes, plus cooling and refrigeration time
Cooking time: 30 minutes
Serves 4

450 g floury potatoes, cut into chunks
650 g poached salmon fillets, flaked
6 spring onions, finely chopped
2 tablespoons chopped flat-leaf parsley or basil
finely grated zest of 1 lemon
1 tablespoon lemon juice
½ teaspoon English mustard
1 egg yolk
salt and freshly ground black pepper
100 g plain flour
1 egg, beaten
125 ml milk
100 g fresh breadcrumbs, made from day-old bread
vegetable oil, for pan-frying
lemon wedges and mayonnaise (see page 205), to serve

1 Cook the potatoes in a large saucepan of boiling salted water for 15–20 minutes, or until tender. Drain and return the potatoes to the pan. Cook over low heat for 1–2 minutes to remove any remaining moisture, then mash well. Allow to cool slightly.

2 In a bowl, combine the mashed potato, flaked fish, spring onion, parsley or basil, lemon zest and juice, mustard and egg yolk. Season well with salt and pepper.

3 Form the mixture into four large patties, or eight smaller ones, and lightly coat in the flour, shaking off any excess.

4 Whisk together the beaten egg and milk in a shallow bowl. Place the breadcrumbs in a second shallow bowl. Dip the fishcakes in the egg mixture and then in the breadcrumbs, making sure they are well coated. Place on a tray lined with baking paper, cover and refrigerate for 20 minutes or until ready to cook.

5 Pour enough oil into a large frying pan to cover the base and pan-fry the salmon cakes over medium heat for 5–6 minutes each side, or until golden. Serve with lemon wedges and a little homemade mayonnaise.

Really Useful Stuff
The simplest way to poach salmon fillets is to wrap them in foil (leaving space for air), add to a pan of cold water and bring slowly to the boil. Simmer for about 3 minutes.

If you like, you can use regular white fish fillets instead of the salmon (or half and half). Make sure you remove any bones in the fillets before poaching.

Crab cakes

These crab cakes are full of flavour as the proportion of crab meat is quite high.

Preparation time: 15 minutes, plus refrigeration time
Cooking time: 15 minutes
Serves 4

500 g fresh crab meat
120 g fresh breadcrumbs, made from day-old bread
3–4 tablespoons mayonnaise
2 tablespoons chopped chives
1 teaspoon Dijon mustard
1 small egg, lightly beaten
salt and freshly ground black pepper
100 g plain flour
vegetable oil, for pan-frying
mayonnaise (see page 205) and lemon wedges, to serve

1 Put the crab meat in a bowl and break it up with a fork. Add the breadcrumbs, mayonnaise, chives, mustard and beaten egg and mix with a fork until combined. Add a little extra mayonnaise if the mixture is dry. Season well with salt and pepper.

2 Form the mixture into eight patties and lightly coat in the flour, shaking off any excess. Transfer to a tray lined with baking paper and refrigerate for at least 30 minutes.

3 Pour the oil into a large heavy-based frying pan to a depth of 1 cm and place over medium heat. The oil will be hot enough when a cube of bread browns in 30 seconds. Add the crab cakes and cook for 3–4 minutes each side, or until golden (you may need to do this in batches). Serve hot with mayonnaise and lemon wedges.

Really Useful Stuff
Tinned crab meat is all right, but frozen and vacuum-packed is better. If you're going to go all out and buy a fresh crab, choose a 'dressed' one (with the meat already taken out and the edible bits arranged back in its shell), or choose a whole boiled crab and ask the fishmonger to pull out the inedible bits for you.

Prawn & chive cakes

I usually chop the prawn meat quite coarsely, so that there are delicious bits of prawn throughout the cakes.

Preparation time: 20 minutes, plus cooling and refrigeration time
Cooking time: 35 minutes
Serves 4

3 large potatoes, quartered
2 tablespoons vegetable oil, plus extra for pan-frying
1 red onion, finely chopped
300 g large uncooked prawns, peeled and chopped
2 tablespoons snipped chives
finely grated zest and juice of ½ lemon
1 egg, lightly beaten
salt and freshly ground black pepper
150 g fresh breadcrumbs
mayonnaise (see page 205) and lemon wedges, to serve

1 Cook the potatoes in a large saucepan of boiling salted water for 15–20 minutes, or until tender. Drain and return the potatoes to the pan. Cook over low heat for 1–2 minutes to remove any remaining moisture, then mash well. Allow to cool.

2 Meanwhile, heat the vegetable oil in a frying pan over medium heat and cook the onion for 5–7 minutes, or until golden. Add the chopped prawns and cook for 1–2 minutes until pink, stirring frequently – take care not to overcook.

3 In a bowl, combine the mashed potato, prawn mixture, chives, lemon zest and juice and beaten egg. Season well.

4 Form the mixture into four patties. Dip the patties in the fresh breadcrumbs, making sure they are well coated, then transfer to a tray lined with baking paper. Cover and refrigerate for at least 30 minutes, or until ready to cook.

5 Preheat the oven to 200°C (Gas Mark 6). Pour enough oil into a large frying pan to cover the base and place over medium heat. Add the prawn cakes and cook for 1–2 minutes each side, or until golden. Transfer to a roasting tray and bake in the oven for 10 minutes, or until cooked through. Serve with lemon wedges and mayonnaise.

Really Useful Stuff
If the prawn cake mixture is too stiff, add a little milk.

Thai fish cakes >

These are classic spicy fish cakes – great as a starter, snack or a hot nibble to have with drinks.

Preparation time: 20 minutes, plus refrigeration time
Cooking time: 15 minutes
Makes about 15

500 g white fish fillets, skin and bones removed
1 egg, beaten
2 tablespoons cornflour
1 tablespoon fish sauce
2 teaspoons red curry paste (see page 41)
1 teaspoon chopped red chilli
2 tablespoons roughly chopped coriander leaves
10 green beans, trimmed and cut into 1 cm lengths (optional)
2 spring onions, chopped
salt
vegetable oil, for pan-frying

Dipping sauce
1 tablespoon sugar
3 tablespoons fish sauce
2 tablespoons lime juice
1 small cucumber, diced
2 long red chillies, finely sliced
1 teaspoon finely chopped coriander leaves

1 Chop the fish into 2 cm pieces, place in a food processor and pulse until coarsely chopped. Add the egg, cornflour, fish sauce, curry paste, chilli and coriander and process until combined.

2 Transfer the mixture to a bowl and add the beans, if using, and spring onion. Mix well and season with a little salt.

3 Form the mixture into small fish cakes using a spoon or wet hands. Place on a tray lined with baking paper and flatten slightly. Cover and refrigerate for 30 minutes.

4 To make the dipping sauce, dissolve the sugar in 2 tablespoons of water in a small bowl. Stir in the fish sauce, lime juice, diced cucumber, chilli and coriander.

5 Pour the oil into a large frying pan to a depth of about 5 mm and place over medium heat. Working in batches, fry the fish cakes for about 2–3 minutes each side or until golden brown, turning once. Drain on kitchen paper and serve with the dipping sauce.

Really Useful Stuff
These fish cakes can be made up to 8 hours ahead of cooking.

Gratins

There is nothing quite like a creamy potato gratin to accompany a much-loved steak or roast chicken dish. I often make gratins to add a bit of variety to grills or roasts, using whatever ingredients are in season.

Hints & Tips

* Root vegetables like potatoes, celeriac, Jerusalem artichokes and parsnips are perfect cooked this way, using either cream or stock, and flavoured with a variety of herbs or spices.

* Celeriac, with its great gnarled celery-flavoured root, works well with strong flavours like feta. I often add some celeriac slices to a potato gratin, as it gives a lovely subtle flavour. The celeriac gratin here is made without any cream to show that root vegetable gratins need not all be rich and creamy.

* Use a good ceramic ovenproof dish so you can serve the gratin at the table. It is a good idea to sit the gratin dish on a baking tray when it is in the oven – this prevents any of the juices bubbling over and sticking to the floor of your oven.

* Gratins can usually be cooked ahead of time and reheated again to serve.

* These recipes are here as a guide only – you can easily replace the ideas with your favourite ingredients.

Potato gratin

This classic creamy, garlicky potato gratin goes perfectly with roast or grilled meat.

Preparation time: 20 minutes
Cooking time: 1½ hours
Serves 6 as a side

600 ml cream
1 bay leaf
salt and freshly ground black pepper
1.5 kg desiree potatoes, peeled
2 cloves garlic, finely chopped

1   Preheat the oven to 170°C (Gas Mark 3) and grease a large, shallow ovenproof dish.

2   Place the cream and bay leaf in a large saucepan and season with pepper. Slowly bring to the boil, then simmer gently for 10 minutes. Remove the bay leaf.

3   Slice the potatoes very thinly (I usually slice the potatoes into the gratin dish as this helps to work out the quantity needed). Add the potato slices to the saucepan of cream, stir well and return the mixture to the boil. Simmer for 2–3 minutes, stirring gently.

4   Spoon a third of the potato mixture into the prepared dish and sprinkle with salt, pepper and a little chopped garlic. Repeat the layering until the dish is full. Cover with foil and bake for 1 hour. Remove the foil and cook for a further 15–20 minutes, or until the top is golden and bubbling, and the potato is tender.

Really Useful Stuff
Cheese goes particularly well with potatoes and cream. Sprinkle the top of the gratin with grated cheddar or parmesan about 15 minutes before the end of cooking and bake, uncovered, until the cheese has melted and is golden.

I don't usually worry too much about peeling the potatoes, especially if I'm using firm-skinned varieties such as desiree.

Leek gratin with gruyère

Leeks and gruyère are a delicious combination. I love to serve this with roast chicken.

Preparation time: 20 minutes
Cooking time: 1½ hours
Serves 6

12 leeks
salt and freshly ground black pepper
385 ml chicken stock
20 g butter, extra
250 ml double cream
125 g grated gruyère

1 Preheat the oven to 160°C (Gas Mark 2–3). Grease a baking dish that will fit the leeks in two layers.

2 Trim the roots from the leeks and most of the green, then cut them in half lengthways. Rinse the leeks to remove any dirt and pat dry with a clean tea towel. Cut into 6–8 cm lengths.

3 Place the leeks in the prepared dish, cut-side down, and season with salt and pepper. Pour on enough stock to cover, dot with butter and bake for about 45 minutes. Cover with foil if the leeks start to colour.

4 Remove from the oven and turn the leeks over. Pour on the cream, cover the dish loosely with foil and bake for a further 30 minutes.

5 Remove the foil and sprinkle with the cheese. Return to the oven until the cheese has melted and is golden.

Really Useful Stuff
You can make this in advance up to the end of step 4. To serve, add the cheese and bake until golden.

Cauliflower with chilli breadcrumbs

Cauliflower roasts suprisingly well. Here, it is sprinkled with spiced breadcrumbs and grated parmesan.

Preparation time: 20 minutes
Cooking time: 20 minutes
Serves 4 as a side

butter, for greasing
1 cauliflower, trimmed and cut into florets
40 g butter, extra
1 clove garlic, crushed
1 long red chilli, finely chopped
80 g fresh breadcrumbs, made from day-old bread
2 tablespoons chopped flat-leaf parsley
salt and freshly ground black pepper
50 g freshly grated parmesan

1 Preheat the oven to 200°C (Gas Mark 6). Grease a baking dish that will hold the cauliflower in two layers.

2 Cook the cauliflower florets in a large saucepan of boiling salted water for 2–3 minutes or until just tender. Be careful not to overcook it – it should still have bite. Drain well and transfer to the prepared dish.

3 Heat the butter in a frying pan over medium heat and cook the garlic and chilli for 1 minute. Tip in the breadcrumbs and fry, stirring frequently, until golden and starting to crisp a little. Stir in the parsley.

4 Season the cauliflower with salt and pepper and scatter with the breadcrumbs. Sprinkle the parmesan over the top and bake for about 10 minutes, or until golden. Serve immediately.

Really Useful Stuff
Make breadcrumbs from day-old bread. Simply remove the crusts and process in a food processor until fine crumbs form.

Broccoli gratin

I have made this with broccoli but you can use a mixture of vegetables – it works especially well with a combination of broccoli and calabrese (Italian sprouting broccoli). The idea is to part-cook the vegetables, then finish them off in the oven under a coating of breadcrumbs, cheese and bacon.

Preparation time: 15 minutes
Cooking time: 30 minutes
Serves 4

500 g broccoli or calabrese, broken into florets
salt and freshly ground black pepper
175 g fresh breadcrumbs, made from day-old bread
175 g finely grated cheddar or gruyère
2 rashers bacon, finely chopped
20 g butter, extra

1 Preheat the oven to 190°C (Gas Mark 5) and lightly grease a gratin dish.

2 Bring a large saucepan of salted water to the boil, add the broccoli or calabrese and simmer for about 3 minutes. Drain well.

3 Arrange the vegetables in the base of the gratin dish, and season lightly with salt and pepper.

4 Combine the breadcrumbs and cheese and sprinkle over the vegetables to cover. Scatter the chopped bacon over the top and dot with butter. Bake for about 25 minutes until crispy and golden.

Really Useful Stuff
You can also add chopped herbs such as chives, parsley or thyme, some chopped garlic or even a little crumbled dried chilli to the breadcrumb mixture as a variation.

Smoked fish gratin

Thanks to my friend Lucas Hollweg for this delicious gratin – smoked fish and cream are natural playmates. Please buy undyed smoked fish where possible.

Preparation time: 20 minutes
Cooking time: 25 minutes
Serves 4

500 g undyed smoked fish fillets, skin and bones removed
150 g spinach leaves
salt and freshly ground black pepper
225 ml double cream
good pinch of cayenne pepper
generous grating of nutmeg
2 teaspoons Dijon mustard
2 teaspoons lemon juice
50 g finely grated parmesan
100 g fresh breadcrumbs, made from day-old bread
20 g butter

1 Preheat the oven to 190°C (Gas Mark 5) and lightly grease a deep gratin dish.

2 Separate the fish into large bite-sized pieces and place in the gratin dish.

3 Bring a large saucepan of salted water to the boil. Add the spinach and as soon as it starts to boil, remove from the heat and drain. Cool under the cold tap, then squeeze hard to remove the moisture. Drape the spinach over the fish and season with a little salt and pepper.

4 Whisk together the cream, spices, mustard, lemon juice and parmesan, then pour over the fish and spinach. Sprinkle the breadcrumbs over the top, season with pepper and dot with the extra butter.

5 Place the gratin dish on a baking sheet (to catch any bits that bubble over) and bake for 20–25 minutes, or until the fish is heated through, the cream is bubbling and the breadcrumbs are golden brown. Serve with a green salad.

Celeriac & feta gratin

Celeriac is a large root vegetable that tastes a little like celery. Its earthy flavour works really well with the feta.

Preparation time: 20 minutes
Cooking time: 1¼ hours
Serves 6 as a side dish

2 celeriac roots
salt and freshly ground black pepper
1 leek, washed and sliced into thin rounds
1 clove garlic, thinly sliced
2 teaspoons snipped chives
100 g feta, crumbled
300 ml chicken or vegetable stock
2–3 tablespoons white wine
butter, for dotting

1 Preheat the oven to 200°C (Gas Mark 6). Lightly grease a gratin dish.

2 Wash and trim the celeriac roots, then peel using a sharp knife. Cut them into quarters, then cut each quarter into thin slices.

3 Layer half the celeriac slices in the prepared dish, seasoning lightly as you go (remember, feta can be quite salty). Top with the leek, garlic, chives and feta, then finish with a layer of the remaining celeriac.

4 Mix together the stock and white wine and pour over the vegetables. Add a little extra stock if needed – you want the liquid to reach just under the top of the celeriac. Dot with a little butter.

5 Cover with foil and bake for 50 minutes. Remove the foil, return to the oven and cook for a further 20 minutes or until the celeriac is golden and the sauce has thickened. Place under a hot grill for a few moments if the gratin is not colouring in the oven. Serve immediately.

Really Useful Stuff
This gratin is also delicious if you leave out the feta and replace the stock with cream and a teaspoonful of Dijon mustard.

A few fresh breadcrumbs sprinkled on top add a lovely crunch to the dish.

Zucchini & tomato gratin ›

This is a great dish for late summer, especially served with roast lamb. You can either arrange the vegetables in rows (pictured) or layer them individually (one of tomato followed by one of zucchini). Either way it tastes great. You can leave out the cheese, if desired.

Preparation time: 20 minutes
Cooking time: 1 hour
Serves 6 as a side dish

2–3 tablespoons olive oil, plus extra for drizzling
1 large onion, sliced
4–5 roma (plum) tomatoes, cut into 4 mm slices
salt and freshly ground black pepper
1 clove garlic, crushed
1 tablespoon chopped thyme
4 zucchini (courgettes), unpeeled, cut into 4 mm slices
125 g grated cheddar (optional)
4 tablespoons freshly grated parmesan (optional)

1 Preheat the oven 180°C (Gas Mark 4).

2 Heat the oil in a large saucepan over low heat. Add the onion and gently fry, stirring occasionally, for 10–15 minutes or until softened and golden. Transfer to an ovenproof gratin or ceramic dish.

3 Arrange a layer of sliced tomato over the onion. Season with salt and pepper and sprinkle with a little crushed garlic and thyme. Next, add a layer of zucchini, seasoning again with salt, pepper, garlic and thyme. Repeat the layers with the remaining ingredients, finishing with a layer of zucchini.

4 Drizzle a little olive oil over the top and sprinkle with the combined cheeses, if using. Bake for 30–40 minutes, or until tender and nicely coloured. Serve immediately.

Ice-cream

Ice-cream must be one of the few dishes in the world that is loved by just about everyone. Making ice-cream at home is easier than you might think, and many of following recipes can be made without an ice-cream machine.

Hints & Tips

Ice-cream bases

Cream or yoghurt: sweetened fruit purée is simply combined with yoghurt or cream and then churned and frozen.

Parfait: this is made by beating a boiling sugar syrup into eggs. Flavourings are added and then lightly whipped cream is folded though the mixture. The inclusion of whipped cream and beaten egg has the double effect of adding air and fat, meaning the mixture doesn't really need churning.

Custard: eggs, sugar and cream are cooked over low heat until thickened, forming a classic custard (see page 46 for custard-making hints). Custard-based ice-creams need mixing and beating during freezing to break up the ice crystals and make the mixture smoother on the tongue. You can achieve this without a machine by partly freezing the mixture and then beating it in a food processor or with an electric mixer, and then re-freezing.

Freezing and churning

Make sure your ice-cream mixture is chilled before churning. Beating the ice-cream either by hand or with a machine breaks down the ice crystals – the more it is beaten while freezing, the finer and creamier the finished texture will be. There are two basic methods for freezing ice-creams: freezing without a machine is called still-freezing, and the action of an ice-cream machine is called stir-freezing.

✳ To still-freeze, pour the chilled ice-cream mixture into a lidded, shallow plastic container (the ice-cream should fill the container to a depth of 4–5 cm). Freeze for 1½ hours, or until frozen around the edges with a soft icy slush in the centre. Either process in a food processor or transfer to a bowl and beat with hand-held electric beaters until the mixture forms a uniform slush. Return to the freezer and repeat twice.

✳ To stir-freeze, pre-chill your machine and start the churn. Pour in the chilled ice-cream mix and churn following the instructions until frozen. Fill your ice-cream machine no more than about three-quarters full (check the manufacturer's instructions). Air is incorporated during the freezing and churning process and the mixture needs room to expand. This aeration process, called overrun, improves the |texture of the ice-cream.

Storage

Store ice-cream in a plastic lidded container, first covering the surface with baking paper.

Serving

✳ After a day or two in the freezer most home-made ice-creams will be rock-hard and need softening to be at their best. This is really important and should be done slowly in the refrigerator (about 20–30 minutes for a tub of ice-cream). It needs to be soft enough to scoop and serve.

✳ If you are serving ice-cream for a dinner party and want to get ahead, scoop the ice-cream into balls and place them on a tray lined with baking paper. Return to the freezer until ready to serve.

✳ If serving in cones, you can have some fun with the decorations: scatter with silver dragees, hundreds and thousands, Smarties, toasted nuts or even crushed chocolate biscuits.

✳ For a simple but delicious dessert, serve home-made ice-cream with crisp biscuits. Try the almond bread (see page 107) or orange and pecan thins (see page 3).

Simple sauces

Chocolate fudge sauce: heat 250 ml cream and 2 tablespoons golden syrup in a small saucepan until simmering. Remove from the heat, add 250 g chopped dark chocolate and whisk until smooth. Serve warm.

Vanilla caramel sauce: heat 200 g chopped butter, 250 g light brown sugar and 200 ml double cream in a saucepan until simmering, stirring constantly. Remove from the heat and stir in 1 teaspoon vanilla extract. Serve warm.

Raspberry sauce: purée 300 g fresh or frozen (thawed) raspberries, 75 g sifted icing sugar and the juice of half a lemon in a blender or food processor. Pass through a sieve to remove the seeds and chill before serving.

Strawberry frozen yoghurt

This is one of the easiest ice-creams to make: simply a matter of adding lightly sweetened puréed fruit to yoghurt. I usually use full-fat yoghurt for frozen yoghurt, which means I can get away with not having to churn it. Ice-creams made with low-fat yoghurt or single cream tend to be a bit icier, as the lower fat content allows ice crystals to form. If you're making this in an ice-cream machine, you can speed up the churning time by partially freezing the purée before combining it with the cream. This type of ice-cream should be eaten within a week of making.

Preparation time: 15 minutes, plus churning and freezing time
Serves 4

400 g strawberries, hulled and roughly chopped
juice of 1 lime
300 g full-fat plain yoghurt
4 tablespoons icing sugar, sifted

1 Purée the strawberries and lime juice in a blender until smooth.

2 Whisk together the yoghurt and sugar in a mixing bowl until light and fluffy. Stir in the fruit purée and mix until smooth. Taste and add extra lime juice or sugar if needed.

3 Freeze in an ice-cream machine if you have one, otherwise pour the mixture into a lidded container and freeze until firm. Remember to soften the frozen yoghurt before serving.

Really Useful Stuff
Add a tablespoon of balsamic vinegar to the basic recipe – it works beautifully with the strawberries.

Try a rasberry ripple version. Make a plain frozen yoghurt by combining 500 g plain yoghurt, 125 g icing sugar and 2 teaspoons vanilla extract and churn until just frozen. Combine 200 g raspberries with 3 tablespoons icing sugar, then swirl the purée through the yoghurt. Freeze until firm.

Vanilla bean ice-cream

The best vanilla ice-cream should be wonderfully creamy and smooth, and the only way to really achieve this is by using a proper ice-cream machine or churn.

Preparation time: 15 minutes, plus churning and freezing time
Cooking time: 15 minutes
Serves 4–6

500 ml milk
1 vanilla bean
6 egg yolks
125 g caster sugar
250 ml cream, lightly whipped

1   Pour the milk into a small saucepan. Using a sharp knife, split the vanilla bean in half lengthways, scrape out the seeds, then add the pod and seeds to the milk. Bring the mixture to simmering point over low heat, then remove from the heat.

2   In a large mixing bowl, whisk the egg yolks and caster sugar for 4–5 minutes, or until the sugar has dissolved and the mixture is thick and pale. Gently whisk the hot milk, including the vanilla pod, into the egg mixture.

3   Return the mixture to the saucepan and cook over low heat, stirring constantly with a wooden spoon, until the mixture thickens slightly and coats the back of the spoon. It is done when you can run your finger down the back of the spoon and a path remains in the mixture for several seconds. Do not allow the mixture to boil or it will curdle. Remove from the heat and strain into a bowl, discarding the vanilla pod. Set aside to cool at room temperature, then chill until ready to proceed.

4   When the custard is cold, whisk in the whipped cream. Churn in an ice-cream machine until firm. Soften before serving.

Really Useful Stuff

Strawberry ice-cream
Omit the vanilla from the basic recipe. Purée 250 g strawberries in a blender or food processor and stir into the chilled custard. Churn in an ice-cream machine, following the manufacturer's instructions.

Simple chocolate ice-cream
Omit the vanilla. Add 2 tablespoons sifted cocoa and 100 g chopped dark chocolate to the milk before heating and proceed with the recipe.

Passionfruit parfait

This is my favourite ice-cream. It has an intense passionfruit flavour that really packs a punch. It can be made without churning if you don't have a machine.

Preparation time: 15 minutes, plus churning and freezing time
Cooking time: 5 minutes
Serves 4–6

8–10 passionfruit
185 g caster sugar
3 large eggs
pinch of salt
300 ml cream

1   Halve the passionfruit and spoon out the pulp. Push the pulp through a small sieve to remove the seeds (save some to add later, if desired).

2   Place the sugar and 100 ml water in a small saucepan and bring to the boil, stirring to dissolve the sugar. Boil steadily for 3 minutes.

3   Meanwhile, beat the eggs and salt with an electric mixer on a medium speed until frothy. Slowly pour the sugar syrup into the egg mixture and continue to beat for 2–3 minutes, or until the mixture has thickened. Stir in the sieved passionfruit and seeds, if using.

4   Whip the cream until soft peaks form, then fold into the passionfruit mixture. Churn in an ice-cream machine if you have one, otherwise pour the mixture into a lidded container and freeze until firm. Remember to soften the parfait before serving.

Really Useful Stuff
It is important to soften this ice-cream by leaving it in the fridge for about 20 minutes before serving.

‹ Orange & chocolate iced pops

Ice-cream scooped into balls, then dipped in chocolate sauce makes a great fun dessert. Orange parfait with a chocolate coating is a delicious blend of flavours, but you can use any combination you like.

Preparation time: 20 minutes, plus churning and freezing time
Cooking time: 5 minutes
Makes 10

185 g caster sugar
100 ml water
3 large eggs
pinch of salt
150 ml concentrated orange juice, chilled
300 ml cream
sprinkles, to serve (optional)

Chocolate coating
250 g good-quality dark chocolate, roughly chopped
1 tablespoon vegetable oil

You will also need
10 paddle-pop sticks (iced lolly sticks)

1   Place the sugar and water in a small saucepan and bring to the boil, stirring to dissolve the sugar. Boil steadily for 3 minutes.

2   Meanwhile, beat the eggs and salt with an electric mixer until frothy. Slowly pour the sugar syrup into the egg mixture and continue to beat for 2–3 minutes, or until the mixture has thickened. Stir in the juice.

3   Whip the cream until soft peaks form, then fold into the orange mixture. Churn in an ice-cream machine if you have one, otherwise pour the mixture into a lidded container and freeze until firm.

4   Place the ice-cream in the fridge to soften and line a baking tray with baking paper. Scoop out 10 balls of ice-cream and insert a stick into each. Place on the prepared tray and return to the freezer to firm.

5   To make the chocolate coating, melt the chocolate in a small heatproof bowl set over a saucepan of just-boiling water. When melted, stir in the oil.

6   Dip each ball of ice-cream into the warm chocolate mixture and scatter with sprinkles, if using. Return the ice-creams to the tray and allow the chocolate to set. The ice-creams are best served immediately as the chocolate will remain nice and shiny. If you are not worried about this and want to make them ahead of time, they can be frozen after dipping.

Really Useful Stuff
For a cheat's version, use good-quality bought ice-cream.

Chocolate & hazelnut semifreddo

Semifreddo is a rich Italian ice-cream that doesn't need churning. I usually make this in a loaf tin, then cut it into slices to serve.

Preparation time: 20 minutes, plus freezing time
Serves 6–8

3 tablespoons runny honey
4 large free-range egg yolks
200 g dark chocolate (70 per cent cocoa solids), melted
100 g skinned toasted hazelnuts, roughly chopped
300 ml cream

1   Line a small loaf tin with plastic wrap, leaving some overhanging the two long sides.

2   Check the honey. If it is not very runny, or you are making the semifreddo on a chilly day, warm it slightly by sitting the jar of honey in a dish of very hot water.

3   In a large mixing bowl, whisk together the egg yolks and honey for 4–5 minutes, until the mixture is thick and pale. Slowly stir in the melted chocolate and then the chopped nuts.

4   Whip the cream until it forms soft peaks then gently fold it into the egg mixture, ensuring there are no streaks.

5   Pour into the prepared loaf tin, cover and freeze overnight. Remove from the freezer and place in the fridge for about 25 minutes before serving. Use the overhanging plastic wrap to help you lift out the semifreddo, then slice and serve.

Rich chocolate truffle ice-cream

This wonderfully rich chocolate ice-cream really benefits from being churned in a machine.

Preparation time: 20 minutes, plus churning and freezing time
Cooking time: 10 minutes
Serves 6–8

250 ml milk
30 g cocoa
1 teaspoon vanilla extract
3 egg yolks
125 g caster sugar
200 g dark chocolate, chopped
400 ml double cream

1 Pour the milk into a small saucepan and stir in the cocoa and vanilla. Bring the mixture to simmering point over low heat.

2 In a large mixing bowl, whisk together the egg yolks and caster sugar for 4–5 minutes, or until the sugar has dissolved and the mixture is thick and pale. Gently and gradually whisk the hot milk into the yolk mixture.

3 Return this mixture to the saucepan and cook over low heat, stirring constantly with a wooden spoon, until the mixture thickens slightly and coats the back of the spoon. It is done when you can run your finger down the back of the spoon and a path remains in the mixture for several seconds. Do not allow the mixture to boil or it will curdle. Remove from the heat and strain into a bowl. Set aside to cool.

4 Meanwhile, place the chocolate in a heatproof bowl. Bring the cream to a simmer in a small saucepan, then pour the hot cream over the chocolate. Stir until the chocolate has melted and the mixture is smooth. Allow to cool.

5 Combine the two mixtures, then cover and place in the fridge to chill. Churn in an ice-cream machine until firm. Soften before serving.

Really Useful Stuff
You can add dark chocolate chips to the mixture before freezing if desired.

This is also good with chopped toasted hazelnuts – add them to the mixture just before churning.

Blackberry & peach ripple terrine

Setting this unusual ice-cream in a loaf tin allows for easy serving – simply turn it out of the tin and slice.

Preparation time: 20 minutes, plus churning and freezing time
Cooking time: 5 minutes
Serves 6–8

3 large ripe peaches
juice of 2 limes
3 tablespoons icing sugar, sifted
360 g caster sugar
200 ml water
5 large eggs
pinch of salt
600 ml cream
250 g blackberries
3 tablespoons icing sugar, sifted, extra

1 Line a small loaf tin with plastic wrap, leaving some overhanging the two long sides.

2 Peel the peaches and remove the stones, then purée the flesh with the lime juice and icing sugar in a blender. Set aside.

3 Place the caster sugar and water in a small saucepan and bring to the boil, stirring to dissolve the sugar. Boil steadily for 3 minutes.

4 Meanwhile, beat the eggs and salt with an electric mixer until frothy. Slowly pour the sugar syrup into the egg mixture and continue to beat for 2–3 minutes, or until the mixture has thickened. Pass the peach purée through a sieve and stir into the mixture.

5 Whip the cream until soft peaks form, then fold the cream into the peach mixture. Churn in an ice-cream machine until almost firm.

6 Blend the blackberries and extra icing sugar to form a purée. Continue to churn the ice-cream, and slowly add the purée until it looks rippled. Remove from the churn and pour into the prepared loaf tin, then cover and freeze overnight. Remove from the freezer and place in the fridge for about 25 minutes before serving. Use the overhanging plastic wrap to help you lift out the terrine, then slice and serve.

Really Useful Stuff
When creating a swirl or ripple, add the ripple sauce after the ice-cream is done and churn for about 30–60 seconds, or until only partially blended. For a more defined swirl, transfer the finished ice-cream to a freezer container, layering it with the sauce. Run a flat-bladed knife through the mixture several times, creating a rippled effect, then freeze immediately.

Jams & preserves

Armed with just a large saucepan and some jars, you can easily turn a few punnets of berries or ripe seasonal fruit into luscious pots of jam. Making an occasional batch of jam is well worth the effort, especially when berries and soft fruit are plentiful. Each of the following recipes yields a relatively small amount, meaning that you end up with just a few jars, and making the process simple.

Hints & Tips

Sugar

Use regular white granulated sugar in most recipes. If using ingredients that are low in pectin, such as strawberries or raspberries, you can use jam or preserving sugar, which contains added pectin to help the jam set.

Pectin

Pectin is the natural agent in fruit that causes jam to set. As most berries are low in pectin, berry jams are sometimes more difficult to set. Personally, I don't mind a soft-set jam, and usually simply add lemon juice, which has high levels of natural pectin.

What size pan?

The recipes given here are for quite small amounts, so there is no need to buy a special jam pan. Just remember that the pan should only be half full when all the ingredients have been added, as you need to allow space in the saucepan when the jam is boiling – the jam spits when it boils, and the extra space keeps your hands and cooker from being spattered. Stainless steel is the best type of pan; avoid aluminium, as it may react with the ingredients.

What is setting point?

Remember that most homemade jams and jellies won't set as firmly as commercial ones. To test if your jam is set, place a saucer in the freezer for a couple of minutes, then take your pan off the heat (after the stipulated boiling time), and place a dollop of the hot jam onto the chilled saucer. Pop the saucer in the fridge for a minute. The dollop should have set and not be runny on the saucer. Run your finger through the dollop – if you can make a line through it (and it wrinkles a little) without the jam running back together, it has reached setting point. If not, return the pan to the heat and continue to cook, testing every 5 minutes, until the jam reaches setting point.

Jars

To sterilise your jars, you can either put them through the dishwasher or wash them in hot soapy water. If hand-washing, rinse the jars with boiling water and then drain on a clean tea towel before using.

To stop all the fruit rising to the surface of the jar, let the pan sit on the bench for 20 minutes before spooning the jam into jars.

Whole strawberry conserve

Don't expect this lovely pink conserve to set as firmly as commercial varieties; it is nice and runny in the French style. If you can find a jam or preserving sugar (which contains pectin), use that for a firmer set.

Preparation time: 20 minutes, plus
**   standing time**
Cooking time: 40 minutes
Makes 1.25 litres

1 kg small to medium strawberries, hulled
900 g granulated sugar
120 ml lemon juice

You will also need
2–3 sterilised glass jars (see opposite)

1   Layer the strawberries and sugar in a large non-metallic bowl, cover with a cloth and leave in a cool place for 12 hours.

2   Tip the berries and sugar into a large saucepan and add the lemon juice. Stir over medium heat until the sugar has dissolved. Bring to the boil and simmer gently for 5 minutes. Set aside for about 30 minutes, stirring occasionally.

3   Return to the boil and boil steadily, uncovered, for 25 minutes. Check for setting point (see opposite), but remember that this jam will not set firmly. Skim off any scum that rises to the surface.

4   Let the jam sit for 20 minutes, then spoon into jars, and seal and label when cool.

Really Useful Stuff

Mixed berry jam
You can use a mixture of berries, rather than just strawberry. Raspberry and strawberry makes a good combination, as does blackberry and strawberry.

Blueberry jam
You can replace the strawberries with blueberries. The addition of a fresh bay leaf to the blueberry jam while boiling gives it a deliciously subtle spiced flavour.

Berry jam with liqueur
Stir 3–4 tablespoons of flavoured liqueur or brandy (such as Cointreau or Grand Marnier) into the jam as it cools.

Peach jam

This really captures the summer flavour of peaches in a jar. If you like, add a vanilla bean when cooking (but remove before bottling).

Preparation time: 20 minutes, plus cooling time
Cooking time: 25 minutes
Makes about 1.5 litres

1 kg ripe yellow-fleshed peaches
60 ml lemon juice
750 g granulated sugar

You will also need
3–4 sterilised glass jars (see page 94)

1 Skin the peaches by first dipping them in boiling water for 1 minute, and then into cold water – the skin should come away easily. Cut them into quarters and remove the stones.

2 Put the fruit in a large saucepan with the lemon juice and 125 ml of water. Simmer gently for about 10 minutes, or until the fruit is soft, stirring well and adding a little water if needed to prevent it catching on the bottom of the pan.

3 Add the sugar and bring to the boil, stirring to dissolve the sugar. Boil rapidly for 10–15 minutes or until the mixture reaches setting point (see page 94).

4 Allow the jam to cool, stir well, then spoon into jars, seal and label.

Really Useful Stuff
This simple jam is delicious with 2 teaspoons of rosewater added at the end of cooking. Alternatively add a little spice: 1 teaspoon of ground cinnamon or ginger or ½ teaspoon of ground cloves or allspice per kilo of fruit. A quarter of a cup of slivered and blanched almonds also makes a nice variation.

Lime marmalade

The intense flavour of this marmalade is achieved by adding the lime peel. It takes a little longer to make than a simple jam, but is well worth the effort.

Preparation time: 30 minutes, plus cooling time
Cooking time: 1¼ hours
Makes about 2 litres

12 limes
1.5 kg granulated sugar

You will also need
a clean square of muslin (or a clean, rinsed Chux or J-cloth), kitchen string, and 4–5 sterilised glass jars (see page 94)

1 Scrub the limes to remove any wax. Peel the fruit using a small, sharp knife or vegetable peeler and then slice the peel thinly. Halve the fruit and squeeze the juice into a large saucepan.

2 Roughly chop the squeezed limes then wrap, together with any pips, in a bag made from a clean square of muslin (or Chux or J-cloth), securing the top with some string. Add to the saucepan, along with the sliced peel and 1.5 litres of water. Bring to the boil then reduce the heat and gently simmer the mixture, uncovered, for 1 hour.

3 Remove the muslin bag from the pan, carefully squeezing any liquid back into the pan. Stir in the sugar and bring the marmalade to the boil, stirring to dissolve the sugar. Boil rapidly for 10 minutes or until setting point is reached (see page 94).

4 Allow the marmalade to cool a little, stir well, then spoon into sterilised jars, and seal and label when cool.

Really Useful Stuff
You can follow the same method to make a three-fruit marmalade. Replace the limes with 1 grapefruit, 3 lemons and 2 large sweet oranges. Cook initially for about 1½ hours, then add the sugar and boil for about 15 minutes, or until setting point is reached.

Simple raspberry jam

This lovely raspberry jam is perfect on freshly baked scones or as a filling for a sponge cake.

Preparation time: 15 minutes, plus cooling time
Cooking time: 1 hour
Makes 1.25 litres

1 kg raspberries or a mixture of berries
100 ml lemon juice
900 g granulated sugar
1 knob butter

You will also need
2–3 sterilised glass jars (see page 94)

1 Put the fruit, lemon juice and 4 tablespoons of water in a large saucepan and simmer over low heat for 15 minutes, or until the fruit is soft.

2 Add the sugar and stir until dissolved. Bring to the boil and boil steadily, uncovered, for 30–40 minutes or until setting point is reached (see page 94).

3 Remove from the heat and stir in the butter. Skim off any scum that rises to the surface.

4 Let the jam sit for 20 minutes, then spoon into sterilised jars and seal and label when cool.

Chilli jelly

This fairly mild chilli jelly uses both long red chillies and capsicums, giving the jelly lots of lovely red speckles.

Preparation time: 15 minutes, plus standing and cooling time
Cooking time: 45 minutes
Makes about 1 litre

8 long red chillies, trimmed
1 kg cooking apples, chopped (cores included)
500 ml cider vinegar
juice of 2 lemons
2 red capsicums (peppers), seeded and roughly chopped
about 800 g granulated sugar

You will also need
4 sterilised glass jars (see page 94)

1 Roughly chop half the chillies and place in a large saucepan with the chopped apple, cider vinegar, lemon juice and 500 ml water. Bring to the boil, then reduce the heat and simmer for about 30 minutes. Pour the liquid and apple pulp into a large strainer or jelly bag set over a large bowl. Leave the mixture to drain for 2–3 hours. Let it drain and drip through naturally; don't be tempted to force the mixture through as this will make the jelly cloudy.

2 Put the chopped capsicum and remaining chilli in a food processor with about 100 ml of the liquid that has drained from the apple pulp and pulse until coarsely chopped. Combine the chilli and capsicum mixture with the remaining liquid that has drained from the apples.

3 Using a measuring jug, measure and transfer the liquid to a large saucepan. For every 500 ml of jelly liquid you will need about 400 g sugar. Add the sugar to the liquid and bring to the boil, stirring to dissolve the sugar. Boil rapidly for 10 minutes.

4 Remove from the heat and set aside to cool for 10 minutes. Stir well, then pour the jelly into sterilised jars, seal and label.

Really Useful Stuff
I use apples for this jelly as they contain lots of natural pectin (the setting agent for jams and jellies). If you can get Bramley or cooking apples (or better still, crab apples) use these as they container higher amounts of pectin than regular apples. If you cannot find cooking apples, use granny smiths.

Meatballs

Flick through any cookbook and you will notice that meatballs are present in some form or another in just about every cuisine. The recipes were usually developed as a way of extending small quantities of tough meat and making it more palatable, or simply as a tasty means of using up leftovers.

Hints & Tips

* A little fat in the meat is necessary to prevent the meatballs from drying out. Look to use a variety of minced meat: veal, beef, pork, chicken, lamb, or even turkey, adding a little fat (such as chopped bacon) if needed. Veal contains very little fat and is often combined with pork.

* To make fresh breadcrumbs, remove the crusts from day-old bread and cut into chunks. Process in a food processor until breadcrumbs form. Store in the fridge for 1–2 days or freeze in a plastic freezer bag until ready to use.

* Rolling the meatballs with damp hands keeps the meat from sticking to your hands, making shaping easier. In some recipes, dusting your hands with flour is more effective. The meatballs should be rolled quite firmly to prevent them from falling apart when cooking.

* Any meatball will benefit from sitting in the refrigerator for a few hours before cooking; it helps them to firm up a little.

* Uncooked meatballs freeze really well. Freeze them in single layers in lidded plastic containers for up to 3 months.

* If you have children, involve them in mixing, rolling and frying the meatballs. It's a great opportunity to teach them a few cooking skills, as well as introducing them to the pleasures of home-cooked food.

Polpette

Time spent in the oven surrounded by a garlicky tomato sauce seems to give these meatballs an edge in this classic Italian recipe.

Preparation time: 20 minutes, plus refrigeration time
Cooking time: 35 minutes
Serves 4

1 thick slice Italian-style bread, crusts removed
milk, for soaking
650 g minced veal (or a combination of minced pork and veal)
2 cloves garlic, finely chopped
4 tablespoons freshly grated parmesan
2 tablespoons chopped flat-leaf parsley, plus extra to garnish
1 teaspoon finely grated lemon zest
1 large egg, lightly beaten
salt and freshly ground black pepper
plain flour, for dusting
2–3 tablespoons olive oil
2 × 400 g tins crushed tomatoes or 500 ml easy no-chop tomato sauce (see page 205)
2 whole cloves garlic, peeled

1   Break the bread into pieces and soak in a little milk for 5–10 minutes. Squeeze dry, then crumble into a large bowl. Add the minced veal, garlic, parmesan, parsley, lemon zest and beaten egg, and mix well. Season with plenty of salt and pepper.

2   To check the seasoning, fry a small amount of the mixture until cooked through and taste it. Adjust the seasoning as needed.

3   Form the mixture into 5 cm balls, then roll them in flour, shaking off any excess. At this stage you can cover and refrigerate the meatballs for up to 4 hours, if desired.

4   Preheat the oven to 200°C (Gas Mark 6). Heat the olive oil in a large ovenproof frying pan over medium heat and cook the meatballs until brown on all sides (you may need to do this in batches). Remove and drain on kitchen paper.

5   Add the crushed tomatoes or sauce and whole garlic cloves to the frying pan, bring to the boil, then reduce the heat and simmer gently for 5 minutes. Return the meatballs to the pan and transfer to the oven. Alternatively, place them in a gratin or small roasting dish. Cook for 20 minutes, turning the meatballs occasionally. Remove the whole garlic cloves and garnish with extra parsley before serving.

Really Useful Stuff
You can also sprinkle the dish with grated mozzarella before baking. If you want to serve spaghetti and meatballs, roll them much smaller. Don't leave out the soaked bread – it seems to make the meatballs less dense.

Sicilian meatballs

The historic combination of Arab rule and its location close to the shipping routes from nearby Africa and Europe has given Sicily's cuisine an exotic mix of sweet and spicy flavours.

Preparation time: 20 minutes, plus refrigeration time
Cooking time: 25 minutes
Serves 4

2 thick slices Italian-style bread, crusts removed
80 g unblanched almonds, roughly chopped
250 g minced beef
250 g minced pork
1 clove garlic, crushed
4 tablespoons milk
50 g freshly grated parmesan or pecorino
1 large egg
40 g currants
40 g pine nuts
1 tablespoon chopped basil
¼ teaspoon ground cinnamon
¼ teaspoon chilli powder
1 teaspoon salt
vegetable oil, for pan-frying

1 Place the bread and almonds in a food processor and process until coarsely ground. Add the beef, pork, garlic, milk, parmesan or pecorino and egg and process until combined. Transfer to a large bowl.

2 Stir the currants, pine nuts, basil, cinnamon, chilli powder and salt into the mixture. Fry a small amount of the mixture until cooked through and taste it. Adjust the seasoning as needed.

3 Form into 5 cm balls, then cover and refrigerate for at least 30 minutes.

4 Heat the oil in a large frying pan over medium heat. Add the meatballs and cook for 10–12 minutes or until brown on all sides and cooked through (you may need to do this in batches). Remove and drain on kitchen paper.

Really Useful Stuff
These meatballs can be made up to 24 hours ahead; they also freeze well.

Thai-style chicken meatballs in lemongrass broth ›

Don't be deterred by the list of ingredients; this dish is simple to make and is a fabulous meal in a bowl.

Preparation time: 30 minutes
Cooking time: 35 minutes
Serves 4

2 long red chillies, roughly chopped
4 cloves garlic, crushed
finely grated zest of 1 lime
2 teaspoons grated ginger
6 spring onions, roughly sliced
handful of mint, roughly chopped
450 g minced chicken
250 g minced pork
salt and freshly ground black pepper
4 tablespoons vegetable oil
4 small bok choy or choy sum, cut into halves or quarters
1 lime, cut into quarters

Lemongrass broth
2 litres chicken stock
3 cm piece ginger, peeled and roughly chopped
1 small red chilli, whole
2 stems lemongrass, crushed
2 tablespoons Thai fish sauce
salt and freshly ground black pepper
½ cup coriander leaves
½ cup mint leaves

1 To make the broth, heat the chicken stock in a large saucepan and add the ginger, chilli and lemongrass. Bring to the boil, then reduce the heat and simmer gently for about 20 minutes.

2 Meanwhile, place the chillies, garlic, lime zest, ginger, spring onion and mint in a food processor and process until it forms a paste. Add the chicken and pork and process, using the pulse action, until combined. Transfer to a bowl and season well with salt and pepper. Fry a small amount of the mixture until cooked through and taste it. Adjust the seasoning as needed.

3 Form the mixture into 2.5 cm balls. Heat the oil in a large frying pan over medium heat, add the meatballs and cook for about 4–5 minutes each side until golden (you may need to do this in batches). Remove and drain on kitchen paper.

4 Remove the ginger, chilli and lemongrass from the broth. Add the bok choy and meatballs and simmer for 6–7 minutes, or until the meatballs are cooked through and the bok choy is tender. Add the fish sauce and season to taste. Spoon into deep bowls, top with the herbs and serve with lime quarters.

Really Useful Stuff
To make this a more substantial dish, add thin noodles to the broth about 5 minutes before serving.

Nigel Slater's chicken & gruyère rissoles

When you cut into these chicken rissoles, a delicious little pool of molten cheese oozes out.

Preparation time: 20 minutes, plus refrigeration time
Cooking time: 40 minutes
Serves 4

2 slices white bread, crusts removed
350 g good-quality herb and pork sausages
400 g minced chicken
2 cloves garlic, crushed
2 tablespoons chopped flat-leaf parsley
2 teaspoons thyme leaves
salt and freshly ground black pepper
120 g gruyère, cut into 8 cubes
2 tablespoons olive oil
juice of 1 lemon
200 ml chicken stock, heated
1 bay leaf

1 Place the bread in a food processor and process to form breadcrumbs.

2 Remove the meat from the sausage casings and add to the processor, along with the chicken, garlic, parsley, thyme and plenty of salt and pepper. Process until combined.

3 To check the seasoning, fry a small amount of the mixture until cooked through and taste it. Adjust the seasoning as needed.

4 Form the mixture into eight rissoles. With your finger make a hole in the centre and insert a cube of gruyère. Reshape into slightly flattened balls, making sure the cheese is completely covered, then cover and refrigerate for 1 hour.

5 Preheat the oven to 200°C (Gas Mark 6). Heat the olive oil in a large frying pan over medium heat, add the meatballs and cook for 3–4 minutes each side (you may need to do this in batches). Transfer to an ovenproof dish in which the rissoles fit snugly and pour on the lemon juice and hot chicken stock to a depth of about 1 cm. Tuck in the bay leaf. Cook in the oven for about 30 minutes, or until the rissoles are nicely coloured and the stock has reduced and thickened a little.

Really Useful Stuff
These are even better reheated the following day, when the flavours in the rissoles have had time to marry.

Spiced Turkish lamb & mint meatballs

This delicious spiced mixture also makes great hamburgers – just flatten them a little before cooking.

Preparation time: 20 minutes, plus refrigeration time
Cooking time: 25 minutes
Serves 4

2 slices white bread, crusts removed
milk, for soaking
1 red onion, finely chopped
3 cloves garlic, crushed
1–2 long red chillies, chopped
4 tablespoons chopped mint
600 g minced lamb
1 teaspoon ground cumin
1 teaspoon ground coriander
finely grated zest of 1 lemon
salt and freshly grated pepper
2 tablespoons olive oil
1 lemon, cut into quarters

Yoghurt dressing
125 ml plain yoghurt
2 tablespoons chopped mint
salt and freshly ground black pepper

1 Break the bread into pieces and soak in a little milk for 5–10 minutes. Squeeze dry, then crumble into a large bowl. Add the onion, garlic, chilli, mint, lamb, cumin, coriander, lemon zest, salt and pepper. Mix well with your hands until combined.

2 To check the seasoning, fry a small amount of the mixture until cooked through and taste it. Adjust the seasoning as needed.

3 Lightly flour your hands and form the mixture into eight balls, then cover and refrigerate for 1 hour.

4 Preheat the oven to 200°C (Gas Mark 6). Heat the olive oil in a large ovenproof frying pan over medium heat, add the meatballs and cook for 3–4 minutes each side. Transfer the pan to the oven and cook for 15 minutes, or until the meatballs are golden and cooked through.

5 To make the yoghurt dressing, mix the yoghurt with the chopped mint. Season well with salt and pepper.

6 Drizzle the yoghurt dressing over the meatballs and serve with lemon wedges.

Really Useful Stuff
These meatballs can be placed on skewers and barbecued, if desired. They are delicious served in pita bread with the yoghurt dressing.

Vegetarian burgers

Proving that burgers do not have to rely on meat or fish to get their flavour, these soft-textured patties are made with fresh herbs, feta and breadcrumbs.

Preparation time: 20 minutes
Cooking time: 15 minutes
Serves 4

1 tablespoon olive oil
1 brown onion, finely chopped
½ long red chilli, chopped
1 clove garlic, chopped
125 g feta, crumbled
1 tablespoon chopped mint
1 tablespoon snipped chives
125 g breadcrumbs, made from day-old bread
3 tablespoons gram flour (chickpea flour)
1 egg, lightly beaten
salt and freshly ground black pepper
safflower oil, for pan-frying

1   Heat the olive oil in a small frying pan and sauté the onion, chilli and garlic for about 5 minutes, or until just softened.

2   Combine the feta, mint, chives, breadcrumbs, gram flour and egg in a large bowl, add the onion mixture and mix well. Season with salt and pepper. Cover and chill the mixture for about 1 hour to firm it up a little.

3   Divide the mixture in half and shape each portion into four small flat patties.

4   Heat a thin layer of safflower oil in a heavy frying pan over medium–low heat. When the oil is hot, add four burgers and cook over low heat for 2–3 minutes until browned. Turn and cook for a further minute or two, or until golden. Remove and keep warm while you cook the remaining burgers.

5   Serve two burgers per person with a little sliced avocado and mayonnaise and a green leaf salad. Also good with spiced tomato relish on the side.

Hamburgers

The best traditional hamburgers are made with all-beef patties. Here I simply add a dash of Worcestershire and a little tomato sauce to the mixture – what could be simpler?

Preparation time: 15 minutes
Cooking time: 10 minutes
Makes 2

250 g minced beef
2 tablespoons tomato ketchup
dash of Worcestershire sauce
salt and freshly ground black pepper
1 tablespoon vegetable oil
butter, for spreading
2 good-quality bread rolls, split in half
50 g rocket leaves
1 ripe tomato, sliced
1 cooked beetroot, sliced

1   Combine the beef, tomato ketchup and Worcestershire sauce in a bowl and season with plenty of salt and pepper. Divide the mixture in half and shape each portion into a 10 cm patty. Do not over-handle the meat – it will toughen the hamburgers.

2   Heat the oil in a heavy frying pan over medium–high heat. When the oil is hot, add the burgers and cook for 2–3 minutes until browned. Turn and cook for a further minute or two, or until well browned and cooked to your liking.

3   Meanwhile, lightly butter the rolls and cover the bottom halves with rocket. Top each with a burger and then a layer of tomato and beetroot. Season lightly and top with the other half of the roll.

Really Useful Stuff
Avoid low-fat minced meat when making burgers, as a little bit of fat will make them juicier. I often add 2 finely chopped rashers of bacon for extra flavour.

Don't forget to offer tomato ketchup, barbecue sauce or mayonnaise with the burgers.

Meringues

Something rather wonderful occurs when you whisk egg whites and sugar together. Despite their reputation for being tricky, meringues can easily be made at home without a lot of fuss or bother. To make the job easy, you will need the help of a trusty bench-top electric mixer or hand-held electric beaters (don't even try to do it by hand) to whisk the egg whites and sugar into those irresistible airy swirls. If the thought of eating such sweet crispy delights fills you with guilt, remember that egg whites are low in fat.

Hints & Tips

✻ To separate an egg, break the egg on the side of a bowl, separating the egg shell into two halves – the yolk will generally sit in the rounder, less pointed half. There are two ways to proceed: either tip the egg into a (very clean) cupped hand, then slightly open your fingers and let the egg white slip through into a bowl, or transfer the yolk back and forth between the two halves of the egg shell, allowing the whites to fall into the bowl.

✻ Make sure the egg whites are at room temperature and free of any specks of egg yolk.

✻ Make sure that the bowl and beaters you are using are spotlessly clean and free of grease – rubbing the inside of the bowl with a cut lemon is a good idea.

✻ If you make meringues on a rainy or humid day, you will probably have to bake them for longer than on a dry day (up to 20 minutes more).

✻ To prevent the meringues from cracking during cooking, do not open the oven door for the first half of the baking time.

✻ Store individual meringues for up to 2 weeks in an airtight container.

Individual meringues

You can serve individual meringues as a tea-time treat (delicious with strawberries) or as an instant dessert with lemon curd or chocolate sauce, served with ice-cream. These meringues store well so are great to make ahead of time. They'll keep in an airtight container for up to 7 days.

Preparation time: 20 minutes, plus cooling time
Cooking time: 40 minutes
Makes 12–15

3 large egg whites
pinch of salt
175 g caster sugar

1   Preheat the oven to 140°C (Gas Mark 1). Line two baking trays with baking paper.

2   Place the egg whites and salt in the clean, dry bowl of an electric mixer. Using the whisk attachment, start on a low speed for 1 minute and then increase the speed to medium and whisk for 2–3 minutes, or until the egg whites form fairly stiff but still moist-looking peaks – if you lift the whisk out of the bowl, the mixture should look fluffy and should cling to the whisk. Continue to whisk, gradually adding the sugar 1 tablespoon at a time. Continue beating and slowly adding the sugar until the mixture is stiff and glossy – this may take 5–10 minutes.

3   If you like, you can add a flavouring at this stage (see left). Fold in your chosen flavouring with a large metal spoon, using large gentle strokes and turning the bowl as you go. Continue until evenly distributed.

4   Using a large metal spoon, spoon free-form shapes onto the prepared trays. Bake for 30–40 minutes (swapping the position of the trays after 20 minutes), or until pale and dry. Turn off the oven and allow the meringues to cool in the oven with the door slightly ajar.

Really useful stuff

Chocolate meringues

Prepare the meringue mixture as far as the end of step 2, when the egg whites are stiff and glossy and all the sugar has been added. Fold 2 tablespoons sifted cocoa and 40 g finely chopped or grated dark chocolate into the mixture. Spoon out and bake as for basic recipe.

Marbled meringues

Prepare the meringue mixture as far as the end of step 2, when the egg whites are stiff and glossy and all the sugar has been added. Spoon 2 heaped tablespoons per meringue onto lined baking sheets. Place a drop or two of pink food colouring in each and, using a skewer, swirl the meringues to create a marbled effect. Bake as for basic recipe.

Chocolate fingers

Prepare the meringue mixture as far as the end of step 2, when the egg whites are stiff and glossy and all the sugar has been added. Fold in 2 tablespoons sifted cocoa. Spoon into a piping bag fitted with a rosette or star nozzle and pipe 7.5 cm fingers onto lined baking trays. Bake for 15–20 minutes. When cool, drizzle with melted chocolate.

‹ Almond bread

This is perfect served alongside creamy desserts
or ice-cream.

Preparation time: 30 minutes, plus cooling time
Cooking time: 1 hour
Makes about 25 slices

200 g whole blanched almonds
5 egg whites
pinch of salt
200 g caster sugar
185 g plain flour, sifted

You will also need
a large loaf tin

1 Preheat the oven to 180°C (Gas Mark 4). Lightly grease the
loaf tin and line it with baking paper, making sure it overhangs
the two long sides.

2 Spread the almonds on a baking tray and lightly toast in the
oven for 2–3 minutes. Remove and leave to cool.

3 Place the egg whites and salt in a clean, dry bowl and whisk
with an electric mixer or hand-held electric beaters until stiff
peaks form. Gradually add the caster sugar, beating well after
each addition. Beat until the mixture is stiff and glossy.

4 Fold in the almonds and flour with a large metal spoon, then
spoon into the prepared loaf tin. Bake for 35–40 minutes, or
until firm and lightly coloured. Reduce the oven temperature
to 140°C (Gas Mark 1).

5 Allow the almond bread to cool in the tin, then slice into
4 mm slices – a serrated knife is good for this. Place the slices
in a single layer on a baking sheet and return to the oven
for 10–15 minutes, or until lightly golden, dry and crisp.
Serve with coffee or as an accompaniment to ice-cream.

Really Useful Stuff
The almond bread is easier to slice if chilled overnight in the fridge
after cooking.

Pavlova

The soft and gooey centre of a classic pavlova is created
by adding a little vinegar and cornflour to the mix.

Preparation time: 25 minutes, plus cooling time
Cooking time: 1¼ hours
Serves 8

4 egg whites
pinch of salt
250 g caster sugar
1 teaspoon white vinegar
½ teaspoon vanilla essence
2 teaspoons cornflour
sweetened whipped cream, to serve
ripe seasonal fruit, to serve

1 Preheat the oven to 120°C (Gas Mark 1). Line a baking tray
with baking paper, then draw a circle 20 cm in diameter in the
middle of the baking paper.

2 Place the egg whites and salt in a clean, dry bowl. Beat with
electric beaters until soft peaks form. Gradually add the caster
sugar, beating well after each addition. Beat until the mixture
is stiff and glossy. Fold in the vinegar, vanilla and cornflour.

3 Heap the mixture onto the circle on the baking paper, shaping
the meringue with a spatula and leaving the centre slightly
hollowed. Cook for 1–1¼ hours, or until crisp and dry on the
outside. Turn off the oven and allow to cool in the oven with
the door ajar.

4 To serve, top with whipped cream and sliced seasonal fruit.

Really Useful Stuff
Traditionally, pavlova is served with strawberries and passionfruit,
but it is also good with whipped cream, lemon curd and mixed berries.

The base may be made a few days ahead and stored in an airtight
container until ready to use.

Bomb Alaska mince pies

This is a simple and delicious way to dress up ready-made mince pies.

Preparation time: 20 minutes
Cooking time: 5 minutes
Makes 12

12 ready-made mince pies
300 ml good-quality vanilla ice-cream
3 egg whites
125 g caster sugar

1 Preheat the oven to 220°C (Gas Mark 7). Remove the pastry 'lids' from the mince pies and top each with 1 rounded tablespoon vanilla ice-cream. Arrange the pies on a small baking tray, then place in the freezer to chill while you make the meringue.

2 Whisk the egg whites in a large clean bowl with electric beaters, until they form soft peaks. Gradually add the caster sugar, whisking well after each addition, and continue to whisk until the mixture is glossy and forms stiff peaks.

3 Remove the tray of mince pies from the freezer, then pipe or spread the meringue over the top of the ice-cream, forming peaked witch's-hat shapes. Bake for 5 minutes, or until lightly browned. Serve immediately.

Coffee & hazelnut kisses

Meringues work well with many flavours. Here, instant coffee powder and chopped hazelnuts make a delicious combination.

Preparation time: 25 minutes, plus cooling time
Cooking time: 20 minutes
Makes about 12–15

3 large egg whites
pinch of salt
175 g caster sugar
1 tablespoon instant coffee powder (not granules)
3 tablespoons finely chopped toasted hazelnuts
125 g dark chocolate, chopped
50 g butter, chopped

1 Preheat the oven to 140°C (Gas Mark 1). Line two baking trays with baking paper.

2 Place the egg whites and a pinch of salt in the bowl of an electric mixer. Using the whisk attachment, start on a low speed for 1 minute and then increase the speed to medium and whisk for 2–3 minutes, or until the egg whites form fairly stiff, but still moist-looking peaks – if you lift the whisk out of the bowl, the mixture should look fluffy and should cling to the whisk. Continue to whisk, gradually adding the sugar 1 tablespoon at a time. Continue beating and slowly adding the sugar, until the mixture is stiff and glossy – this may take 5–10 minutes.

3 Fold in the instant coffee and chopped hazelnuts with a large metal spoon, using large gentle strokes and turning the bowl as you go. Continue until evenly distributed.

4 Spoon the mixture into a piping bag with a star nozzle and pipe stars onto the prepared baking sheets. Bake for about 15–20 minutes until pale and dry.

5 Meanwhile, melt the chocolate and butter in a bowl set over a pan of very hot water, stirring until smooth. Set aside to cool, then beat with a wooden spoon until smooth and fluffy.

6 When the meringues have cooled, sandwich them together with a little of the chocolate mixture.

Really Useful Stuff

It's a good idea to make the meringues the day before you want to serve. Then make the chocolate filling a couple of hours ahead, and sandwich together just before serving.

Muffins & small cakes

A simple muffin recipe can turn anyone into a great baker. What could be easier than combining everyday ingredients, spooning the batter into paper cases and then baking it for about 20 minutes? Muffins are the only cakes I know where lumps in the batter are a good thing. And they're so versatile – there's a variation to suit all tastes, whether sweet or savoury. Once you've mastered muffins, do give cupcakes and madeleines a go: they're perfect for an afternoon-tea treat.

Hints & Tips

✱ The most important rule when making muffins is not to overmix the batter. It doesn't need to be smooth – for once, lumps are allowed. Mix gently with a large metal spoon until the ingredients are just combined.

✱ Buttermilk adds acidity to the mixture which helps the raising agents to act. If you can't find buttermilk, use a mixture of half plain yoghurt and half skim milk, or sour regular milk by stirring in 2 teaspoons of lemon juice.

✱ When baking cakes and sweet dishes, I use unsalted butter.

✱ No paper muffin cases to hand? Make your own by cutting circles of baking paper about 3–4 cm wider than the size of the cups in the tin. Grease the tin with a little soft butter (to help the paper stick) and line the cups with the circles, leaving the folded edges standing up – the effect is irregular and attractive.

✱ If you like the idea of fresh muffins for breakfast, the batter can be spooned into the tin and refrigerated overnight before baking in the morning. You can also spoon the batter into the paper cases and then freeze them. Cook from frozen, adding a few extra minutes to the cooking time.

✱ If there is a down-side to muffins, it has to be their poor keeping quality, so bake and serve warm. Friands will happily keep for up to 2 days.

✱ You can make a crumble topping for muffins or small cakes by combining 60 g chopped pecans, 100 g light brown sugar, 50 g plain flour, 3 heaped tablespoons rolled oats (porridge oats) and 50 g melted butter. Sprinkle over the batter before baking.

Classic blueberry muffins

These are classic American-style muffins. So easy to make – the ingredients simply need a gentle mix.

Preparation time: 15 minutes
Cooking time: 25 minutes
Makes 12

310 g plain flour
2 teaspoons baking powder
½ teaspoon bicarbonate of soda
pinch of salt
200 g caster sugar
finely grated zest of ½ orange
300 ml buttermilk
2 eggs
1 teaspoon vanilla essence
125 g unsalted butter, melted
200 g fresh or frozen blueberries

You will also need
a 12-hole muffin tin

1   Preheat the oven to 190°C (Gas Mark 5). Grease the muffin tin and line with paper muffin cases.

2   Sift the flour, baking powder, bicarbonate of soda and salt into a mixing bowl. Stir in the sugar and the orange zest and make a well in the centre.

3   Whisk together the buttermilk, eggs, vanilla and melted butter. Pour into the dry ingredients and stir with a wooden spoon until the ingredients are just combined. Do not overmix – the batter should not be smooth. Add the fruit and lightly fold to combine (again, do not overmix).

4   Spoon the mixture into the muffin cases and bake for 20–25 minutes, or until the tops are firm and golden and a skewer inserted into the centre of a muffin comes out clean. Allow to cool in the tin for 5 minutes before turning out onto a wire rack. Serve warm.

Really Useful Stuff
The blueberries can be replaced with raspberries or blackberries or even strawberries to make a whole variety of berry muffins – you can even combine berries, if desired.

If using frozen berries, don't thaw them first – use straight from the freezer.

Chocolate chip muffins

The chocolate chips and chopped nuts give each mouthful a delicious burst of flavour.

Preparation time: 15 minutes
Cooking time: 20 minutes
Makes 12

300 g self-raising flour
125 g caster sugar
pinch of salt
100 g unsalted butter, chilled and diced
100 g dark chocolate chips, plus extra to decorate
50 g finely chopped almonds or hazelnuts (optional)
2 eggs
about 175 ml buttermilk

You will also need
a 12-hole muffin tin

1 Preheat the oven to 200°C (Gas Mark 6). Grease the muffin tin and line with paper muffin cases.

2 Sift the flour, sugar and salt into a mixing bowl. Using your fingertips, rub the butter into the flour until the mixture resembles coarse breadcrumbs. Stir in the chocolate chips and nuts, if using.

3 Break the eggs into a measuring jug and beat lightly, then pour in enough buttermilk to make 250 ml. Add the egg mixture to the bowl and mix with a large metal spoon until the dough comes together (it will be quite sticky). Take care not to overmix.

4 Spoon the dough into the muffin cases, then sprinkle extra chocolate chips over the top. Bake for about 20 minutes or until firm to the touch. Remove from the oven, leave in the tin for a few minutes then transfer to a wire rack.

Really Useful Stuff
These muffins can be made with dark, milk or white chocolate.

You can also replace 3 tablespoons of the flour with cocoa powder.

Pistachio & white chocolate friands

Pistachios work perfectly with white chocolate and also add an interesting colour to the finished friands. Make sure you buy ready-shelled, unsalted pistachios.

Preparation time: 20 minutes
Cooking time: 30 minutes
Makes 8

100 g unsalted pistachio kernels
125 g icing sugar, sifted, plus extra to serve
50 g plain flour, sifted
2 teaspoons finely grated lemon zest
100 g unsalted butter
100 g white chocolate, chopped
5 egg whites

You will also need
8 friand tins or baby brioche tins

1 Preheat the oven to 180°C (Gas Mark 4). Lightly grease the tins.

2 Place the nuts and half the icing sugar in a food processor and process until the nuts are finely ground. Transfer to a mixing bowl. Add the flour, zest and remaining icing sugar.

3 Melt the butter and chopped chocolate in a small saucepan over low heat, stirring occasionally until smooth.

4 Lightly beat the egg whites with a fork until just fluffy and pour into the bowl with the dry ingredients. Add the melted butter and chocolate and mix with a wooden spoon until smooth. The mixture will be quite wet, but this is fine.

5 Spoon the mixture into the prepared tins until three-quarters full. Bake for 20–25 minutes, or until golden, risen and firm to the touch. Allow to cool in the tins for 10 minutes before turning out onto a wire rack to cool completely. Dust with icing sugar before serving.

Really Useful Stuff
These little cakes can also be made in baby loaf tins or muffin tins. Specialist cookware shops stock a variety of small tins.

The cooking time may vary slightly depending on the tin you use – just keep an eye on them: they are ready when golden and firm to the touch. Don't open the oven door until they look ready.

Other nuts work well with this recipe – try using the same quantity of ground pecans, almonds or hazelnuts.

Simple lemon cupcakes

Baking a lovely batch of cakes really can be this easy.
One word of advice: make sure the butter is very soft.

Preparation time: 10 minutes
Cooking time: 20 minutes
Makes 12

175 g unsalted butter, softened at room temperature
175 g caster sugar
3 eggs, lightly beaten
finely grated zest of 1 lemon
175 g self-raising flour
1 teaspoon baking powder

You will also need
a 12-hole muffin tin or cupcake tin

1 Preheat the oven to 170°C (Gas Mark 3). Line the tin with paper cases.

2 Place the butter, sugar, egg and lemon zest in a large mixing bowl. Sift in the flour and baking powder and use a large wooden spoon to beat until the mixture just comes together (don't overbeat).

3 Spoon the mixture into the paper cases and bake for about 20 minutes, or until golden and firm to the touch. A skewer inserted into the centre of a cake should come out clean. Leave in the tin for a few minutes before turning out onto a wire rack to cool. Dust with icing sugar or spread with fresh strawberry icing (see below).

Really Useful Stuff
You can make a delicious orange cake simply by replacing the lemon zest with orange zest.

To make fresh strawberry icing, put 4 hulled and halved strawberries in a bowl and mash with a fork. Sift 240 g icing sugar over the strawberries and mix well. Add enough hot water (about 1–2 teaspoons) to produce a spreadable consistency.

Orange madeleines

I have a bit of a reputation for my afternoon teas, and much of the credit must go to these delicious little sponge cakes. The traditional shell-shaped madeleine trays are definitely worth the investment.

Preparation time: 10 minutes
Cooking time: 10 minutes
Makes 18

2 eggs
60 g caster sugar, plus extra to serve
finely grated zest of ½ orange
4 tablespoons plain flour
50 g unsalted butter, melted

You will also need
a madeleine tin

1 Preheat the oven to 180°C (Gas Mark 4). Lightly grease the tin and dust with flour.

2 Whisk together the eggs, sugar and orange zest for about 3–4 minutes, or until the sugar has dissolved and the mixture has increased in volume and is thick and pale.

3 Sift the flour on top and fold in gently with a large metal spoon. Stir in the melted butter until just combined.

4 Spoon the mixture into each hole until three-quarters full (depending on the size of your tin, you may need to do this in two batches). Bake for 8–10 minutes, or until risen and firm to the touch. Leave in the tin for a few minutes, then transfer to a wire rack. Sprinkle lightly with caster sugar while still warm and serve within a couple of hours of baking.

Really Useful Stuff
Make chocolate madeleines by sifting a heaped tablespoon of cocoa with the flour and omitting the orange zest. Dust the madeleine tin with sifted cocoa rather than flour before baking.

You can also make these in a shallow patty tin, though because they are slightly larger, this quantity of mixture will only make 12 cakes.

Rock cakes

I was sent off to school most days with one of these in my lunchbox – baking and eating them again has made me realise how lucky I was! This recipe comes from my mum's handwritten cookbook from the early 1960s.

Preparation time: 20 minutes
Cooking time: 15 minutes
Makes 12

225 g self-raising flour
½ teaspoon baking powder
pinch of salt
125 g unsalted butter, chilled and diced
80 g sugar
200 g sultanas
1 teaspoon finely grated lemon or orange zest
1 large egg
2–3 tablespoons milk

1 Preheat the oven to 190°C (Gas Mark 5). Lightly grease a baking sheet.

2 Sift the flour, baking powder and salt into a large bowl. Using your fingertips, rub the butter into the flour until the mixture resembles coarse breadcrumbs. Stir in the sugar, sultanas and grated zest.

3 Mix together the egg and milk and pour into the dry ingredients. Mix with a wooden spoon until the mixture comes together (it should be fairly stiff, but add a little extra milk if needed).

4 Spoon mounds of dough about the size of a golf ball onto the prepared baking sheet, leaving room for spreading, and bake for 12–15 minutes or until golden. Transfer to a wire rack to cool. Best served plain or buttered with mugs of tea.

Really Useful Stuff
You can use either sultanas or currants in this recipe. And mixed peel makes a nice addition – add about 2 tablespoons, if desired.

Cheese & chive muffins ›

These muffins are great as snacks or in a lunchbox, but they also go really well with soup. I often make them in mini muffin tins to accompany tomato soup.

Preparation time: 15 minutes
Cooking time: 30 minutes
Makes 12

350 g self-raising flour
½ teaspoon bicarbonate of soda
salt and freshly ground black pepper
2 teaspoons snipped chives
75 g feta, cut into 5 mm cubes
50 g freshly grated parmesan
150 g grated cheddar
300 ml buttermilk
2 eggs, lightly beaten
100 g unsalted butter, melted

You will also need
a 12-hole muffin tin

1 Preheat the oven to 190°C (Gas Mark 5). Grease the muffin tin or line with paper muffin cases.

2 Sift the flour, bicarbonate of soda and a pinch of salt into a mixing bowl. Stir in the chives, feta, parmesan, a couple of grindings of black pepper and most of the cheddar (reserve a little for sprinkling). Make a well in the centre.

3 Whisk together the buttermilk, egg and melted butter. Pour into the dry ingredients and stir until the ingredients are just combined. Do not overmix – the batter should not be smooth.

4 Spoon the mixture into the muffin cases and sprinkle with the remaining cheddar. Bake for 25–30 minutes, or until the tops are golden and a skewer inserted into the centre of a muffin comes out clean. Leave in the tin for 5 minutes before turning out onto a wire rack.

Really Useful Stuff
If you don't have any buttermilk, use 300 ml milk soured with 1 teaspoon lemon juice.

These muffins are best eaten the day they are made, and are delicious with a little butter.

Omelettes & frittatas

To me, simple egg dishes like omelettes and frittatas are perfect 'fast food'. Even the best-quality organic eggs are reasonably inexpensive, making any egg dish nice and affordable. Eggs are a terrific vehicle for a wide range of flavours, from mushrooms and bacon to asparagus and smoked salmon, so whatever your mood you'll find a recipe to suit.

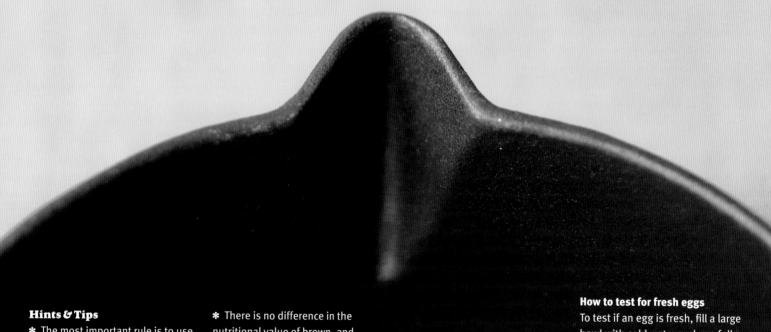

Hints & Tips

* The most important rule is to use the best eggs you can find – the difference in flavour is enormous. Ideally, look for free-range organic eggs at a local market.

* Look beyond hen eggs. There are a few small producers now selling bantam, duck, pheasant and quail eggs (in season) – look out for them at produce markets. You can use a couple of hen eggs and then add one or two of these (depending on the size of the eggs) as a variation. There are no hard and fast rules.

* There is no difference in the nutritional value of brown- and white-shelled eggs – the colour of the shell is simply determined by the breed of the hen.

* Eggs should be stored at a constant temperature, preferably below 8°C.

* Although special omelette pans are available, any heavy, non-stick frying pan will make a good omelette.

* An omelette will not sit even for a minute, so don't cook it until you are ready to eat it.

* Depending on your taste, you can serve an omelette runny in the middle, moist or firmly cooked – it is only a matter of adjusting the cooking time. Do remember that it will continue to firm slightly after cooking.

* If making omelettes for a few people, I tend to undercook the first few and keep them warm in a low oven – they have usually firmed up perfectly by the time I'm ready to serve.

How to test for fresh eggs

To test if an egg is fresh, fill a large bowl with cold water and carefully place an egg in the water. A very fresh egg will immediately sink to the bottom and lie flat on its side. As the egg starts to lose freshness (and more air enters the egg), it will begin to stand upright with its smaller end lying on the bottom of the bowl (if it does this it will still be OK to eat). If the egg fully floats in the water and does not touch the bottom of the bowl at all, it should be discarded as it is unlikely to be very fresh.

Classic herb omelette

This is my favourite Sunday night treat after a big lunch, or a simple weeknight dinner if I have had a busy day testing recipes and just want something easy and delicious for supper. Buy the best organic eggs you can find.

Preparation time: 5 minutes
Cooking time: 5 minutes
Makes 1

15 g butter
3 large organic eggs
salt and freshly ground black pepper
1–2 tablespoons chopped herbs
   (chives, chervil, parsley or basil)

You will also need
a small non-stick frying pan

1 Melt the butter in a small non-stick frying pan over medium heat.

2 Meanwhile, quickly beat the eggs in a bowl. Season well with salt and pepper and add the chopped herbs.

3 When the butter has stopped foaming, add the beaten egg to the pan. Move it around the pan with a fork until it begins to set. Tip the pan a little and lift the edges of the omelette, so that any runny egg flows underneath and starts to set. This will take less than a minute. If you are adding a filling (see below for suggestions), place this over one half of the omelette now.

4 Ease the fork or a spatula under the edge of the omelette and, tilting the pan slightly, fold it in half. Cook for 30–60 seconds, then slide the omelette onto a plate. The eggs should be completely cooked on the outside, but still creamy and soft in the centre.

Really Useful Stuff
Good fillings for omelettes include cheese, crumbled crisp bacon, grilled mushrooms, steamed asparagus, tomato and basil, and smoked salmon.

Mascarpone, zucchini & parmesan frittata

Equally delicious warm or cold, frittata is perfect picnic fare. It makes a more-ish snack, and is also good cut into small pieces and served as part of an antipasto platter, or with drinks.

Preparation time: 10 minutes
Cooking time: 25 minutes
Serves 4

1 tablespoon olive oil
1 zucchini (courgette), trimmed and
    sliced into 5 mm thick rounds
6 large organic eggs
150 g mascarpone
1 tablespoon chopped flat-leaf parsley
125 g freshly grated parmesan
salt and freshly ground black pepper

1 Preheat the oven to 190°C (Gas Mark 5). Heat the oil in a large ovenproof frying pan over medium heat and sauté the zucchini for 3–4 minutes. Remove the pan from the heat.

2 Whisk together the eggs and mascarpone until just combined, then stir in the parsley and three-quarters of the parmesan. Season with salt and pepper.

3 Place the frying pan with the zucchini back on the heat and pour in the egg mixture. Reduce the heat to low and cook, stirring once or twice, for 7–8 minutes – the bottom should be firm and the top a little soft. Sprinkle with the remaining parmesan.

4 Place the pan in the oven and cook for 5–10 minutes, until the top is puffed and set and the cheese is golden. Serve straight from the pan or place a large flat plate over the top of the pan and invert the frittata onto it. Serve warm or at room temperature with a rocket salad.

Really Useful Stuff
Replace the zucchini with 100 g baby English spinach leaves if desired, or leave out the mascarpone and use 125 ml cream instead.

Try incorporating sautéed mushrooms, cooked asparagus, prosciutto, drained marinated artichokes, feta, goat's cheese or cooked potato slices. Variations on this recipe are only limited by the ingredients you happen to have to hand.

Tortilla Española ›

I prefer to eat tortilla hot, but a good tortilla is also enjoyable cold or at room temperature.

Preparation time: 20 minutes
Cooking time: 1 hour
Serves 6

olive oil, for pan-frying
700 g onions, finely sliced
700 g potatoes
5 organic eggs
salt and freshly ground black pepper

You will also need
a small non-stick blini pan or 23–25 cm non-stick frying pan

1 Heat 4 tablespoons of olive oil in a deep, medium frying pan over low heat. Add the onion and cook slowly, stirring occasionally, for about 30 minutes until soft and golden.

2 Meanwhile, peel the potatoes and slice into 1 cm rounds. Add the potatoes to the onion and turn up the heat a little. Cook for 10–15 minutes until the potatoes are soft and golden, but not crispy, stirring frequently and breaking them up with a spatula. When the mixture becomes a brown mush, take off the heat and drain well on kitchen paper. Allow to cool slightly.

3 Beat the eggs in a large bowl. Add the potato and onion mix and season well with salt and pepper. Heat 1 teaspoon of olive oil in the non-stick pan over medium heat and add a sixth of the mixture. Cook for about 2 minutes, gently pushing the back of the spatula around the edge of the tortilla to create a rounded edge.

4 Invert the tortilla onto a plate, then slide it back into the pan and cook the other side for about 2 minutes – it should still be nice and runny in the middle. Turn out on to a warm plate and keep warm. Repeat to make the remaining tortillas, then serve immediately.

Really Useful Stuff
You can make a delicious prawn tortilla by replacing half the potatoes with prawns. Cook half the amount of potatoes as above, and then add cooked and peeled prawns when the potato and onion mixture has been removed from the heat.

Pancakes

Whoever invented pancakes was a very clever soul, and someone I am greatly indebted to. Who would have thought that a combination of flour, milk and eggs (plus a little butter) could produce my best-loved Sunday breakfast – a stack of American-style pancakes drizzled in maple syrup. And what's more, these versatile goodies are comfortable being thick or thin with sweet or savoury flavourings. Once you've learnt the basics, the possibilities are endless.

Hints & Tips

✴ When making crêpes and pancakes, I use a non-stick frying pan with a base measurement of 16 cm.

✴ Many people recommend letting your batter rest for an hour or two before cooking. Sometimes I do let it rest (mainly because I want to get prepared ahead of time) but if I'm in a hurry I don't bother, and the results are pretty much the same. If you are making ahead, you may need to add a little extra liquid to the batter before cooking.

✴ Buttermilk makes a good substitute for regular milk in pancake batter – it gives them a little extra rise as well as an interesting flavour.

✴ When cooking classic American-style pancakes, you generally don't need to grease a non-stick pan, but it helps to rub the pan with some buttered kitchen paper before cooking the first batch. With crêpes or English-style pancakes, you may need to grease the pan after every third crêpe.

✴ I usually start by making a small pancake or crêpe first to test the batter, heat and timing – this one is the cook's treat!

✴ You may have to adjust the temperature as you go – reduce the heat a little after you have cooked the first few crêpes or pancakes.

✴ Pancakes and crêpes can be cooked ahead of time and reheated to serve. You can do this on a low heat in the microwave (with baking paper between the pancakes), or cover them with foil and warm in a low oven, or stack them on a heatproof plate, cover with foil and set over a pan of barely simmering water.

✴ Cooked pancakes and crêpes also freeze very well. Place a layer of baking paper between the pancakes, wrap in plastic and freeze for up to 2 months.

Basic crêpes

These simple crêpes are at their best sprinkled with sugar and drizzled with lemon juice.

Preparation time: 10 minutes
Cooking time: 15 minutes
Makes 6–8

150 g plain flour
pinch of salt
2 eggs, lightly beaten
320 ml milk
30 g butter, melted, plus extra for greasing

1 Sift the flour and salt into a bowl, and make a well in the centre.

2 In a separate bowl, combine the beaten egg, milk and melted butter. Gradually pour the wet ingredients into the dry ingredients and mix until a smooth batter forms. Alternatively, whiz the ingredients in a food processor or use a stick blender. The consistency should be similar to pouring cream, so add a little extra milk if needed.

3 Lightly grease a small non-stick frying pan (use kitchen paper spread with a little butter) and place over medium heat for 2–3 minutes.

4 Ladle the batter into the pan, and tilt the pan until the base is thinly coated. Cook for about 1 minute, or until bubbles appear on the top and the underside is golden. The edges should start to brown and crisp. Using a spatula, flip the crêpe over and cook for a further 45–60 seconds. Turn out onto a warm plate and keep warm while you cook the remaining crêpes, greasing the pan after every three crêpes.

Really Useful Stuff

For sweet crêpes, add 1–2 teaspoons sugar to the flour before adding the egg mixture. Serve with maple syrup or a squeeze of lemon juice and a sprinkling of sugar.

For savoury crêpes, fill them with ratatouille or mushrooms cooked in a little cream.

Crêpes with ham & pesto

These make a terrific brunch or lunch dish. Serve simply with a few salad leaves.

Preparation time: 20 minutes
Cooking time: 40 minutes
Serves 4

200 g plain flour
½ teaspoon salt
3 eggs, beaten
375 ml milk
200 g pesto (see page 206)
16 thin slices ham
40 g butter, melted, plus extra for greasing
50 g gruyère, freshly grated
50 g freshly grated parmesan
freshly ground black pepper

1   Sift the flour and salt into a mixing bowl. Combine the beaten egg and milk and mix into the flour. Add extra liquid if needed – the batter should be the consistency of pouring cream.

2   Grease a small non-stick frying pan (use kitchen paper spread with a little butter) and place over medium heat for 1 minute. Ladle 2–3 tablespoons of batter into the pan and tilt the pan until the base is thinly coated. Cook for 1–2 minutes, or until bubbles appear on the top and the underside is golden. The edges should start to brown and crisp. Using a spatula, flip the crêpe over and cook for a further 45–60 seconds before turning out. Repeat with the remaining batter to make 16 crêpes.

3   Preheat oven to 180°C (Gas Mark 4) and grease an ovenproof dish with butter.

4   Spread each crêpe with some pesto and place a slice of ham on top. Fold in half, then in half again and finally fold once more, making a triangle shape. Layer the crêpes in the prepared dish, drizzle with melted butter and sprinkle with the combined cheeses. Season with pepper and bake for about 15 minutes or until the crêpes are heated through and the cheese has melted.

Really Useful Stuff
You can make the batter up to 2 hours before using. You can also make the crêpes ahead of time, then fill and bake when ready to serve.

Classic American-style pancakes ›

The mixture for these classic pancakes (or drop scones) can be made well in advance – even the night before – and cooked when hungry eaters have taken their place at the table.

Preparation time: 10 minutes
Cooking time: 25 minutes
Makes 6–8

250 g plain flour
pinch of salt
2 teaspoons bicarbonate of soda
3 tablespoons caster sugar
2 eggs, lightly beaten
250–300 ml buttermilk, or milk soured with
    a squeeze of lemon juice
40 g butter, melted, plus extra for greasing
maple syrup, to serve

1   Sift the flour, salt and bicarbonate of soda into a bowl. Stir in the sugar and make a well in the centre.

2   In a separate bowl, combine the beaten egg, milk and melted butter. Gently stir the wet ingredients into the dry ingredients and mix just enough to moisten the batter (a few lumps won't matter). Add a little extra milk if the batter seems thick – it should be the consistency of double cream or drinking yoghurt.

3   Preheat the oven to 150°C (Gas Mark 2). Grease a large non-stick frying pan with a little butter (use kitchen paper spread with a little butter) and place over medium heat for 2–3 minutes. Ladle enough batter into the pan to form a pancake about 10 cm in diameter (cook 3–4 pancakes at a time, depending on the size of your pan). Cook for about 2–3 minutes, or until bubbles appear on the top and the underside is golden. Using a spatula, flip the pancake over and cook for a further minute or so before turning out. Keep warm in the oven while you make the rest (the mixture makes about 24 pancakes). Serve warm in short stacks with maple syrup.

Really Useful Stuff

Blueberry pancakes
Add 1 cup of blueberries to the batter just before cooking.

Banana pancakes
Slice one or two ripe bananas into thin rounds. After pouring the batter into the pan, place two or three rounds onto the pancake, pressing on them lightly. Gently turn and cook the other side. You may need to cook the pancakes over a lower heat as the fruit can burn easily.

Savoury pancakes
Add whatever you have to hand – a little grated zucchini (courgette), chopped fresh herbs or spring onions added to the batter all make delicious variations.

Basic waffles

Admittedly you need a waffle maker for this recipe, but I assure you it's worth putting one on your Christmas list. These are sensational.

Preparation time: 15 minutes
Cooking time: 20 minutes
Makes about 16

250 g plain flour
pinch of salt
1 teaspoon bicarbonate of soda
2 teaspoons caster sugar
2 eggs, separated
250 ml milk
30 g melted butter
1 teaspoon vanilla extract
fresh berries, to serve
maple syrup, to serve

You will also need
an electric waffle maker

1 Sift the flour, salt and bicarbonate of soda into a large bowl. Stir in the sugar and make a well in the centre.

2 In a separate bowl, combine the egg yolks, milk, melted butter and vanilla. Gently stir the wet ingredients into the dry ingredients and mix with a wooden spoon until combined; the batter will be slightly lumpy.

3 Beat the egg whites with hand-held electric beaters until they form stiff peaks, then fold into the batter with a large metal spoon.

4 Preheat an electric waffle maker. Pour 3–4 tablespoons of batter into the centre of the waffle plates. Close the lid, without locking the handle, and cook the waffles for about 3 minutes or until golden. Do not open the waffle maker during the first minute of cooking. Remove and keep warm while you make the remaining waffles. Serve with berries and maple syrup.

Really Useful Stuff
When folding the stiff egg whites into the batter, mix through a large spoonful of the whites first. This will slacken the mixture, making it much easier to fold in the remaining egg whites.

Blinis

Blinis are the traditional way to serve caviar or salmon roe, topped with a dollop of crème fraîche or sour cream. The yeast gives them a light texture and the buckwheat flour gives them their distinctive flavour. The recipe below is adapted from a recipe by British food writer Delia Smith.

Preparation time: 10 minutes, plus standing time
Cooking time: 20 minutes
Makes about 24

50 g buckwheat flour
175 g white bread flour
1 teaspoon salt
1 × 7 g sachet (2 teaspoons) dried yeast
200 ml crème fraîche
225 ml milk
2 large eggs, separated
softened butter, for greasing

1 Sift both flours and the salt into a bowl, and stir in the dried yeast. Make a well in the centre.

2 Warm the crème fraîche and milk gently over low heat – it should just be tepid. Pour the warm milk and the egg yolks into the flour mixture and whisk with a balloon whisk until the mixture is smooth. Cover the bowl with a damp tea towel or plastic wrap and leave in warm place for 1 hour until the mixture is spongy and bubbles have formed.

3 Use hand-held electric beaters to whisk the egg whites until they form stiff peaks, then gently fold the whites into the batter. Cover and leave for a further hour.

4 Lightly grease a small, heavy, non-stick frying pan (use kitchen paper spread with a little butter) and place over medium heat for 2–3 minutes. Using about 2 tablespoons of mixture for each blini, cook for about 2 minutes, or until firm and just golden, then flip over with a spatula and cook the other side for 1 minute. Repeat with the remaining batter. Serve warm or cold.

Really Useful Stuff
Buckwheat is a member of the rhubarb family with angular brown seeds which are ground to produce a speckled flour with a rich nutty flavour. As buckwheat is not a grain, the flour does not contain gluten, so it is usually used in conjunction with other flours in cooking.

Pasta

Dried pasta is the Italian version of fast food – it fits the bill perfectly when you want to get good food on the table with as little fuss as possible. The recipes are inspired by fresh seasonal ingredients mixed with a few goodies from the store cupboard. And is there a better way to combat cool nights and short days than a large dish of baked pasta? The thought of bubbling sauce topped with a golden crusty cheese and breadcrumb topping is irresistible to me. Sure, baked pasta dishes are more weekend fare than fast weeknight suppers, but the reward gained in the eating is well worth the extra time it takes to prepare.

Hints & Tips

∗ Only buy good-quality dried pasta – the surface should be slightly rough rather than glossy and smooth. The sauce adheres better when the pasta is a little textured.

∗ Try a few different shapes. There are no hard and fast rules, but generally long, thin pasta such as spaghetti and linguine work well with delicate sauces, whereas shapes such as penne or farfalle are better suited to a more robust or chunky sauce.

∗ Cook the pasta in a large saucepan of rapidly boiling, salted water (no oil) and start testing it about 1 minute before the recommended time by tasting a piece – it should be tender, but with a slight 'bite' (al dente). Drain the pasta well and add the sauce immediately.

∗ Allow 100 g of dried pasta per person.

∗ In spring and summer avoid slow-cooked sauces and try a bit of 'assembly-line' cooking, where good-quality fresh ingredients are simply tossed through the pasta and then the whole dish is drizzled with extra virgin olive oil and scattered with parmesan. Examples include spaghetti with garlic, chilli and olive oil (see opposite) or spaghettini with crab and basil (see page 128).

∗ Baked pasta should be cooked in an earthenware or ovenproof china dish that can be brought to the table. The pasta can also be frozen in the ceramic dish (wrapped in foil and plastic) and then thawed and heated at a later date.

∗ Baked pasta dishes can generally be prepared up to 8 hours ahead of time and stored in the fridge. Before serving, place in a preheated oven for about 30 minutes or until heated through.

Spaghetti with garlic, chilli & olive oil

This is the simplest and speediest of all pasta dishes: olive oil is infused with garlic and chilli, and then stirred through hot pasta. Your kitchen will be filled with the heady aroma of garlic.

Preparation time: 10 minutes
Cooking time: 10 minutes
Serves 4

400 g dried spaghetti
100 ml olive oil
3 cloves garlic, finely chopped
1–2 long red chillies, seeded and finely chopped
2 tablespoons chopped flat-leaf parsley
salt and freshly ground black pepper
freshly grated parmesan, to serve

1 Bring a large saucepan of salted water to the boil, add the pasta and boil rapidly until al dente (check the cooking time on the packet).

2 While the pasta is cooking, combine the olive oil, garlic and chilli in a small saucepan. Cook over very low heat for 7–8 minutes to allow the oil to absorb the flavours. The oil should barely simmer, and the garlic should colour slightly, but don't let it burn.

3 Drain the cooked pasta and return it to the saucepan. Pour the oil mixture over the top and add the parsley. Toss thoroughly with tongs and season with salt and pepper. Serve immediately with freshly grated parmesan.

Really Useful Stuff
You can vary this dish by using chopped fresh basil or rocket in place of the parsley. A squeeze of lemon juice is also good.

Grated zucchini (courgette) stirred through with the chilli and oil is also a great addition.

Spaghettini with crab & basil

This recipe is beautifully simple – just stir the crab and basil into the hot pasta and serve.

Preparation time: 10 minutes
Cooking time: 10 minutes
Serves 4

400 g spaghettini or other fine pasta
400 g fresh cooked crab meat
1 long red chilli, finely sliced
1 clove garlic, crushed
finely grated zest of 1 lemon
juice of ½ lemon
2 tablespoons extra virgin olive oil, plus extra to serve (optional)
sea salt and freshly ground black pepper
2 tablespoons torn basil

1 Bring a large saucepan of salted water to the boil, add the pasta and boil rapidly until al dente (check the cooking time on the packet).

2 Meanwhile, combine the crab meat, chilli, garlic and lemon zest in a bowl. Stir in the lemon juice and olive oil and season well. Mix with a fork to flake the crab meat.

3 Drain the cooked pasta and return it to the saucepan. Add the crab mixture and basil and stir to combine. Drizzle with a little extra olive oil, if desired. Check the seasoning and add extra lemon juice, salt or pepper if you think it needs it. Serve immediately.

Really Useful Stuff
You can replace the crab with a tin of tuna – use the oil from the tin to replace the oil in the recipe. A handful of chopped rocket also makes a delicious addition.

Farfalle with spring vegetables ›

This is a great way to make use of an abundance of fresh asparagus. A small amount of cream in the sauce adds a nice richness, without being heavy.

Preparation time: 15 minutes
Cooking time: 15 minutes
Serves 2

200 g farfalle or penne
12 stems asparagus
1 tablespoon olive oil
150 g peas (thawed if frozen)
4–5 tablespoons cream
finely grated zest and juice of ½ lemon
salt and freshly ground black pepper
20 basil leaves, roughly chopped
2 tablespoons chopped flat-leaf parsley
freshly grated parmesan, to serve

1 Bring a large saucepan of salted water to the boil, add the pasta and boil rapidly until al dente (check the cooking time on the packet).

2 Meanwhile, trim the asparagus, cutting off any woody ends. Cut any thick stems in half lengthways, then cut into 10–12 cm lengths. Heat the oil in a large frying pan over medium heat and cook the asparagus, tossing, for about 2 minutes. Add the peas and cook, stirring, until the vegetables have softened slightly and are bright green. Keep warm over low heat.

3 A few minutes before the pasta is ready, add the cream and lemon juice to the vegetables and boil until the cream has reduced and coats the vegetables. Season to taste.

4 Drain the cooked pasta and return it to the saucepan. Pour the vegetables and sauce over the pasta and stir in the herbs and lemon zest. Serve immediately with freshly grated parmesan.

Really Useful Stuff
To make a super-quick version of this recipe, leave out the asparagus and use 250 g frozen peas, thawed. You could also add grated zucchini (courgette) at the end of the vegetable cooking time.

‹ Lasagne with mushrooms

You can make a very tasty lasagne without meat. Here the mushrooms give a lovely earthy flavour.

Preparation time: 30 minutes
Cooking time: 45 minutes
Serves 4–6

80 g butter
6 tablespoons plain flour
1.2 litres milk
2 eggs, beaten
350 g freshly grated parmesan
10 fresh lasagne sheets (see note below)
salt and freshly ground black pepper
½ teaspoon cayenne pepper
a few knobs of butter

Mushroom filling
25 g butter
1 onion, finely chopped
500 g mushrooms, sliced
2 teaspoons chopped marjoram or thyme

1   Preheat the oven to 190°C (Gas Mark 5) and grease a shallow ovenproof dish.

2   Melt the butter in a large saucepan over medium heat. Sprinkle on the flour, stir with a wooden spoon and cook for 1–2 minutes until the flour has browned slightly. Gradually pour in the milk, whisking constantly until there are no lumps. Bring to the boil, then reduce the heat and simmer, stirring, for 3–4 minutes until thickened. Take off the heat and stir in the beaten egg and two-thirds of the parmesan.

3   To make the filling, melt the butter in a large frying pan over medium heat and sauté the onion for about 5 minutes. Add the mushrooms and cook, stirring often, for 7 minutes until tender and just coloured. Stir in the herbs.

4   Spoon a thin layer of the cheese sauce onto the base of the prepared dish. Place a layer of lasagne sheets on the sauce (cutting to fit the base if needed), then spoon on a layer of mushrooms. Season with salt and pepper, and repeat to make as make as many layers as you have ingredients (or space) for. Finish with a layer of sauce, then sprinkle with the remaining parmesan and the cayenne pepper, and top with a few knobs of butter. Bake for 20–30 minutes or until bubbling and nicely browned on top.

Really Useful Stuff
Try using a variety of mushrooms, especially in autumn when there are lots of different types about. Include a handful of dried mushrooms as they add a more intense flavour – remember to soak them in a little warm water for 30 minutes first. Drain well (reserving the soaking liquid), then dry them on kitchen paper and sauté along with the other mushrooms. Use the soaking liquid in place of some of the milk when making the white sauce.

You can use homemade, dried or fresh lasagne sheets for these recipes. I always cook dried lasagne sheets first by dropping them into a large saucepan of boiling salted water for about 5 minutes. A quick dip in a bowl of cold water stops the cooking, then I lay the sheets on a clean tea towel or kitchen paper to drain.

Mrs Maietta's tomato lasagne

This beautifully simple lasagne was a favourite of a friend of mine's Italian grandmother. Mrs Maietta grew up in Naples and then moved to New York in the 1930s. I love the way this dish retains the old-world simplicity of a Neapolitan cook and blends with the New World, using ingredients such as tinned tomatoes.

Preparation time: 20 minutes
Cooking time: 1 ¼ hours
Serves 6

3–4 tablespoons olive oil
3 onions, sliced
1 clove garlic, finely chopped
3 × 400 g tins chopped tomatoes
salt and freshly ground black pepper
butter, for greasing
500 g fresh ricotta
1 egg
1 tablespoon chopped basil
pinch of nutmeg
100 g grated parmesan
400 g fresh lasagne sheets
300 g mozzarella, sliced

1   Heat the oil in a large saucepan and cook the onion and garlic for about 5 minutes until tender. Add the tomatoes and bring to the boil, then reduce the heat and simmer gently for about 30 minutes. Season with salt and pepper.

2   Preheat the oven to 190°C (Gas Mark 5). Grease a 28 × 23 cm ceramic ovenproof dish with a little butter.

3   Combine the ricotta, egg, basil, nutmeg and 2 tablespoons of parmesan in a bowl and season to taste.

4   Spread a couple of tablespoons of the tomato sauce across the base of the lasagne dish, then top with a layer of lasagne sheets. Cover with a layer of the ricotta mixture, and some slices of mozzarella. Repeat until all the ingredients have been used, finishing with a layer of pasta well covered with the remaining tomato sauce. Sprinkle with the remaining parmesan and bake for 35–40 minutes, or until heated through and golden.

Really Useful Stuff
This can easily be made ahead of time and chilled for up to 24 hours before cooking and serving.

Penne with spicy tomato & sausage sauce

Penne works best with a chunky sauce like this one. Use Italian-style sausages if you can find them.

Preparation time: 15 minutes
Cooking time: 25 minutes
Serves 4

2 tablespoons olive oil
4 rashers streaky bacon, chopped
1 large onion, finely chopped
2 cloves garlic, crushed
2 × 400 g tins chopped tomatoes
1–2 whole red chillies
6 Italian-style sausages, cut into 3 cm lengths
salt and freshly ground black pepper
400 g penne
3 tablespoons chopped flat-leaf parsley
freshly grated parmesan, to serve

1   Heat the oil in a large saucepan over medium heat and cook the bacon, onion and garlic for 5 minutes, stirring occasionally. Add the chopped tomatoes and chillies and bring to the boil. Add the sausages, then reduce the heat and simmer, covered, for 20 minutes.

2   Take the lid off the pan and boil for a further 5 minutes to reduce the sauce slightly. Season to taste with salt and pepper.

3   Meanwhile, bring a large saucepan of salted water to the boil, add the penne and boil rapidly until al dente (check the cooking time on the packet).

4   Drain the cooked pasta and return it to the saucepan. Remove the chillies from the sauce, then pour it over the penne. Stir in the parsley and serve with freshly grated parmesan.

Really Useful Stuff
To give this dish an extra kick, make it with spicy sausages.
The sauce can be made in large quantities and frozen, if desired.

Linguine with mascarpone & ham

The mascarpone gives this creamy sauce a lovely consistency without having to reduce or thicken it.

Preparation time: 10 minutes
Cooking time: 10 minutes
Serves 4

400 g linguine
125 g mascarpone
knob of unsalted butter
3 tablespoons freshly grated parmesan, plus extra to serve
100 g thickly cut leg ham, cut into strips
salt and freshly ground black pepper
handful of basil, torn

1   Bring a large saucepan of salted water to the boil, add the linguine and boil rapidly until al dente (check the cooking time on the packet).

2   Meanwhile, warm the mascarpone, butter, parmesan and ham in a small saucepan over low heat. Season well with salt and pepper.

3   Drain the cooked pasta and return it to the saucepan. Pour the sauce over the pasta and stir in the basil. Serve with freshly grated parmesan.

Really Useful Stuff
Try to source the ham from a butcher or deli that cuts it freshly off the bone. Ask for thick slices.

Pappardelle with chicken ragu

Thick ribbons of flat pasta are perfect with this robust, meaty sauce.

Preparation time: 20 minutes
Cooking time: 1 hour
Serves 4

2 tablespoons olive oil
150 g pancetta, cut into dice
1 onion, finely chopped
1 clove garlic, crushed
1 carrot, chopped
185 g mushrooms, thinly sliced
3 Italian-style sausages, casings removed
750 g boneless, skinless chicken thighs, cut into 1 cm pieces
400 g tin chopped tomatoes
500 ml chicken stock
1 bay leaf
400 g pappardelle or other wide, flat pasta
salt and freshly ground black pepper
freshly grated parmesan, to serve

1 Heat the oil in a large saucepan over medium heat and cook the pancetta, onion, garlic, carrot, mushrooms and sausage meat for about 8 minutes, stirring occasionally and breaking up the sausage meat with a fork. Add the chicken, chopped tomatoes, stock and bay leaf. Bring to the boil, then reduce the heat and simmer gently for about 50 minutes, stirring occasionally. Add a little extra stock if the sauce is too thick.

2 Meanwhile, bring a large saucepan of salted water to the boil, add the pappardelle and boil rapidly until al dente (check the cooking time on the packet).

3 Drain the cooked pasta and return it to the saucepan. Stir in the sauce and season to taste. Serve with freshly grated parmesan.

Really Useful Stuff
Make a larger batch of the sauce and freeze the leftovers for another use.

Macaroni cheese

No pasta chapter would be complete without a recipe for macaroni cheese. This one is rich and deliciously cheesy, just as it should be.

Preparation time: 10 minutes, plus standing time
Cooking time: 50 minutes
Serves 4

1.5 litres milk
1 bay leaf
400 g macaroni
75 g butter
4 tablespoons plain flour
250 g grated mature cheddar
2 teaspoons Dijon mustard
salt and freshly ground black pepper
50 g freshly grated parmesan
60 g fresh breadcrumbs, made from day-old bread

1 Preheat the oven to 190°C (Gas Mark 5).

2 Place the milk and bay leaf in a large saucepan over low heat and bring to just under the boil. Remove from the heat and set aside for 10 minutes to allow the flavours to infuse. Take out the bay leaf.

3 Bring a large saucepan of salted water to the boil, add the macaroni and boil rapidly until al dente (check the cooking time on the packet). Drain and place in a large bowl.

4 Meanwhile, melt the butter in a large saucepan over medium heat. Sprinkle on the flour, stir with a wooden spoon and cook for 1–2 minutes until the flour has browned slightly. Gradually pour in the warm milk, whisking constantly until there are no lumps. Bring to the boil, then reduce the heat and simmer, stirring, for 3–4 minutes until thickened.

5 Pour the white sauce over the pasta. Add the cheddar and mustard and stir until combined. Season to taste with salt and pepper. Spoon the mixture into a large, shallow ovenproof dish, and scatter the parmesan and breadcrumbs over the top. Bake for 35–40 minutes or until golden and heated through.

Really Useful Stuff
A little chopped bacon makes a delicious addition to the topping – finely chop 4 rashers of streaky bacon and mix with the parmesan and breadcrumbs before sprinkling over the top.

Baked penne with capsicums

The idea for this dish came from my favourite Italian food writer, Anna Del Conte. Anna is both a wonderful teacher and a brilliant cook, and I have learnt to cook many, many dishes from the pages of her books. I have been lucky enough to work with her on several occasions, and this is my simplified adaption of one of her classic baked pasta dishes.

Preparation time: 30 minutes
Cooking time: 40 minutes
Serve 4

750 g mixed yellow, green and red capsicums (peppers)
1 teaspoon dried oregano
salt and freshly ground black pepper
320 g penne
2 tablespoons extra virgin olive oil, plus extra for drizzling
2 cloves garlic, finely sliced
2 anchovies, chopped
4 tablespoons fresh breadcrumbs, made from day-old bread
2 tablespoons chopped flat-leaf parsley
2 tablespoons roughly torn basil
1 long red chilli, finely chopped
12 black olives, pitted and sliced
50 g freshly grated parmesan

1   Char the capsicums by either cooking them on a ribbed grill plate over high heat or placing the capsicums, a few at a time, directly on the flame of a large gas burner on your stove. Heat for 10–12 minutes or until evenly charred on all sides, turning every few minutes.

2   When the capsicums are cool enough to handle, remove the skins – they will slide off easily. Don't rinse the roasted capsicums under the tap or all the delicious juices will be lost. Simply cut them in half, remove the veins and seeds and slice into 1 cm strips. Place in a bowl and add the oregano. Season with salt and pepper.

3   Bring a large saucepan of salted water to the boil, add the penne and boil rapidly until al dente (check the cooking time on the packet).

4   Preheat the oven to 190°C (Gas Mark 5).

5   While the pasta is cooking, heat the olive oil in a frying pan over medium heat and cook the garlic and anchovies, stirring, for 2 minutes. Add the breadcrumbs, parsley, basil, chilli and olives and cook, stirring, for about 2 minutes. Season to taste.

6   Drain the pasta, reserving some of the water. Return the pasta to the pan and add the breadcrumb mixture and about 2 tablespoons of the reserved pasta water. Mix thoroughly, adding a little extra water if the pasta seems dry. Stir in the parmesan.

7   Spoon half the pasta into a medium ovenproof dish and top with half the capsicum. Repeat with another layer of pasta and capsicum, and drizzle a little extra virgin olive oil over the top. Bake for about 20 minutes, or until heated through.

Really Useful Stuff
You can find roasted and skinned capsicums in some Italian delis; it's fine to use these instead of grilling your own. And of course, the recipe works just as well with just one type of capsicum, rather than the three colours.

Spinach & ricotta cannelloni ›

Using fresh lasagne sheets makes this delicious dish so easy to make.

Preparation time: 25 minutes
Cooking time: 25 minutes
Serves 4

500 g ricotta
150 g baby English spinach leaves, chopped
2 tablespoons roughly chopped basil
1 clove garlic, crushed
¼ teaspoon grated nutmeg
salt and freshly ground black pepper
6–8 fresh lasagne sheets
500 ml easy, no-chop tomato sauce (see page 205)
50 g freshly grated parmesan

You will also need
an 18 × 25 cm ovenproof dish

1   Preheat the oven to 200°C (Gas Mark 6).

2   Put the ricotta in a bowl and break it up with a fork. Add the spinach, basil and garlic and mix well. Sprinkle with the nutmeg and season well with salt and pepper.

3   Cut each lasagne sheet in half. Spread 2–3 tablespoons of the mixture down the centre of each sheet and then roll into a tube, overlapping the edges slightly.

4   Spread a layer of tomato sauce over the base of the ovenproof dish. Place the cannelloni tubes, seam-side down, in a single layer in the dish. Pour the remaining sauce over the top, sprinkle with parmesan and bake for 20–25 minutes or until the pasta is tender and the cheese is golden.

Really Useful Stuff
There are lots of good prepared tomato sauces available these days. If you want to save yourself some time, buy one of these instead of making your own. Having said that, the recipe on page 205 is so easy and delicious it's worth the little bit of extra effort.

Pastry

We all know that you can buy ready-made pastry in most supermarkets, but an infinitely better version can be made at home by hand or with the help of your trusty food processor. Contrary to popular belief, making pastry is not difficult, and when you've tasted the results you'll be so pleased you took the time.

Hints & Tips

* The kitchen, utensils and working surfaces must be cool. Pastry doesn't like warmth.
* Weigh and measure the ingredients as accurately as possible.
* Never overwork the dough or handle it too much; make it quickly and keep it well chilled. Once the dough is made, don't be tempted to knead it – simply pat into a flattened disc shape, wrap in plastic wrap and chill.
* The easiest way to roll out the pastry is to place the dough between two sheets of baking paper and to use a large rolling pin. The paper prevents the dough sticking to the surface, making it easier to handle. Give the pastry a quarter-turn every time you roll it – this helps to keep the shape as round as possible.

* Make sure fillings are cold or at room temperature before topping with pastry. If you try to put lovely chilled homemade pastry over a warm filling, the pastry will soften, be more difficult to work with and the finished pastry may not be as crisp.
* Always use real butter where butter is called for – margarine or softened butter blends will not give the same results. If a recipe lists lard in the ingredients, real butter may be used instead, but do try to use lard when required – it gives the pastry a really good crispness.
* Uncooked pastry can be wrapped and stored in the fridge for 2 days or in the freezer for up to a month. If storing puff pastry, always stack the pastry or any leftover trimmings in layers. If you roll the leftover bits of dough into a ball, you will lose the layers and the pastry won't rise.

To line a pie or flan tin

* If you have rolled the pastry between two sheets of baking paper, remove the top sheet, and then invert the pastry over the tin. Once the pastry is in the tin, quickly lift up the sides so they don't become broken or cut by the edges of the tin. Use a small ball of leftover dough to help press the pastry into the corners and edges of the tin. Trim away any excess with a small, sharp knife.
* If working on a lightly floured surface, roll the pastry to the suggested thickness, lightly roll it around the rolling pin and then carefully unroll it over the tin. Continue as above.

Baking blind

* To blind bake, line the tin with pastry and then line the pastry with foil or baking paper, leaving some overhanging the tin. Half-fill the pastry case with a layer of pie weights (available in cookware shops), uncooked dried beans or rice and bake at 200°C (Gas Mark 6) for 15 minutes. Remove the weights and foil and bake the pastry case for a further 10 minutes, or until dry and lightly coloured.

Glazing

* To give your finished pastry a lovely shine, brush it with beaten egg or milk before baking. I usually prefer beaten egg as it gives both a good shine and a lovely golden colour.

The simplest shortcrust pastry

Shortcrust is the pastry to use when you are making fruit pies, quiches and sweet or savoury tarts.

**Preparation time: 20 minutes,
 plus refrigeration time
Makes enough for the base and top
 of a 20 cm pie**

**350 g plain flour
¼ teaspoon salt
175 g butter, chilled and diced
about 100 ml chilled water**

1   Sift the flour and salt into a large bowl. With your fingertips, rub the butter into the flour until it resembles coarse breadcrumbs. Using a large fork or palette knife, stir in enough water to make the pastry come together in clumps. If there is still dry flour in the bowl, you may need to add a little extra water.

2   Gather the dough and gently press together into a ball (don't knead). Flatten slightly into a disc, then wrap in plastic wrap and refrigerate for 30 minutes before using.

Really Useful Stuff

If you would rather make this by machine, put the flour, salt and diced butter in a food processor and pulse until the mixture resembles coarse breadcrumbs. Add the chilled water and pulse until the mixture just clumps together in a ball – it is important not to overwork the dough. Add a little extra water if the dough doesn't clump together. Press gently into a ball and flatten slightly to a disc. Wrap in plastic wrap and refrigerate for 30 minutes before using.

Sweet shortcrust pastry

Sweet shortcrust is enriched with a little added sugar and a beaten egg, which makes it perfect for sweet tarts. To make it, add 1 tablespoon of caster sugar to the flour. Add 1 beaten egg yolk and 3–4 tablespoons of chilled water to the mixture and follow the basic recipe.

Rough puff pastry

There are a few ways to simplify the process of making puff pastry. This method works well and will give you a good flaky pastry, though not as light as a classic puff (see page 140). Here, you cut the butter into the flour and make a simple buttery dough, then roll, fold and turn it a few times.

Preparation time: 25 minutes, plus resting and refrigeration time
Makes enough to top 2 medium pies

250 g plain flour
½ teaspoon salt
175 g butter, chilled but pliable
about 150 ml chilled water

1   Sift the flour and salt into a large bowl. Roughly chop the butter into 1.5 cm dice, add to the bowl and rub them in roughly. You want to see bits of butter.

2   Make a well in the centre and pour in about two-thirds of the cold water, mixing with a large knife or palette knife until you have a firm, rough dough. Add a little extra water if needed, but the dough should be on the dry side. Gently press together into a ball, wrap in plastic wrap and refrigerate for 30 minutes.

3   Turn the dough out onto a lightly floured board, shape gently to form a rectangle, then roll out to make a rectangle that is about three times longer than it is wide (about 20 × 60 cm). Try to keep edges straight. The butter should have a marbled effect in the pastry.

4   Fold one third of the dough into the middle and then the other third on top. Give the dough a quarter turn and roll out again to three times the length. Fold as before, then cover with plastic wrap and refrigerate for at least 30 minutes before using.

Choux pastry

Choux pastry is used for both savoury (gougères) and sweet pastries (chocolate éclairs, choux buns and profiteroles). It is made in a saucepan and uses heat and air to make it rise. In fact, the pastry rises considerably when cooked, leaving a hollow in the centre that is perfect for filling.

Preparation time: 15 minutes
Cooking time: 10 minutes
Makes enough for 12–15 choux puffs or profiteroles

150 g plain flour
good pinch of salt
100 g unsalted butter, chopped
150 ml milk
4 eggs

1   Sift the flour and salt into a bowl.

2   Heat the butter and milk in a large saucepan over medium heat. When the butter has melted, bring to the boil, then take the pan off the heat and add the flour. Beat with a wooden spoon until the mixture is smooth and leaves the sides of the hot pan.

3   Return the pan to the heat for 1 minute, stirring constantly – this will remove any excess moisture. Transfer the dough to a large mixing bowl. Add the eggs one at a time, beating well after each addition with a wooden spoon. The dough should appear shiny and the mixture should be able to drop off a spoon – you may not need to add all the egg.

4   Alternatively, transfer the mixture to a food processor and while the mixture is still warm, add the eggs and process using the pulse action until just combined. Do not overmix!

5   If not using immediately, brush the top of the dough with a little milk or beaten egg, then cover with plastic wrap to prevent it from drying out.

Really Useful Stuff
Sprinkle the lined baking tray with a little water before adding the dough – this creates steam which will help the pastry rise.

When piping the pastry onto baking trays, leave plenty of space between each one as the pastry will more than double in size while cooking.

Gougères›
Once all the eggs have been added to the dough, mix in 75 g grated gruyère, emmenthal or cheddar. Drop or pipe tablespoons of the mixture onto a baking tray lined with baking paper. Sprinkle with a little extra cheese and bake in a preheated 190°C (Gas Mark 5) oven for 15–20 minutes, or until golden and puffed. They should be dry on the outside but still a little soft on the inside. Makes about 30.

Cheat's flaky pastry

This quick version of flaky pastry is useful when you don't have much time, but you need a crisp, buttery crust for a savoury pie or sausage roll.

Preparation time: 20 minutes, plus refrigeration time
Makes enough to cover a 28 cm pie dish

200 g plain flour
¼ teaspoon salt
125 g butter, frozen for 30 minutes before use
2–3 tablespoons chilled water

1   Sift the flour and salt into a large bowl. Using the largest holes of a grater, grate the frozen butter into the flour. Gently mix with a palette knife or spatula, making sure that all the pieces of butter are coated in flour – the butter should be left in chunky grated pieces, not worked into the dough.

2   Add about 2 tablespoons of the chilled water and mix in with the knife. The pastry should come together in clumps – add a little extra water if necessary. When the dough holds together, gently press it into a ball and flatten slightly to form a disc. Gently roll out the pastry to a rectangle about 1 cm thick. Mark the pastry in thirds, then fold one end up and the other down over it – envelope style. Press the ends together to seal. Wrap in plastic wrap and refrigerate for at least 30 minutes. Repeat the rolling, folding and chilling once more. Make sure the pastry is chilled before using.

Really Useful Stuff

When making the flaky pastry, the thing to remember is not to overwork the dough or handle it too much. Make it quickly and keep it well chilled.

It is important to use frozen butter and to handle the dough as little as possible – use the wrapping paper to hold the butter while grating it.

Flaky pastry is best rolled quite thin.

Any leftover pastry can be placed in a freezer bag and frozen for up to 1 month.

Puff pastry

Classic puff pastry begins with a simple dough that is rolled out and wrapped around a slab of butter. The dough is then repeatedly rolled, folded, turned and chilled. While this is time-consuming, the method distributes the butter evenly in sheets throughout the dough. When the pastry bakes, the moisture in all the layers of butter creates steam, causing the dough to puff and separate into many layers.

Preparation time: 1 hour, plus refrigeration time
Makes enough to cover 2 medium pies

250 g plain flour
pinch of salt
30 g lard or butter, chilled and diced
about 120 ml chilled water
175 g butter, chilled

1   Sift the flour and salt into a large bowl. With your fingertips, rub the lard or butter into the flour until it resembles coarse breadcrumbs. Using a large fork, stir in enough water to make a soft dough (you may need to add a little extra water). Gently press together into a ball, wrap in plastic wrap and refrigerate for 30 minutes.

2   Put the butter between two pieces of baking paper and flatten out with a rolling pin to form a 10 × 7.5 cm rectangle.

3   Roll out the chilled dough to a rectangle that measures 25 × 12.5 cm.

4   Take the butter out of the paper and put on the dough rectangle. Fold both ends of the dough to the centre to enclose the butter completely. Press the edges to seal. Refrigerate for 15 minutes.

5   Roll out the dough on a floured surface to make a rectangle that is three times longer than it is wide. Fold one third into the middle and then the other third on top. Seal the edges and give the pastry a quarter turn. Repeat this rolling and folding once more, then wrap in plastic wrap and rest in the refrigerator for 30 minutes.

6   Repeat this rolling, folding and turning twice more, then cover and rest in the refrigerator for another 30 minutes. Repeat this step again (the pastry will have been rolled and folded six times altogether) and refrigerate for 30 minutes before using.

Really Useful Stuff

It is important that the pastry is well chilled otherwise it will become greasy and tough when baked. Also the butter might come through the surface – if this happens, dab on a little flour.

Roll with short, sharp strokes – if you roll the pastry with long strokes, any air bubbles may break the surface of the dough.

If at any time the butter starts to ooze out of the pastry when rolling, put it back in the fridge until firm.

Pies

Could anything be more perfect than a crispy, golden pastry topping covering a delicious, soft, comforting filling? Pies may take a little time to prepare but your efforts are amply rewarded when you take that first delectable bite. And the beauty is that you can make them ahead of time for a main meal or dessert. The filling and the pastry can usually be made the day before, meaning all you have to do when you're ready to eat is assemble and bake until golden.

Hints & Tips

✳ Although I am no longer one of those cooks that has to do it all myself, I always make my own shortcrust pastry. Truthfully, homemade shortcrust tastes much better than ready-made varieties, and it doesn't take very long to make.

✳ When it comes to puff pastry, I am happy to cheat a little and use ready-rolled. You may find that one of those frozen squares fits your pie dish but it never seems to be quite thick enough or large enough for mine. These days it seems to be impossible to buy a block of ready-made puff pastry that you can roll yourself, so I usually brush three of the thawed squares with a little melted butter and then firmly press them together. Refrigerate for 15 minutes, then carefully roll out the pastry to a size and thickness that suits. Try to keep the scraps layered as it is these layers of pastry that cause it to rise.

✳ I always try to have the pastry made well ahead of time and keep it in the refrigerator until needed; 375 g pastry (pastry made with 250 g flour and 125 g butter) is plenty for a top-crusted pie, with leftovers for decoration.

✳ The filling needs to be cold before being covered with pastry so make it ahead of time as well, if time permits.

✳ Handle the pastry carefully and as little as possible. If it becomes soft or sticky, return it to the fridge.

✳ I usually roll out the pastry between two sheets of baking paper. This prevents the pastry sticking to the work surface, and also makes it easier to transfer to the pie.

✳ Use a pie funnel if you have one – it helps to release the steam that builds up under the pastry, giving you a crisper pastry. Place in the centre of the pie dish, then cut a cross in the middle of the pastry lid large enough to accommodate the funnel.

✳ Use any scraps of pastry to decorate the pie. Cut them into leaves or letters of the alphabet or whatever takes your fancy, and stick them to the top of the pie with a little beaten egg.

✳ For a lovely, shiny finish, brush the pastry with a little beaten egg before cooking.

✳ Make sure the oven is preheated before adding the pie. You need a good hot oven to set the pastry.

✳ When making a double-crusted pie (that is, one that has a pastry base and lid), use a round metal pie dish, as this will help the pastry on the base become crisp. I usually use shortcrust on the base and puff on the top, simply because puff pastry is designed to rise.

✳ When making pot pies or a top-crusted deep-dish pie, look for deep ceramic pie dishes, usually oval or round with an edge.

✳ Pies cope very well with being frozen. I usually assemble a pie and freeze it uncooked until needed. Thaw the pie in the fridge before baking.

Vegetable pot pies

Preparation time: 20 minutes
Cooking time: 1½ hours
Serves 8

4 potatoes, peeled
3 medium sweet potatoes, scrubbed
1 butternut pumpkin, peeled
4 zucchini (courgettes)
6 carrots, scrubbed
3 red onions, cut into thin wedges
1–2 tablespoons olive oil
salt and freshly ground black pepper
1.5 litres milk
1 bay leaf
75 g butter
4 tablespoons plain flour
250 g grated mature cheddar
1 tablespoon chopped chives
380 g block puff pastry (see page 140) or
    4 sheets ready-rolled puff pastry, thawed
    if frozen
1 egg, beaten

1 Preheat the oven to 200°C (Gas Mark 6).

2 Cut the potatoes, sweet pototoes and
   pumpkin into 2 cm chunks. Top and tail
   the zucchini and carrots and cut into
   similar-sized pieces. Place the vegetables
   in two large roasting tins, add the onion
   wedges and drizzle with a little olive oil.
   Roast, turning occasionally, for about
   50 minutes or until soft and nicely
   coloured (remove the pumpkin early if
   needed). Season well and divide among
   eight individual ovenproof dishes. Place
   the dishes on a large baking sheet.

3 Meanwhile, gently bring the milk and bay
   leaf to just under the boil. Remove from
   the heat and set aside for 10 minutes for
   the flavours to infuse.

4 Melt the butter in a large saucepan and
   sprinkle with the flour. Stir with a wooden
   spoon and cook over medium heat for
   1 minute, or until the flour has browned
   slightly. Gradually pour in the milk and
   bay leaf, whisking constantly until there
   are no lumps. Bring to the boil, then
   simmer, stirring, for about 5 minutes until
   the sauce thickens. Add the cheese and
   chives and stir until melted and combined.
   Remove the bay leaf.

5 Spoon the cheese sauce into the dishes
   until the vegetables are partially covered.

6 Cut the pastry into squares a little
   larger than the dishes. Place over the
   filling, letting the corners overhang the
   dishes – there is no need to trim. Decorate
   with the pastry scraps. Brush with beaten
   egg and bake for about 35 minutes, or until
   the pastry is golden.

Really Useful Stuff
Vary this recipe by using other
vegetables – parsnips and Jerusalem
artichokes roast well, as does asparagus.

Use any leftover pastry to add the first
letter of your guests' names to the pie top,
giving them the personal touch.

Little prawn & pea pasties

Although not traditional, prawns, peas and potatoes make a delicious filling for these portable handfuls. They are perfect hot or cold.

Preparation time: 25 minutes
Cooking time: 40 minutes
Makes 14

40 g butter
2 leeks, washed and sliced
1 large potato, cut into 1 cm cubes
100 g frozen peas, thawed
100 ml cream
50 ml white wine
350 g cooked medium prawns, peeled, deveined and roughly chopped
2 tablespoons chopped flat-leaf parsley
1 tablespoon chopped chives
finely grated zest of 1 lemon
salt and freshly ground black pepper
700 g shortcrust pastry (see page 137) or 7 sheets ready-rolled shortcrust pastry, thawed if frozen
1 egg, beaten

1   Preheat the oven to 200°C (Gas Mark 6) and line two baking trays with baking paper.

2   Heat the butter in a large saucepan over medium heat and cook the leek, potato and peas for about 4 minutes, then add the cream and wine. Cook for 5 minutes, or until the leek has softened and the wine has evaporated. Remove from the heat and add the prawns, herbs and lemon zest. Season well with salt and pepper.

3   Cut the pastry in half. Roll out each half and cut seven 15 cm rounds from each half (you need 14 rounds in all). If you are using ready-rolled sheets, cut out two 15 cm rounds from each sheet.

4   Place 2 tablespoons of the prawn mixture in the centre of each pastry round. Brush the edges with a little beaten egg, then bring the edges together on the top and seal by pressing with your fingers, shaping and crimping the top like a classic pasty. Repeat with the remaining dough to make 14 pasties. If you are making these ahead of time, cover and refrigerate until ready to cook.

5   Brush the pasties with beaten egg and place on the prepared trays. Bake for 25–30 minutes, or until golden.

Really Useful Stuff
The prawn and pea mixture also makes a good filling for a classic pie. Line a metal pie tin with pastry, fill with the prawn and pea mixture then top with a pastry lid. Bake in a preheated 180°C (Gas Mark 4) oven for about 40 minutes or until the pastry is golden.

Angela Boggiano's scallop & crab pies ›

I call my friend Angela Boggiano 'the pie queen', and I have spent many happy hours as taster during the writing and testing of her recipes. It really makes sense to use the scallop shells as pie dishes for these tasty individual pies. Just give them a good scrub once you've removed the scallops.

Preparation time: 20 minutes
Cooking time: 25 minutes
Makes 4

20 g butter
2 golden shallots, chopped
6 thin rashers pancetta or bacon, finely chopped
8 large scallops, including the coral (roe)
150 g fresh cooked crab meat
pinch of cayenne pepper
finely grated zest of ½ lemon
2 tablespoons finely chopped flat-leaf parsley
3 tablespoons fromage frais
salt and freshly ground black pepper
380 g block puff pastry (see page 140) or 4 sheets ready-rolled puff pastry, thawed if frozen
milk, for glazing

You will also need
4 cleaned and dried scallop shells or small ramekins

1   Preheat the oven to 200°C (Gas Mark 6).

2   Heat the butter in a small frying pan over low heat and cook the pancetta or bacon for a few minutes until the fat starts to run. Add the shallots and cook for a further 3–4 minutes.

3   Meanwhile, slice each scallop horizontally into three rounds and halve the coral. Place the sliced scallops, corals and crab meat in a bowl and stir in the pancetta and shallot mixture, cayenne pepper, lemon zest and parsley. Add the fromage frais and season well with salt and pepper.

4   Divide the mixture among four cleaned and dried scallop shells and place on a baking tray.

5   If using a block of pastry, roll it out to a thickness of 3 mm; if using ready-rolled pastry, lay out the sheets on the bench. Cut out four rounds of pastry about 1 cm larger than the shells. Place the pastry rounds loosely over each shell, then press down on the shell edge to shape. Cut away any excess pastry and brush with a little milk. Bake for 15 minutes or until the pastry is puffed and golden. Serve immediately.

Really Useful Stuff
If you were unable to buy scallops on the shell, ask your fishmonger to keep some shells aside for you. Otherwise, you can spoon the filling into small soufflé dishes or ramekins and place the pastry rounds on top.

Lamb shank pie

This recipe was inspired by genius Sean Moran, an Australian chef with a small but perfectly formed restaurant at Bondi Beach. After overcooking lamb shanks one day, he rescued them and turned them into the stars of a most memorable pie.

Preparation time: 20 minutes
Cooking time: 2 hours
Serves 6

50 g plain flour
salt and freshly ground black pepper
6 large lamb shanks
3 tablespoons olive oil
2 carrots, sliced into rounds
4 red onions, quartered
8 cloves garlic, sliced
750 ml full-bodied red wine
300 ml beef stock (see page 230)
2 bay leaves
2 tablespoons finely chopped rosemary
3 tablespoons redcurrant jelly
1 quantity rough puff pastry (see page 138)
1 egg, beaten

1 Season the flour with salt and pepper, then dust the shanks with the seasoned flour. Reserve the remaining flour.

2 Heat half the oil in a large saucepan or heavy-based casserole dish over medium heat and brown the shanks all over (you may need to do this in batches). Remove and set aside.

3 Heat the remaining oil in the saucepan and cook the carrot, onion and garlic, stirring frequently, for 3–4 minutes or until lightly coloured. Sprinkle with the reserved flour and cook for a further minute. Add the wine, stock, bay leaves, rosemary and redcurrant jelly. Return all the shanks to the pan and bring to the boil. Reduce the heat and simmer, covered, over low heat for about 2 hours, or until the meat falls off the bone and the sauce is rich and thickened.

4 Remove the shanks from the pan and, when cool enough to handle, flake the meat into small pieces. Return the meat to the pan. Reserve one of the bones and discard the rest.

5 Preheat the oven to 200°C (Gas Mark 6).

6 Spoon the lamb filling into a large, deep ceramic pie dish. Use the reserved bone as a pie funnel and place in the centre of the dish.

7 Roll out the pastry to a thickness of 4 mm and to a size about 4 cm larger than the pie dish. Cut off a 2 cm strip of pastry and place this along the edge of the pie dish, brushing the edge of the dish with a little water to help secure the pastry. Cut a cross in the middle of the remaining pastry (for the bone to poke through) and place the pastry lid over the pie filling, sliding the cross in the middle over the bone. Press down the pastry edges with your thumb and forefinger. Trim off any excess, then brush with beaten egg. Bake for 35–40 minutes, or until the pastry is golden and crisp.

Really Useful Stuff
You can change the seasoning to suit your preference. For instance, chilli, cumin and fresh mint will give the pie a Middle Eastern flavour.

Chicken & bacon pie

I usually make this with frozen ready-rolled sheets of puff pastry, but often find that the sheets are not quite big enough to fit the top of my favourite pie dish. If you have the same problem, you can remedy this by placing three pastry sheets on top of one another and then rolling a few times with a rolling pin until large enough to cover your dish.

Preparation time: 20 minutes
Cooking time: 2¼ hours
Serves 4–6

1 × 2 kg chicken, rinsed
2 onions, quartered
2 carrots, chopped
1 bay leaf
1 tablespoon olive oil
4 rashers bacon, chopped
2 leeks, washed and sliced
50 g butter
2 tablespoons plain flour
1 tablespoon chopped chives or flat-leaf parsley
salt and freshly ground black pepper
180 g block puff pastry (see page 140) or 3 sheets
    ready-rolled puff pastry, thawed if frozen
1 egg, beaten

1 Place the chicken, onion, carrot and bay leaf in a large saucepan. Cover with cold water and bring to the boil. Skim off any fat, then reduce the heat and simmer very gently for 1 hour.

2 Remove the chicken and set aside to cool. Strain the broth, discarding the solids, and return to the saucepan. Boil rapidly for about 20 minutes until it has reduced to about 375 ml. Set aside.

3 Remove the meat from the chicken, discarding the skin, and cut into bite-sized pieces and place in a bowl.

4 Heat the oil in a frying pan over medium heat and cook the bacon and leek, stirring, for 5–7 minutes or until tender. Add to the chicken meat.

5 Melt the butter in a saucepan over medium heat. Stir in the flour and cook for 1 minute. Whisk in the reduced broth, bring to the boil and whisk until thickened and smooth. Add enough of the sauce to the chicken mixture to moisten it. Stir in the herbs and season well, then leave to cool.

6 Preheat the oven to 190°C (Gas Mark 5). Spoon the filling into a large ceramic pie dish. Join and roll out the pastry, if necessary (see introduction) until large enough to cover the pie. Brush the edges of the dish with beaten egg. Cover with the pastry, pressing down on the edges to seal. Trim away any excess and cut it into shapes to decorate the top. Brush with beaten egg and bake for 40–45 minutes, or until the pastry is golden.

Really Useful Stuff
If you like a wet pie filling, add more of the sauce to the chicken mixture before spooning it into the pie dish.

If you want to start the pie ahead of time, make the filling up to 2 days ahead and refrigerate until needed.

Don't add the pastry lid more than about 2 hours before cooking or it may go soggy. Keep chilled until ready to cook.

Spinach, feta & mint pie

The addition of fresh mint, parsley and pine nuts makes this classic pie much more interesting.

Preparation time: 20 minutes
Cooking time: 45 minutes
Serves 4

500 g baby English spinach leaves
100 g butter
1 small brown onion, chopped
3 spring onions, sliced
2 cloves garlic, crushed
200 g feta, crumbled
3 tablespoons pine nuts, toasted
2 eggs, beaten
2 tablespoons chopped mint
2 tablespoons chopped flat-leaf parsley
salt and freshly ground black pepper
6 large sheets filo pastry, thawed if frozen
pinch of nutmeg or allspice

You will also need
a 23 cm square ovenproof dish

1   Place the spinach in a large colander in a clean sink and pour on a large kettle of boiling water. Rinse with cold water and then pick up the spinach and squeeze it firmly to remove any moisture (you may need to do this in batches). Chop the spinach.

2   Heat 30 g butter in a large frying pan over medium heat and cook the onion, spring onion and garlic, stirring occasionally, for about 7 minutes or until the onion has softened. Transfer to a large mixing bowl.

3   Give the spinach another squeeze then add to the bowl, along with the feta, pine nuts, eggs and herbs. Season to taste with salt and pepper.

4   Preheat the oven to 190°C (Gas Mark 5).

5   Melt the remaining butter. Grease the base of the ovenproof dish. Arrange a sheet of filo pastry in the base of the dish, allowing some overhang and brush with melted butter. Add two more layers of pastry, brushing each sheet with butter. Spoon in the filling, spread it out evenly and sprinkle with the nutmeg or allspice. Fold in the overhang, then top with three layers of pastry, brushing each with a little butter. Trim the pastry if necessary to fit the dish. Score the top of the pie into squares with a sharp knife and bake for about 25–35 minutes, or until the pastry is golden.

Blackberry & apple pie ›

I like to use pastry just on the top of this pie as the blackberries give out a lot of juice, which would make a pastry base soggy. This works well in a ceramic pie dish.

Preparation time: 30 minutes, plus refrigeration time
Cooking time: 40 minutes
Serves 6–8

650 g blackberries
2–3 tablespoons caster sugar, to taste
finely grated zest of ½ orange
3 dessert apples, peeled and cored
1 egg, beaten
sugar, for sprinkling

Shortcrust pastry
300 g plain flour
1 tablespoon caster sugar
pinch of salt
150 g butter
1 egg yolk, beaten
3–4 tablespoons chilled water

You will also need
a 22 cm pie dish

1   Make sweet shortcrust pastry, following the directions on page 137. Refrigerate for 30 minutes before using.

2   Roll out the pastry between two sheets of baking paper to a size large enough to cover the pie dish. Refrigerate between the sheets of paper on a flat tray for 30 minutes.

3   Preheat the oven to 180°C (Gas Mark 4).

4   Place the blackberries in a bowl and add the caster sugar and orange zest. Dice the apples into 2 cm pieces and stir into the blackberries.

5   Fill the base of the pie dish with the blackberry and apple mixture and insert a pie funnel, if using. Brush the edge of the pie dish with a little beaten egg. Make a cross in the centre of the pastry for the pie funnel then cover the fruit with the pastry. Press the edges together to seal. Brush the pastry with beaten egg and sprinkle lightly with sugar.

6   Bake for about 40 minutes, or until the pastry is golden and crisp. Serve warm with cream, custard or ice-cream.

Really Useful Stuff
This is the formula for all sorts of delicious fruit pies. Peaches and blackberries make a nice combination – use about 350 g of each (adding too many berries will make the pie quite wet as the berries give out a lot of liquid when cooking). You can also add other fruits to apple – apple and pear work well together.

‹ Macadamia & coconut tart

Macadamia nuts are delicious in baking, especially when teamed with golden syrup and coconut. Walnuts could also be used, if preferred.

Preparation time: 30 minutes, plus refrigeration time
Cooking time: 1 hour
Serves 8

200 g unsalted macadamias
4 heaped tablespoons shredded or flaked coconut
4 large eggs, beaten
150 g brown sugar
125 g butter, melted
4 tablespoons golden syrup or honey
3 tablespoons cream
finely grated zest of 1 lemon

Shortcrust pastry
300 g plain flour
2 tablespoons caster sugar
pinch of salt
150 g butter
1 egg yolk, beaten
3–4 tablespoons chilled water

You will also need
a 23 cm loose-based tart tin

1   Make sweet shortcrust pastry, following the directions on page 137. Refrigerate for 30 minutes before using.

2   Roll out the pastry between two sheets of baking paper to fit the tart tin. Grease the tin, then line with the pastry, pressing it into the edges. Trim any excess pastry and refrigerate for 30 minutes.

3   Preheat the oven to 200°C (Gas Mark 6).

4   Line the pastry with foil or baking paper, leaving some overhanging the tin. Half-fill the pastry case with a layer of pie weights, uncooked dried beans or rice and bake for 15 minutes. Remove the weights and foil and bake the pastry case for a further 10 minutes, or until dry and lightly coloured. Allow to cool.

5   Reduce the oven temperature to 180°C (Gas Mark 4). Toast the macadamias and coconut on separate baking trays in the oven for about 5–10 minutes until golden, shaking the trays occasionally. Set aside to cool.

6   Beat the eggs and sugar with a whisk, then add the melted butter, golden syrup and cream and beat until smooth. Stir in the lemon zest. Roughly chop the nuts, then stir the nuts and coconut into the egg mixture. Pour into the cooled pastry case and bake for about 20–25 minutes, or until set. Serve warm with double cream or ice-cream, if desired.

Stuffed pears wrapped in pastry

These make a wonderful dessert for an autumn or winter dinner party. The individually wrapped pears look sensational when baked, and may be decorated with leftover pastry cut into leaves, if desired.

Preparation time: 40 minutes, plus refrigeration time
Cooking time: 35 minutes
Makes 4

4 ripe pears (with stalks if available)
2 tablespoons raisins, chopped
1 tablespoon roughly chopped pecans
1 tablespoon brown sugar
20 g unsalted butter, softened at room temperature
1 tablespoon ground almonds
½ teaspoon ground ginger
1 egg, beaten
demerara or raw sugar, for sprinkling

Shortcrust pastry
300 g plain flour
2 tablespoons caster sugar
pinch of salt
150 g butter
1 egg yolk, beaten
3–4 tablespoons chilled water

1   Make sweet shortcrust pastry, following the directions on page 137. Refrigerate for 30 minutes before using.

2   Roll out the pastry between two sheets of baking paper to a thickness of 2–3 mm. Cut four squares large enough to wrap each pear, and return the pastry to the fridge until ready to use. Save any scraps for decorating.

3   Peel the pears and halve them vertically. Use a teaspoon to scoop out the seeds and cores.

4   Place the raisins, pecans, sugar, butter, ground almonds and ginger in a bowl and mix until well combined. Divide the mixture among the pear halves, then place the two halves back together.

5   Place a pear in the centre of a pastry square, bring two adjacent corners together, then bring the other two sides together. Brush the pastry with beaten egg, then press the four flaps of pastry to the pear. Repeat with the remaining pears and pastry. Cut out leaf shapes from the pastry scraps and use to decorate. Brush with a little more egg and sprinkle with demerara or raw sugar. Place the finished pears on a baking tray and refrigerate for 30 minutes.

6   Preheat the oven to 200°C (Gas Mark 6).

7   Bake the pears for 30–35 minutes, or until golden. Serve warm with cream or ice-cream.

Banana tarte tatin

Bananas make a delicious change from the classic apple version of this dish.

Preparation time: 20 minutes
Cooking time: 40 minutes
Serves 6

250 g ready-rolled puff pastry
100 g unsalted butter, chopped
185 g caster sugar
6 bananas, peeled and cut into 5 cm lengths on an angle
crushed seeds from 4 cardamom pods

You will also need
a heavy 26 cm frying pan with an ovenproof or removable handle

1 Roll out the pastry between two sheets of baking paper to a size 1 cm larger in diameter than the frying pan. Refrigerate between the sheets of paper on a flat tray until needed.

2 Preheat the oven to 200°C (Gas Mark 6).

3 Place the frying pan over medium heat and add the butter and sugar. Cook for about 5–10 minutes, until the mixture caramelises and turns golden brown – be careful not to burn the sugar. Remove from the heat.

4 Arrange the banana pieces in the pan in a single, snug layer, and sprinkle the cardamom over the top. Place the pastry on top of the bananas and tuck in loosely around the edges.

5 Bake for about 25–30 minutes, or until the pastry is golden and crisp. Remove and allow to sit for 5 minutes, then pour off any excess caramel into a jug. Place a round serving plate upside-down on top of the pastry and gently turn both over to unmould the tart. Drizzle the excess caramel over the top and serve with yoghurt or ice-cream.

Really Useful Stuff
This also works beautifully with pears (peeled and quartered)
or mango (cut into thick slices).

Blueberry meringue pie

As much as I love lemon meringue pie, I also like to make changes. Using a blueberry filling under those clouds of meringue is a favourite variation.

Preparation time: 30 minutes, plus refrigeration time
Cooking time: 1 hour
Serves 6–8

600 g blueberries
150 g sugar
finely grated zest and juice of 1 lemon
pinch of allspice
2 tablespoons cornflour

Shortcrust pastry
300 g plain flour
1 tablespoon caster sugar
pinch of salt
150 g butter
1 egg yolk, beaten
3–4 tablespoons chilled water

Meringue topping
4 large egg whites
¼ teaspoon cream of tartar
150 g caster sugar

You will also need
a 23 cm ceramic or metal pie dish

1 Make sweet shortcrust pastry, following the directions on page 137. Refrigerate for 30 minutes before using.

2 Roll out the pastry between two sheets of baking paper until large enough to fit the pie dish. Grease the dish, then line with the pastry, pressing it into the edges. Trim any excess pastry and refrigerate for 30 minutes.

3 Preheat the oven to 200°C (Gas Mark 6).

4 Line the pastry with foil or baking paper, leaving some overhanging the dish. Half-fill the pastry case with a layer of pie weights, uncooked dried beans or rice and bake for 15 minutes. Remove the weights and foil and bake the pastry case for a further 10 minutes, or until dry and lightly coloured. Allow to cool.

5 Combine the blueberries, sugar, lemon zest, juice and allspice in a large saucepan. Place over medium heat and cook, stirring to dissolve the sugar, for 10–15 minutes or until the juices have started to run. Mix the cornflour with a little water to make a paste and add to the blueberries. Continue to cook, stirring frequently, for about 5 minutes or until the mixture has thickened. Set aside to cool, then spoon into the pie shell.

6 To make the meringue topping, beat the egg whites and cream of tartar until stiff peaks form. Gradually beat in the caster sugar, then continue to beat until the meringue is thick and shiny.

7 Cover the pie with the meringue, making peaks with the back of a spoon. Bake for 10–15 minutes, or until the meringue is golden. Serve warm or cold with whipped cream.

Pizza

Roll up your sleeves! How long is it since you enjoyed the satisfaction of kneading and rolling dough? Making pizza from scratch is not difficult – it's lots of fun for kids and adults alike. Have a pizza party . . . Present your fellow diners with small dough bases and a choice of toppings and let everyone make their dream pizza. Serve with large bowls of salad.

Hints & Tips

* For ease, I have used dried yeast in the dough recipe. Reconstitute the yeast with a teaspoon of sugar in a jug of tepid water until frothy. This way you can make sure the yeast is working before you add it to the flour.
* Strong white bread-making flour is best for making pizza. It contains a high proportion of gluten, which is what makes the dough flexible and allows the bread to rise.
* You can make the pizza base up to 12 hours before you want to bake it. The trick is to make the dough and let it rise slowly in the fridge, as chilled dough rises very slowly. When you're ready to make the pizza, simply remove the dough from the fridge and punch it down to get rid of any air. Let it come to room temperature, then knead lightly and roll out or stretch into shape.

* A good pizza base should have a little bit of chew, so don't roll out the dough any thinner than 4 mm.
* The less topping you have the crisper the pizza will be . . . so a pizza base topped with garlic and olive oil should be nice and crusty.
* If you have any leftover dough, you can form it into pizza bases, part-bake them for about 10 minutes and then freeze them. To use, simply thaw, add the topping and bake until ready. This seems to work better than freezing uncooked pizza dough.
* Using a rolling pin to stretch the dough into shape is frowned upon by the professionals, but I always say to do what is easiest for you. If you want to stretch the dough by hand, use your palm or knuckles and push it slowly into shape. Initially it will recoil, but let it rest for a few minutes and then stretch again. Flour your knuckles if necessary.

* Always drain mozzarella well before using. Put the slices in a colander and press gently with your fist to remove any excess moisture. Pat dry with kitchen paper.
* Make sure the oven is properly preheated – the dough needs a real blast of heat to set the crust.
* To get a good crisp crust on your pizzas, bake them directly on pizza baking stones (available in specialist cookware shops) or on a large unglazed terracotta tile (available from tile shops). These are a worthwhile investment if you make pizzas often. Place them on the bottom shelf of the oven – and remember it will take longer to preheat the oven when using a tile (about 40 minutes). Assemble the pizza on a tray sprinkled with cornmeal or polenta and then slide it off the tray onto the tile and bake.

Pizza dough

Making your own pizza base is really simple. You can do most of the kneading with an electric mixer if you like.

Preparation time: 20 minutes,
  plus standing time
Cooking time: 20 minutes
Makes two 30 cm or three 23 cm pizza bases

1 × 7 g sachet (2 teaspoons) dried yeast
1 teaspoon sugar
350 g strong white bread flour
½ teaspoon salt
2 tablespoons olive oil
cornmeal or polenta, for sprinkling

1 To make the base, put the yeast and sugar in a jug with 200 ml of tepid water. Set aside for 10 minutes, or until it froths. Place the flour and salt in a large mixing bowl. Make a well in the centre, add the yeast mixture and olive oil and mix until a firm dough forms. Knead on a lightly floured surface for 5–7 minutes, or until smooth and elastic.

2 Alternatively, to save time and muscle power, you can put all the ingredients in the bowl of an electric mixer and beat on a medium speed for about 7 minutes using a dough hook. Turn out and knead on a lightly floured surface for a minute or two.

3 Place the dough in a lightly oiled bowl, cover with plastic wrap and stand in a warm place for 1–1½ hours, or until the dough has doubled in size. If you want to make the dough ahead of time, once you get to this stage, cover with plastic wrap and refrigerate for up to 12 hours. Then bring back to room temperature and proceed as below.

4 Preheat the oven to 210°C (Gas Mark 6–7) and lightly oil two or three metal pizza trays and sprinkle with a little cornmeal. Punch down the dough with your fist to release the air, divide into two or three equal portions and either roll out or stretch to a thickness of about 4 mm. Transfer to the prepared pizza trays and add toppings of your choice. Bake for 15 minutes, then slide the pizzas off the trays onto the oven shelf and cook for a further 5 minutes, to crisp up the base.

Really Useful Stuff
I often make a double batch of dough. Any extra can be rolled out and partly baked (see opposite), then wrapped in plastic wrap and stored in the freezer.

Toppings

The most important rule for pizza toppings is that less is definitely more – don't overload your pizzas. And don't forget to drain mozzarella well before adding it to a pizza. Here are a few ideas.

Margherita

A real classic – spread each pizza base with a layer of tomato pizza sauce, then top with slices of mozzarella. Sprinkle with torn basil leaves before serving.

Garlic

Brush each pizza base liberally with some olive oil (extra virgin is best), then scatter with thinly sliced garlic cloves and sprinkle with sea salt. You can also add some roughly chopped rosemary and a sprinkling of freshly grated parmesan or even some chopped anchovies, if desired.

Four seasons

Spread the dough with a thin layer of tomato pizza sauce then top with thin slices of prosciutto or parma ham, slices of drained bottled or tinned artichokes and halved and pitted black olives.

Pizza bianca

Brush the dough with extra virgin olive oil and sprinkle with freshly grated parmesan. Finish with some thinly sliced mushrooms that have been tossed with olive oil.

Spicy sausage

Spread your pizza base with tomato sauce and then top with slices of mozzarella, slices of pepperoni or spiced salami-style sausage and a sprinkling of thyme leaves.

Artichoke

Brush the pizza base with extra virgin olive oil and then roughly cover with sliced mozzarella. Drain a 100 g jar of artichokes and break the artichokes into smallish pieces. Spread these over the top of the pizza. Top with a few cherry tomatoes.

Easy homemade tomato sauce for pizza

I always keep a few tins of tomatoes in the cupboard for simple recipes like this. Using tinned tomatoes makes this sauce ridiculously easy to make.

Preparation time: 10 minutes, plus standing time
Cooking time: 30 minutes
Makes enough for 4 pizzas

2 × 400 g tins chopped or crushed tomatoes
2 cloves garlic, crushed
3 tablespoons olive oil
salt and freshly ground black pepper

1   Drain the tomatoes in a large fine sieve over a mixing bowl for about 10 minutes. Discard the liquid.

2   Transfer the tomato pulp, garlic and olive oil to a large saucepan and cook over low heat, stirring frequently, for 20–30 minutes, or until reduced and thick. Season to taste with salt and freshly ground black pepper.

3   Store in a sealed container in the fridge for 4 days, or freeze any leftovers.

Really Useful Stuff
Draining the tomatoes gets rid of excess liquid, allowing the sauce to thicken more quickly when cooking. Although not traditional, I sometimes add a little chopped basil or some dried chilli.

‹ Simple mozzarella & tomato pizza

This recipe proves that simple need not be boring. I love the classic combination of tomato and mozzarella. Use cherry tomatoes for their lovely sweet flavour and scatter with torn basil leaves if desired.

Preparation time: 15 minutes
Cooking time: 20 minutes
Makes 1

cornmeal or polenta, for sprinkling
½ quantity pizza dough (see page 155)
1 tablespoon olive oil
1 clove garlic, chopped
250 g mozzarella, thinly sliced
100 g cherry tomatoes, halved
salt and freshly ground black pepper
extra virgin olive oil, to serve

1   Preheat the oven to 220°C (Gas Mark 7). Lightly oil a metal pizza tray and sprinkle with a little cornmeal or polenta. Roll out or stretch the dough to a thickness of 4 mm and place on the tray.

2   Brush the pizza dough with olive oil and sprinkle with chopped garlic. Top with sliced mozzarella, leaving a 2 cm border around the edge. Scatter the cherry tomatoes over the top and season well with salt and freshly ground black pepper.

3   Bake for 15 minutes, or until the dough is golden around the edges and the cheese has melted and is lightly coloured. Then slide the pizza off the tray onto the oven shelf and cook for a further 5–7 minutes, to crisp up the base. Drizzle with a little oil before serving.

Really Useful Stuff

Salad pizza
When the pizza come out of the oven, top with a handful of lightly dressed salad leaves and serve immediately.

Buffalo mozzarella
Look for mozzarella made from buffalo milk – it is slightly more expensive, but deliciously flavoured and worth every penny. Buffalo mozzarella works well with the recipe above where there are only a few ingredients.

Prosciutto or parma ham
Add thin slices of prosciutto or parma ham to the pizza about halfway through the cooking. It will crisp slightly and add great flavour and texture.

Individual pizzettes
One batch of dough will make about 18 baby pizzettes. Cut out rounds of dough with a biscuit cutter, then top with a slice of mozzarella and few halved cherry tomatoes. Bake for about 15 minutes.

Green pizza

Again, simplicity reigns supreme. The pesto replaces a tomato sauce and the anchovies perfectly complement the mozzarella.

Preparation time: 15 minutes
Cooking time: 20 minutes
Makes 1

cornmeal or polenta, for sprinkling
½ quantity pizza dough (see page 155)
2–3 tablespoons fresh pesto (see note on page 206)
2 cloves garlic, finely chopped
4 anchovy fillets, drained and roughly chopped
300 g mozzarella, sliced
1 tablespoons chopped capers
salt and freshly ground pepper
extra virgin olive oil, to drizzle
handful of rocket leaves, lightly dressed

1   Preheat the oven to 220°C (Gas Mark 7). Lightly oil a metal pizza tray and sprinkle with a little cornmeal or polenta. Roll out or stretch the dough to a thickness of 4 mm and place on the tray.

2   Spread the pesto over the pizza dough and sprinkle with chopped garlic and anchovies. Top with sliced mozzarella, leaving a 2 cm border around the edge. Scatter with the capers and season well with salt and freshly ground black pepper. Drizzle with a little olive oil.

3   Bake for 15 minutes, or until the dough is golden around the edges and the cheese has melted and is lightly coloured. Slide the pizza off the tray onto the oven shelf and cook for a further 5–7 minutes, to crisp up the base.

4   When the pizza comes out of the oven, top with the rocket leaves and serve immediately.

Really Useful Stuff

Spinach & olives
Quickly cook 500 g of spinach in a frying pan with a little oil until wilted, then squeeze dry and roughly chop. Brush the dough with a little olive oil, then top with the chopped spinach. Sprinkle with slices of mozzarella and some small black olives.

Potato pizza
Top the pizza base with some paper-thin slices of potato, strips of pancetta, chopped rosemary and freshly grated parmesan.

Roast butternut & feta
Peel, chop and roast a small butternut pumpkin until tender. Arrange the roasted butternut pieces over a pizza base, then scatter with rosemary, crumbled feta and chopped mozzarella. Sprinkle with a little freshly grated parmesan.

Fig & honey pizzas

Pizza doesn't always have to be savoury. Figs, honey and mascarpone make a delicious sweet topping.

Preparation time: 20 minutes, plus standing time
Cooking time: 20 minutes
Makes 8

400 g soft dried figs, halved
cornmeal or polenta, for sprinkling
1 quantity pizza dough (see page 155), made with
   2 tablespoons brown sugar added to the flour
250 g mascarpone
50 g walnuts, roughly chopped
2 tablespoons demerara or raw sugar
runny honey, to drizzle

1 Place the figs in a bowl and cover with boiling water. Leave for about 20 minutes to soften.

2 Preheat the oven to 200°C (Gas Mark 6). Sprinkle a large baking tray with a little cornmeal or polenta.

3 After the dough's first rise, punch it down, knead lightly and then divide into eight equal portions. Roll out or press each piece of dough into a round about 10 cm in diameter. Lay the rounds on the baking tray.

4 Drain the figs, then dry them with a little kitchen paper.

5 Spread each round of dough with some mascarpone, leaving a 1 cm border. Arrange the figs on top of the mascarpone, pressing them gently into the dough. Sprinkle each pizza with the walnuts, a little sugar and a drizzle of honey.

6 Bake for about 20 minutes, or until golden and the base is crisp. Serve warm.

Really Useful Stuff
You can also use ripe fresh figs when in season. Cut them into quarters and arrange on top

Apple & cinnamon
Cut 3 peeled eating or granny smith apples into 5 mm slices (about the same thickness as the pizza dough). Roll or stretch ½ quantity of pizza dough into a rectangle about 28 × 20 cm and arrange the apple slices on top, slightly overlapping the slices and leaving a 2 cm border. Sprinkle with a little caster sugar and ground cinnamon and bake until golden.

Calzone ›

Calzone are Italian-style turnovers made with pizza dough. The filling is usually more substantial than a pizza topping. Serve hot, or eat at room temperature at your next picnic.

Preparation time: 20 minutes
Cooking time: 25 minutes
Makes 2

cornmeal or polenta, for sprinkling
125 g salami, sliced
125 g fresh ricotta
300 g mozzarella, drained and chopped
2 roma (plum) tomatoes, diced
2 tablespoons chopped flat-leaf parsley
6–8 basil leaves
salt and freshly ground black pepper
1 quantity pizza dough (see page 155)
1–2 tablespoons olive oil

1 Preheat the oven to 220°C (Gas Mark 7). Sprinkle a large baking tray with a little cornmeal or polenta.

2 Combine the salami, ricotta, mozzarella, tomato, parsley and basil leaves in a large bowl. Season to taste with salt and freshly ground black pepper.

3 Divide the dough into two portions, then roll each portion out to a 28 cm round. Transfer to the prepared baking tray, then brush each round with a little olive oil.

4 Divide the filling mixture into two and place over half of each base, leaving a 2 cm border around the edges. Brush the edges with a little water and then fold the other half of the base over the filling to make a half-moon shape. Seal the edges by crimping them between your fingers. Brush the calzone with a little olive oil, sprinkle with cornmeal or polenta, then bake for 20–25 minutes, or until golden. Cool slightly and serve.

Really Useful Stuff

Goat's cheese & herb filling
Combine about 150 g each of coarsely chopped goat's cheese and mozzarella with 2–3 tablespoons chopped flat-leaf parsley or chives, and some thinly sliced ham or prosciutto. Season well.

Cherry tomato & mozzarella filling
Combine 300 g halved cherry tomatoes, 200 g mozzarella, 2–3 tablespoons freshly grated parmesan and some torn basil leaves. This makes a great vegetarian filling.

Pot-roasts

There is something immensely satisfying about producing a complete meal in one pot. In addition to the obvious benefits in the washing-up department, the results of pot-roasting can be stunning. It's one of the easiest, most delicious kinds of home cooking there is.

Hints & Tips

* Pot-roasting was used mainly for stove-top cooking before ovens were readily available. I usually prefer to cook them in a low oven as the heat is more even and can be better controlled. You can still use the hob if you are able to get the heat down very low – the pot-roast should barely simmer as it cooks.

* Use a good, heavy, flameproof casserole dish and make sure the meat sits fairly snugly in the dish. You need to have a good tight fit so that none of the steam escapes. Covering the pan with greaseproof paper before adding the lid can help. I use a large cast-iron Le Creuset that I've had for about 10 years – this type of dish is perfect as the stove-top searing and slow-roasting in the oven can be done in the same pot.

* Usually the meat is seared a little first and then it sits on a bed of roughly chopped vegetables. A little liquid is added (not too much as the meat will give out its own juices), then the meat cooks away gently in the steam and juices created in the sealed dish.

* The vegetables cooked in a pot-roast usually become very soft. Some cooks discard them, but I love them as they are full of flavour. You can also mash them slightly to thicken the sauce.

Really Useful Stuff
The carrots will be quite soft when the dish
is ready to serve. I like them like this, but
if you prefer them a little firmer, then add
them about 30 minutes before the end of the
cooking time.

Pot-roast chicken

As a general observation about all
ingredients, but particularly chicken, you
really do get what you pay for. When it
comes to buying a whole chicken, I would
rather pay almost double the price for top
quality and eat it less often. The success of
this recipe depends almost entirely on the
quality of the ingredients used.

Preparation time: 15 minutes
Cooking time: 2 hours
Serves 4–6

2 tablespoons vegetable oil
150 g pancetta or thick-cut bacon, diced
1 clove garlic, crushed
2 leeks, washed and sliced into rounds
1 × 2 kg chicken, rinsed
500 ml chicken stock
4 sprigs thyme
2 bay leaves
8 small carrots, scrubbed
sea salt and freshly ground black pepper
6 slices prosciutto, grilled until crisp

1   Preheat the oven to 180°C (Gas Mark 4).

2   Heat the oil in a large, heatproof
    casserole dish over medium heat and cook
    the pancetta, garlic and leek, stirring
    occasionally, for 5–10 minutes or until the
    leek has softened.

3   Add the chicken to the casserole, breast-
    side up, and pour in the stock to a depth
    of 2 cm. Tuck in the thyme, bay leaves and
    carrots and season the chicken breast with
    a little salt and pepper. Cover tightly with
    foil or with a lid, and cook in the oven for
    1¾ hours, basting occasionally with the
    pan juices. Remove the lid for the last
    20 minutes to allow the chicken to brown.

4   Remove the chicken and vegetables to a
    warm dish. Skim any fat off the sauce, then
    taste and adjust the seasoning if needed.
    If the sauce is too thin, place the casserole
    dish over high heat and boil until reduced
    to the desired consistency. Remove the
    thyme and bay leaves and transfer the
    sauce to a jug. Serve the chicken and
    vegetables with the sauce and crisp slices
    of prosciutto.

Slow-roast pork

This is the dish I cook when I want maximum impact for feeding a large group – it is big in flavour and the meat simply melts in the mouth.

Preparation time: 15 minutes
Cooking time: 16 hours
Serves 8–10

2 teaspoons sea salt
6 cloves garlic, chopped
2.5 cm piece ginger, grated
2 teaspoons dried chilli flakes
1 tablespoon brown sugar
2 tablespoons olive oil
2–3 tablespoons sherry vinegar
1 large rolled shoulder of pork (about 5–6 kg), skin scored
2 granny smith apples, peeled and cut into 2 cm chunks
2 leeks, washed and sliced into 1 cm rounds
375 ml apple cider or dry apple juice
2 bay leaves

1 Preheat the oven to 220°C (Gas Mark 7).

2 Pound the salt, garlic, ginger, chilli, sugar, olive oil and 2 tablespoons of vinegar in a mortar and pestle (or process in a small food processor) until the mixture forms a thick paste. Add a little more vinegar if needed.

3 Rub the paste all over the top of the pork, rubbing it well into the scored fat. Place the pork, skin-side up, in a large casserole dish and roast uncovered for 30 minutes.

4 Remove from the oven and reduce the temperature to 120°C (Gas Mark 1). Spoon off any fat from the bottom of the dish, then add the apple, leek, cider and bay leaves. Put the lid on and return to the oven for at least 10 hours – up to 15 hours, if you have the time. Check occasionally to make sure the meat is not colouring too much, especially after 10 hours.

5 Remove the lid and increase the temperature to 220°C (Gas Mark 7). Roast for a further 30 minutes, or until nicely coloured. Check occasionally to make sure the apples and liquid don't dry out – add a little water or cider if needed.

6 Transfer the pork to a warm dish and cover with foil, then remove any fat from the sauce with a spoon. Cut the pork into thick slices, spoon on the sauce and apples and serve with mashed potato and peas.

Really Useful Stuff
I usually start this the night before I want to serve it. Don't attempt to cook it for the stated length of time unless you are using a large piece of pork. Reduce the time if you are cooking a smaller piece – anything under 2.5 kg will need about 4–5 hours.

Pork shoulder is a great cut for this recipe. The meat is fattier than meat from the hind quarters and tends to be tastier because the fat lubricates the meat as it cooks. It is also cheaper. Buy decent pork from your butcher and avoid anything labelled as 'lean'.

Pot-roast lamb with gremolata ›

This is comfort food with attitude – the chilli adds a little spice and the gremolata freshens the taste.

Preparation time: 15 minutes
Cooking time: 4¼ hours
Serves 4–6

2 tablespoons vegetable oil
150 g pancetta, diced
2 cloves garlic, crushed
1 brown onion, finely sliced
3 sticks celery, sliced
1 boned and rolled shoulder of lamb
400 g tin chopped Italian tomatoes
125 ml red wine
250 ml beef or chicken stock
1 large red chilli, whole
2 sprigs rosemary
400 g tin cannellini beans, drained and rinsed
salt and freshly ground black pepper

Gremolata
1 clove garlic, finely chopped
1 tablespoon finely chopped flat-leaf parsley
1 tablespoon finely chopped mint
finely grated zest of 1 lemon

1 Preheat the oven to 160°C (Gas Mark 2–3).

2 Heat the oil in the large flameproof casserole dish over medium heat and cook the pancetta, garlic, onion and celery, stirring occasionally, for 6–7 minutes or until tender but not coloured.

3 Add the lamb, then stir in the chopped tomatoes, wine and stock. Bring to the boil, then tuck the chilli and rosemary sprigs into the pot. Cover and cook in the oven for about 4 hours, checking occasionally to make sure there is enough liquid in the casserole. Remove the lid and increase the temperature to 180°C (Gas Mark 4) for the last 20 minutes.

4 Meanwhile, to make the gremolata, combine all the ingredients in a small bowl.

5 Transfer the lamb to a warm plate and cover with foil. Skim off any fat from the sauce. Add the cannellini beans to the sauce, adding a little extra stock or water if it is dry. Stir over low heat until warmed through, then season to taste with salt and pepper. Cut the lamb in thick slices and serve with the sauce. Sprinkle with the gremolata just before serving.

Really Useful Stuff
The Italians often freshen up the taste and appearance of slow-cooked meat dishes with a sprinkling of gremolata – a feisty combination of parsley, lemon and garlic. I use it often, and with the addition of a little chopped mint, it is the perfect way to season pot-roasted lamb. Comfort food with attitude!

Puddings

I'm not going to pretend I don't know that most of us have a love/hate relationship with puddings and desserts. But the truth is that on a cold winter's night a shiny healthy apple just doesn't cut it when compared with a memory-nudging bread and butter pudding. I'm not suggesting you eat this sort of thing all the time, but surely we're allowed every now and then?

Hints & Tips

Pudding basins

✳ Pudding basins are usually made of ceramic or metal. I tend to use ceramic for larger puddings and small metal moulds for individual serves.

✳ The sizes are general given by volume. To check the capacity of your basin, simply fill it with water, then transfer the water to a measuring jug.

✳ To cover a pudding basin, cut a large square of baking paper and the same-sized square of foil (the square should be about 12 cm larger than the diameter of the basin). Place the two squares on top of each other then fold and pleat in the centre (the pleats should be about 1.5 cm wide). Place over the basin, paper-side down, and seal tightly with string.

✳ To make it easier to remove the pudding basin from the pan of hot water, make a little handle from string. Tie the string firmly around the rim of the basin, then loop it over the top of the basin (like a bucket handle) and tie firmly.

Really Useful Stuff
You can warm a few tablespoons of golden syrup in a small saucepan and serve as extra sauce, if desired.

Golden syrup pudding

This recipe comes from my grandmother's handwritten recipe book. Wonderfully sticky, this good old-fashioned pudding is well worth reviving as an occasional treat.

Preparation time: 20 minutes
Cooking time: 1¼ hours
Serves 6–8

50 g butter, plus extra for greasing
125 g caster sugar
1 teaspoon vanilla extract
2 large eggs
175 g self-raising flour
1 teaspoon baking powder
2–3 tablespoons milk
3–4 tablespoons golden syrup

You will also need
a 1.25 litre pudding basin

1   Preheat the oven to 180°C (Gas Mark 4). Lightly grease a 1.25 litre pudding basin.

2   Place the butter, sugar and vanilla extract in a bowl and beat until pale and fluffy. Add the eggs, one at a time, beating well after each one.

3   Sift in the flour and baking powder and gently fold in using a large metal spoon. Stir in 2 tablespoons of milk. Add a little extra, if needed – the mixture should be soft enough to fall off a spoon.

4   Cover the base of the prepared basin with golden syrup. Carefully spoon in the batter. Cut squares of baking paper and foil (see opposite) and cover the top with the squares, paper-side down. Seal tightly with string. Place the pudding in a deep baking tin and pour in enough very hot (but not boiling) water to come one third of the way up the side of the basin. Cover the baking tin with foil and cook in the centre of the oven for 1–1¼ hours, or until the pudding has risen and is firm to the touch. Serve hot with custard (see page 47).

Steamed blackberry jam pudding

This old-fashioned jam pudding has been a family favourite for years. Just the thing for a cold night.

Preparation time: 20 minutes
Cooking time: 1¼ hours
Serves 8

125 g butter, softened at room temperature,
    plus extra for greasing
125 g caster sugar
1 teaspoon vanilla extract
finely grated zest of ½ lemon
4 eggs
250 g self-raising flour
2–4 tablespoons milk
6 tablespoons blackberry jam
175 g blackberries

You will also need
a 1.25 litre pudding basin

1   Preheat the oven to 180°C (Gas Mark 4). Lightly grease a 1.25 litre pudding basin.

2   Place the butter, sugar, vanilla extract and lemon zest in a bowl and beat until pale and fluffy. Add the eggs, one at a time, beating well after each one.

3   Sift in the flour and gently fold it in using a large metal spoon. Stir in 2 tablespoons of milk. Add a little extra, if needed – the mixture should be soft enough to fall off a spoon.

4   Cover the base of the prepared pudding basin with half the jam and half the berries, then spoon in the batter. Cover the top with pleated foil and seal tightly with string. Place the pudding basin in a deep roasting tin and pour enough very hot (not boiling) water into the tin to come one third of the way up the side of the basin. Cook in the centre of the oven for 1–1¼ hours, or until the pudding has risen and is firm to the touch.

5   While the pudding is steaming, make a sauce by simmering the remaining berries and jam in a small saucepan for about 3–4 minutes, or until syrupy.

6   To serve, turn out the pudding and pour the sauce over the top. Serve hot with custard (see page 47).

Really Useful Stuff
You can use this recipe to make many different-flavoured puddings. For a simple variation, try other kinds of berries and jam. You can also just use jam, such as apricot jam or marmalade, and leave the fruit out altogether.

Fruity bread & butter pudding

I would usually advise against playing with classic recipes, but in this case a handful of blackberries does make a delicious variation.

Preparation time: 20 minutes, plus standing time
Cooking time: 50 minutes
Serves 4

6 slices panettone or other light fruit bread
40 g unsalted butter, softened at room temperature
100 g blackberries or blueberries, thawed if frozen
4 eggs
125 g caster sugar
1 teaspoon vanilla essence
1 teaspoon finely grated lemon zest
250 ml full-fat milk
500 ml cream
2 teaspoons demerara or raw sugar

You will also need
a deep 1.5 litre ovenproof dish

1   Remove the crusts and butter the panettone, then cut into pieces about 5 × 9 cm. Arrange the bread in two layers in the ovenproof dish, layering the berries between the bread.

2   Whisk together the eggs, sugar, vanilla, lemon zest, milk and cream. Pour the mixture over the bread and sprinkle with the sugar. Make sure there is enough liquid to cover the bread – add a little extra milk or cream if necessary. Set aside for 30 minutes to allow the bread to soak up the liquid a little.

3   Preheat the oven to 180°C (Gas Mark 4).

4   Place the dish in a large roasting tin and transfer to the oven. Fill the tin with enough very hot (not boiling) water to come halfway up the side of the dish. Bake for 45–50 minutes, or until the custard is set and the bread is slightly puffed and golden on top. Serve warm or hot.

Really Useful Stuff
You can easily leave out the berries if desired, or replace them with dried fruit such as sultanas or chopped dried apricots or figs.

Play around with the flavours. Add a sprinkle of ground ginger, freshly grated nutmeg, ground cinnamon or allspice to the cream mixture as a variation.

Classic Christmas pudding

This is my favourite Katie Stewart recipe – she very cleverly uses butter instead of the more traditional suet, with brilliant results. This is best made a few months ahead so the flavours have time to develop, then simply steamed on Christmas day.

Preparation time: 25 minutes, plus standing time
Cooking time: 5 hours
Serves 8–10

125 g self-raising flour
1 teaspoon mixed spice
a pinch of salt
75 g fresh white breadcrumbs, made from day-old bread
50 g flaked almonds
350 g mixed dried fruit
1 granny smith apple, peeled, cored and coarsely grated
2 large eggs
finely grated zest and juice of 1 lemon
1 tablespoon black treacle
185 g brown sugar
125 g butter
2 tablespoons brandy or rum

You will also need
a 1.2 litre pudding basin

1 Sift the flour, mixed spice and salt into a large mixing bowl. Add the breadcrumbs, flaked almonds, dried fruit and grated apple.

2 In a jug, combine the eggs, lemon zest, juice and treacle.

3 Melt the sugar and butter in a saucepan over low heat.

4 Pour the egg mixture and the butter mixture into the dry ingredients and mix well. Cover with a cloth and set aside for 1 hour.

5 Preheat the oven to 150°C (Gas Mark 2) and grease a 1.2 litre pudding basin.

6 Stir the batter, then spoon into the pudding basin, ensuring the top is level. Cover with buttered baking paper containing a few small pleats, then cover the top of the basin with pleated foil and secure with string. Place the pudding in a deep roasting tin and pour boiling water into the tin to a depth of 2.5 cm. Cover the roasting tin with a tent of foil and cook for 4–5 hours.

7 Let the pudding cool completely. Remove the coverings, then spoon on the brandy or rum, and re-cover with fresh baking paper and foil. Store somewhere cool for up to 4 months – the refrigerator is a good place.

8 To serve the pudding, let it come to room temperature, then re-cover with buttered baking paper and secure with foil, and steam for 2 hours as above.

Really Useful Stuff
To serve with flaming brandy, heat about 2 tablespoons of brandy in a small saucepan over low heat. When the brandy is warm, tilt the saucepan on its side a little and bring a flame close to the brandy. It should immediately catch on fire. Carefully pour the brandy over the pudding and take it to the table.

Sticky banana pudding

This sticky banana pudding is sweet and comforting. For best results, make sure you use really ripe bananas.

Preparation time: 20 minutes
Cooking time: 45 minutes
Serves 6–8

175 g pitted dates, chopped
1 teaspoon bicarbonate of soda
60 g unsalted butter, softened at room temperature
185 g caster sugar
2 eggs, lightly beaten
220 g self-raising flour
1 teaspoon vanilla extract
3 very ripe bananas, mashed with a fork

banana caramel sauce
125 g unsalted butter, cubed
150g brown sugar
200 ml cream
1 banana, finely chopped

You will also need
a 20 cm square cake tin

1 Preheat the oven to 180°C (Gas Mark 4). Grease the cake tin and line the base and sides with baking paper.

2 Place the dates in a bowl, add the bicarbonate of soda and pour on 300 ml boiling water. Set aside.

3 Beat the softened butter and caster sugar until pale and fluffy. Add the beaten eggs, a bit at a time, beating well after each addition. Sift in the flour. Add the dates and their juice, then the vanilla and the mashed banana and mix well (the mixture will be quite wet).

4 Pour into the prepared tin and bake for 35–45 minutes, or until risen and firm to touch. A skewer inserted in the centre should come out clean.

5 Just before the pudding is ready, make the sauce by placing the butter, brown sugar and cream in a small saucepan. Bring to the boil, then reduce the heat and simmer for 5 minutes. Remove from the heat and stir in the chopped banana.

6 Turn the pudding out of the tin and cut into squares. Serve with the hot sauce and cream or ice-cream.

Really Useful Stuff
You can make individual puddings by baking the mixture in six small pudding basins or dariole moulds. Bake for 20–25 minutes.

This pudding can be made ahead of time and reheated in the oven to serve (don't make the sauce until ready to serve). Any leftovers are delicious served cold with tea or coffee.

Rice & risotto

I used to avoid cooking rice, simply because I was not confident about it. Then I put my mind to it, learnt the very best methods (and a few tricks) – and now I cook it all the time. A good risotto is a comforting, creamy concoction, with just a hint of bite in the rice. The trick is in the stirring, which releases the starch and gives the dish its magical texture. Master the basic recipe and you will never be more than half an hour away from the very best store-cupboard supper.

Hints & Tips

Types of rice
Basmati: a lovely aromatic, nut-like and delicately flavoured long-grain rice, mainly used in Indian cooking and the one to use for a pilaf. Regular long-grain rice varieties and cooked basmati grains are free-flowing rather than sticky.

Jasmine: another type of long-grain rice, originally grown in Thailand and served as an accompaniment to Thai food. It has a lovely nutty aroma.

Risotto rice: there are three types of risotto rice – carnaroli, vialone nano and arborio. Arborio is universally available and is a large-grained rice (superfino) with a high level of surface starch. This means it breaks down to give a creamy texture and a dense, sticky risotto. Vialone nano has smaller, round grains (semifino) which keep their shape better during cooking, giving a risotto with more bite. It works well when you are stirring in robust ingredients as the grains are less likely to break down. Carnaroli is known as the

king of risotto rice. It is a superfino grain that produces a creamy texture but it retains some bite – perfect for simple risottos with few ingredients.

Risotto
* The better the stock, the better the risotto. If at all possible, use homemade stock – the gelatine in a homemade chicken stock, for example, helps to give risotto a lovely texture as well as flavour (see page 229).
* As a general guide, you will need about 500 ml stock to 100 g rice, but the amount will vary depending on the type of rice you are using and the heat of the pan. About 20 minutes after you start adding the stock, the risotto should be ready – when cooked, the grains should fall easily from a spoon, and the liquid should have thickened to a creamy consistency. You can have it soupy and creamy or drier and stickier, depending on preference – just take it off the heat when it reaches your preferred consistency.

* Stirring a risotto is part of the ritual for me. I like to stir, ladle the stock, watch the pan and become absorbed by it all – it's a nice way to forget the stress of the day. You don't have to be a slave to the process though; a perfectly good risotto can be made by stirring every now and then, as long as you keep an eye on the saucepan and add more stock frequently. You never want to drown the rice with the liquid, but don't let it dry out either.
* Don't be tempted to leave out the butter at the end. Called 'mantecare', this process of adding the butter softens and marries all the flavours. I sometimes use crème fraîche in place of the butter, giving the risotto a lovely creamy finish.
* Let the risotto rest for 5 minutes before serving – this is an essential part of the process and allows the flavours to settle.

* I often make a larger batch of risotto than I need so that I can play with the leftovers. Sometimes I layer the remaining risotto in an ovenproof dish with taleggio or mozzarella and breadcrumbs and bake until golden, or I transform it into arancini (see page 176).
* Traditionally risotto is served alone, as a dish before the main course, but it also makes a great accompaniment. For example, a Milanese is often served with osso bucco, and the pea and lemon risotto goes particularly well with roast chicken or guinea fowl.

Perfect steamed rice

To make perfect steamed rice, use the absorption method. Choose long-grain rice such as basmati that will separate into fluffy, individual grains when cooked. This makes a delicious accompaniment to braised food, Indian dishes or roast meats.

Cooking time: 15 minutes, plus standing time
Serves 4

200 g basmati or long-grain rice
½ teaspoon salt

1 Place the rice, salt and 600 ml water in a large saucepan and bring to the boil over high heat. Stir once, then reduce the heat to the lowest setting and cover with a tight-fitting lid. Cook for 15 minutes.

2 Check that all the water has been absorbed – if not, cook for another couple of minutes. Remove from the heat and rest, covered, for 5–10 minutes. Fluff the rice with a fork before serving.

Really Useful Stuff

As a basic rule of thumb, use 50 g rice and 150 ml water per person.

200 g uncooked rice will give about 250 g cooked rice.

Don't be tempted to stir the rice while it cooks as this releases the starch and makes it sticky.

Serve plain or toss through herbs, spices or cooked vegetables, such as onion and mushrooms.

Italian baked rice with fontina & parmesan

This is based on a recipe by Australian writer Loukie Werle from her wonderful book *Splendido*, which unfortunately is no longer in print.

Preparation time: 15 minutes
Cooking time: 35 minutes
Serves 4

30 g butter, plus extra for greasing
400 g arborio rice
250 g fontina or gruyère cheese, thinly sliced
4 tablespoons cream
salt and freshly ground black pepper
125 g freshly grated parmesan

You will also need
a 1.5 litre baking dish

1 Preheat the oven to 190°C (Gas Mark 5) and lightly grease the dish.

2 Cook the rice in a large saucepan of boiling salted water for about 11 minutes, or until just al dente. Drain and spread half the rice in the prepared baking dish.

3 Arrange half the fontina or gruyère over the rice, top with half the cream and dot with half the butter. Season with salt and pepper. Cover with the remaining rice and top with the remaining fontina, cream and butter. Sprinkle with the parmesan and bake for about 25 minutes, or until golden. Serve hot.

Simple rice pilaf

A pilaf is type of rice dish where the grains are sautéed briefly in butter, then simmered in stock or water with various seasonings. This is a great basic, lightly spiced pilaf that makes a perfect accompaniment to Indian food.

Preparation time: 5 minutes
Cooking time: 20 minutes
Serves 4–6

250 g basmati rice
3 tablespoons vegetable oil
1 cinnamon stick
6 cloves
6 cardamom pods
1 tablespoon cumin seeds
600 ml chicken or vegetable stock (see pages 229 and 231), brought to a simmer

1 Preheat the oven to 170°C (Gas Mark 3).

2 Rinse the rice in cold water and drain in a colander.

3 Heat the oil in a large saucepan with an ovenproof handle over medium heat. Add the cinnamon stick, cloves, cardamom and cumin seeds and stir for a few seconds until aromatic. Reduce the temperature slightly, add the rice and cook, stirring constantly, for about 1 minute or until well coated.

4 Add the simmering stock to the pan, then simmer for 3–5 minutes. Cover with a tight-fitting lid and transfer the pan to the oven. Bake for 10–15 minutes – the stock should be absorbed and the rice should be just tender. Fluff the rice with a fork before serving.

Really Useful Stuff

Pilaf with herbs
Add 1 chopped onion and 1 crushed clove garlic to the oil in the basic method and cook until softened. Proceed with the basic recipe, stirring in 2 tablespoons chopped flat-leaf parsley and 1 tablespoon chopped mint at the end of the cooking time. Fluff up a little with a fork before serving.

Leek & saffron pilaf
Add 1 thinly sliced leek and 1 crushed clove garlic to the oil in the basic method and cook until softened. Add a pinch of saffron and 1 bay leaf when adding the stock. Proceed with the basic recipe. Remove and discard the bay leaf before serving. Fluff up a little with a fork and sprinkle with chopped parsley before serving.

Capsicum & cumin pilaf
Add 1 chopped onion, 1 chopped red capsicum (pepper) and 1 crushed clove garlic to the oil in the basic method and cook until softened. Add ½ teaspoon ground cumin to the rice before adding the stock. Proceed with the basic recipe. Fluff up with a fork before serving.

Persian rice with pistachio & dill

This recipe was given to me by my neighbour, Elsa. The pistachio and dill are a great combination – perfect with grilled chicken or fish. The rice should have a nice golden crust stuck to the bottom of the pan (definitely my favourite part of the dish).

Preparation time: 10 minutes
Cooking time: 35 minutes
Serves 6–8

400 g basmati rice
75 g butter
2–3 tablespoons chopped dill
120 g unsalted pistachios, roughly chopped
salt and freshly ground black pepper

1　Rinse the rice in cold water and drain in a colander. Cook in a large saucepan of boiling salted water for about 5 minutes, then drain well.

2　Dry the saucepan, then add the butter and melt over medium heat. Spoon layers of rice, dill and pistachios over the butter in a loose pile, finishing with a rice layer and seasoning lightly as you go. Using the handle of a wooden spoon, make five or six holes through the rice, touching the bottom of the pan (like little tunnels).

3　Place a clean tea towel over the saucepan, then cover with a lid (lift the corners of the tea towel onto the top of the pan to avoid them catching on the flame). Place over low heat and cook for 25–30 minutes or until the rice is tender and a crust has formed on the bottom of the pan.

4　To serve, spoon the rice onto a platter. Dip the pan in a bowl or sink of cold water for about 30 seconds to help to loosen the crust, then remove the crust with a metal spoon and serve on top of the rice.

Fried rice

The rule with fried rice is to keep it simple – the 'less is more' approach works here.

Preparation time: 10 minutes
Cooking time: 10 minutes
Serves 4

1 tablespoon vegetable oil
2 eggs, lightly beaten
2 tablespoons peanut oil
5 spring onions, chopped
1 clove garlic, crushed
80 g frozen peas, thawed
1 tablespoon grated ginger
4 rashers smoked bacon, chopped
500 g cooked rice, chilled
1 tablespoon soy sauce or XO sauce
salt and freshly ground white pepper

1　Heat the vegetable oil in a wok over medium–high heat, add the beaten egg and swirl to coat the wok. When set, turn out onto a board and allow to cool. Cut into strips.

2　Heat the peanut oil in the wok, add the spring onion, garlic, peas, ginger and bacon and stir-fry quickly for 3–4 minutes. Add the rice and egg strips and stir-fry vigorously until heated through, breaking up any lumps of rice as you go. Stir in the soy sauce or XO sauce until well combined. Season with salt and white pepper, and serve immediately.

Really Useful Stuff
Always begin with cold rice – in fact, I usually cook it the day before. To make 500 g cooked rice, boil 400 g long-grain rice in a large saucepan of boiling salted water for 10–15 minutes, or until tender. When cooked, drain and rinse, then store overnight in the refrigerator.

XO sauce is a spicy sauce made with chillies and dried seafood. It is often used in Cantonese cooking.

Peeled cooked prawns added towards the end of the cooking time are also delicious.

Risotto with roast butternut pumpkin

Roast pumpkin adds a gorgeous flavour and colour to this simple risotto. Serve as a main or as a side dish with roast meat.

Preparation time: 25 minutes
Cooking time: 30 minutes
Serves 4

1 small butternut pumpkin, peeled, seeds removed and cut into 2 cm pieces
1 clove garlic, crushed
1–2 tablespoons olive oil
salt and freshly ground black pepper
1.2 litres chicken or vegetable stock
60 g butter
1 onion, finely chopped
250 g risotto rice
100 ml dry white wine
60 g freshly grated parmesan

1 Preheat the oven to 200°C (Gas Mark 6) and grease a large roasting tray. Place the chopped pumpkin and garlic in a large bowl. Add the oil, sprinkle with salt and pepper and mix well. Transfer to the prepared tray and roast for about 30 minutes, or until the vegetables have softened and coloured.

2 Meanwhile, bring the stock to a gentle simmer in a large saucepan.

3 Heat half the butter in a large heavy-based saucepan over medium heat, add the onion and cook, stirring, for 5 minutes. The onion should soften but not change colour. Add the rice and stir to coat in the butter. Add the wine and cook, stirring, until most of it has evaporated.

4 Add enough of the simmering stock to just cover the rice. Stir frequently, and wait until the rice has absorbed most of the stock before adding any more. Repeat the process, stirring well and adding stock until the rice is cooked (if you run out of stock, continue with simmering water). The whole process will take about 18–25 minutes. Taste the rice – it should be soft but still retain a little bite.

5 Remove the pan from the heat and stir in the grated parmesan and remaining butter. Cover and allow to rest for 5 minutes. Stir in the pumpkin just before serving.

Really Useful Stuff
Roasting the butternut give is a delicious flavour, but if you are in a hurry, you can simply cook it in the simmering stock while you are making the risotto.

Basic risotto

This is my really useful basic risotto – delicious as it is, but also a great base for variations.

Preparation time: 10 minutes
Cooking time: 30 minutes
Serves 4

1.2 litres chicken or vegetable stock
60 g butter
1 onion, finely chopped
250 g risotto rice
100 ml dry white wine
60 g freshly grated parmesan

1 Bring the stock to a gentle simmer in a large saucepan.

2 Heat half the butter in a large heavy-based saucepan over medium heat, add the onion and cook, stirring, for 5 minutes. The onion should soften but not change colour. Add the rice and stir to coat in the butter. Add the wine and cook, stirring, until most of it has evaporated.

3 Add enough of the simmering stock to just cover the rice. Stir frequently, and wait until the rice has absorbed most of the stock before adding any more. Repeat the process, stirring well and adding stock until the rice is cooked (if you run out of stock, continue with simmering water). The whole process will take about 18–25 minutes. Taste the rice – it should be soft but still retain a little bite.

4 Remove the pan from the heat and stir in the grated parmesan and remaining butter. Cover and allow to rest for 5 minutes before serving.

Really Useful Stuff

Risotto alla Milanese
The traditional accompaniment for osso bucco, this is made by adding a large pinch of saffron strands to the risotto with the stock.

Pea & lemon risotto ›
Add the finely grated zest of one lemon to the pan when you add the rice. Blanch fresh or frozen peas in the simmering stock and stir in halfway through the risotto cooking time.

Mushroom risotto
Sauté 300 g of seasonal mushrooms in a little butter or oil and stir through the risotto at the end of cooking. Delicious garnished with snipped chives.

Arancini

These are so good it's worth making a big batch of plain risotto just to have the leftovers.

Preparation time: 20 minutes, plus refrigeration time
Cooking time: 20 minutes
Makes about 12

350 g cold leftover risotto
125 g good-quality mozzarella, cut into 12 cubes
100 g plain flour
2 eggs, beaten
200 g breadcrumbs, made from day-old bread
salt and freshly ground black pepper
vegetable oil, for deep-frying

1   Take about 2 large tablespoons of the risotto and shape with your hands into a flattened disc. Place a piece of mozzarella in the centre and squeeze the risotto around the cheese to form a firm ball. Repeat with the remaining ingredients.

2   Line a baking tray with baking paper. Place the flour, beaten egg and breadcrumbs in three separate shallow bowls. Season the flour with a little salt and pepper. Roll the arancini in the flour, then in the egg and finally in the breadcrumbs. Shake off any excess breadcrumbs and set aside on the prepared tray. Refrigerate for 20 minutes.

3   Pour the oil into a deep-fryer or deep saucepan to a depth of about 5 cm and heat to 180°C (a cube of bread dropped in the oil will brown in 15 seconds). Gently lower two or three arancini into the oil and fry for about 5 minutes, until golden, turning with a slotted spoon. Remove and drain on kitchen paper. Keep warm while you cook the remaining batches. Serve immediately with a simple tomato sauce, if desired (see page 205).

Really Useful Stuff
Make sure the risotto you are using is no more than two days old; cooked rice doesn't keep well. Look for buffalo mozzarella if you can find it – the flavour is much more interesting.

Prawn & zucchini risotto›

I love this recipe. It looks pretty on the plate and has a wonderful combination of flavours. The zucchini should be just tender when the risotto is ready.

Preparation time: 20 minutes
Cooking time: 35 minutes
Serves 4

1.5 litres chicken or fish stock
350 g uncooked medium prawns
3 tablespoons olive oil
1 onion, chopped
1 clove garlic, chopped
2 zucchini (courgettes), diced
300 g risotto rice
1 tablespoon chopped flat-leaf parsley
2–3 tablespoons crème fraîche
salt and freshly ground black pepper

1   Bring the stock to a gentle simmer in a large saucepan.

2   Peel the prawns, adding the heads and shells to the stock for extra flavour, if desired. Slice the prawns in half lengthways, and remove the veins.

3   Heat half the oil in a large heavy-based saucepan over medium heat and fry the prawns, stirring, for 1–2 minutes until pink and cooked. Remove from the pan. Heat the remaining oil and cook the onion, garlic and zucchini for about 5 minutes, or until soft but not coloured. Add the rice and stir gently for 1 minute to coat with the oil.

4   Add enough of the simmering stock to just cover the rice (don't worry about straining the stock – just work around the heads and shells with your ladle). Stir frequently, and wait until the rice has absorbed most of the stock before adding any more. Repeat the process, stirring well and adding stock until the rice is cooked (if you run out of stock, continue with simmering water). The whole process will take about 18–25 minutes. Taste the rice – it should be soft but still retain a little bite.

5   Remove from the heat and stir in the prawns, parsley and crème fraîche. Season to taste with salt and pepper, then cover and allow to rest for 5 minutes before serving.

Roast dinners

The fad and fashions of food always keep me on my toes – new ingredients, cuisines and techniques are always there to be discovered and adapted. Roasts, for good reason, never seem to go out of fashion and will always be part of my repertoire, whatever the season. And why not? With one roasting tin, a minimum of fuss and a little prodding and turning you can easily turn out a fantastic meal. It's worth taking the trouble to warm the plates before serving – just 2–3 minutes in the oven will do the trick.

Hints & Tips

✳ Buy the best chicken you can afford. I won't settle for anything that isn't at least free-range (locally produced and organic is ideal) and that hasn't had the sun on its back for at least some of its life. The only way to get a good bird is to be choosy: buy from a local growers' market (where you can chat to the farmer) or from a good butcher. Good-quality chicken is expensive – and rightly so.

✳ I never bother with a chicken under 2 kg. The bigger the better, I say, as there are lots of useful ways to serve any leftovers, such as in a risotto or for a salad or pasta dish, and the carcass can be used to make stock or soup.

✳ Trussing helps a bird to keep its shape during cooking. With the bird breast-side up, bring the string under the parson's nose, cross the string around the top of the parson's nose and then bring it over the ends of the legs and tie firmly – make sure the legs are tied well together, sealing the cavity of the bird.

✳ Always rest your chicken after cooking. It will still be steaming hot after 30 minutes. Resting is extremely important as it allows all the juices to settle and the texture of the flesh to relax. Rest it breast-side down so the juices settle back into the breast.

✳ Buy good-quality aged beef. Good butchers will age their beef by hanging it in their cool room for up to 28 days. The hanging both increases the flavour and loosens the texture of the meat, making it tastier and more tender.

✳ Remove the meat from the fridge about 30 minutes before cooking – this gives it time to return to room temperature.

✳ If necessary, tie the meat with string to give it an even shape, which allows for even cooking.

✳ During cooking, baste the meat with the juices from the pan, using a large metal spoon.

Roasting times

If the roasting time is not given in a recipe, weigh the meat and calculate the cooking time as given below. If the meat is to be stuffed, you need to do this before weighing and calculating the cooking time. If you have a meat thermometer, insert it into the thickest part of the roast – but not in contact with the bone. For beef and lamb, the temperature should read: rare 50°C; medium 60°C; well done 70°C. For pork, the temperature should read 75°C.

Beef rib, sirloin or rump

Give the meat 30 minutes at 220°C (Gas Mark 7), then reduce the heat to 170°C (Gas Mark 3) and cook for:
rare: 10 minutes per 500 g
medium: 13–15 minutes per 500 g
well done: 20 minutes per 500 g.

Beef fillet

A fillet of beef is the most tender piece of beef (also the most expensive and with less flavour than other cuts). Roast a 1 kg piece in a 200°C (Gas Mark 6) oven for 30–35 minutes, or until a roasting thermometer inserted into the centre reads 50°C for rare or 60°C for medium. Make sure you let it rest after cooking. I like to spread a fillet of beef with a little Dijon mustard before roasting.

Lamb leg, shoulder or saddle

Give the meat 20 minutes at 220°C (Gas Mark 7), then reduce the heat to 170°C (Gas Mark 3) and cook for:
rare: 10 minutes per 500 g – though I much prefer perfectly pink medium;
medium: 15 minutes per 500 g;
well done: 20 minutes per 500 g.

Pork

Calculate the cooking time by allowing 25 minutes for every 500 g, plus an extra 20 minutes.

Roast chicken

I usually make good use of the space in the roasting tin (use a large one) and place whole scrubbed carrots around the chicken. Turn the carrots occasionally as they roast.

Preparation time: 10 minutes, plus resting time
Cooking time: 1 hour 20 minutes
Serves 4

1 × 2–2.5 kg free-range chicken
1 lemon, halved
1 clove garlic, unpeeled
a few sprigs thyme
4 rashers streaky bacon
1 tablespoon olive oil
salt and freshly ground black pepper

You will also need
kitchen string

1 Preheat the oven to 180°C (Gas Mark 4).

2 Rinse the chicken and pat dry with kitchen paper. Place in a baking tin and squeeze the juice of half a lemon over the bird. Place the other lemon half inside the cavity, along with the garlic clove and thyme sprigs. Use a length of string to truss the bird (see opposite). Cover the breast of the chicken with the bacon rashers, and drizzle olive oil over the legs and thighs.

3 Transfer to the oven and roast for about 15 minutes, then lift off the bacon and set aside. Using tongs and a large spoon, turn the bird over, then return to the oven and roast for a further 50 minutes.

4 Increase the heat to 200°C (Gas Mark 6) and turn the chicken again (it should be breast-side-up). Remove the string. Season the breasts with salt and pepper, then return to the oven and roast for a further 10–15 minutes, or until nicely golden. Check if the chicken is cooked by piercing the flesh between the thigh and leg – if the juices run clear, it's ready.

5 Transfer the roasted chicken to a warm dish, breast-side-down, and rest in a warm place for 30 minutes (yes, 30 minutes) while you make the gravy and finish off the vegetables. Return the bacon to the oven for 10 minutes to crisp before serving.

Really Useful Stuff

Stuffing is a good way to make a roast chicken go a little further. I never stuff the cavity as this just tends to increase the cooking time and dry out the breast. Instead, I usually roll the stuffing into balls and roast in a 180°C (Gas Mark 4) oven while the chicken is resting.

To make herb and nut stuffing, melt 120 g butter in a large frying pan over medium heat and cook 1 chopped red onion and 6 chopped rashers of bacon for about 7 minutes until tender. Transfer to a bowl and combine with 250 g fresh breadcrumbs, 3 tablespoons chopped sage and parsley, 100 g chopped hazelnuts, 100 g chopped pecans, the finely grated zest and juice of ½ orange and the leaves from 12–14 thyme sprigs. Season well with salt and freshly ground black pepper

To make a simple gravy, pour off the fat from the baking tin and place the tin over medium heat. Add about 125 ml wine and 350 ml chicken stock, stir well with a wooden spoon and scrape any bits stuck to the bottom, incorporating them into the gravy. Bring to the boil and simmer until the gravy has reduced and slightly thickened. Season to taste with salt and freshly ground black pepper. Alternatively, have a look at the red wine gravy recipe on page 204.

Five-spice roast chicken

Every so often I like to vary the flavours of a classic roast chicken – here it is rubbed with a Chinese-style spice mix.

Preparation time: 20 minutes, plus standing time
Cooking time: 1¼ hours
Serves 4

1 teaspoon whole black peppercorns
1 tablespoon Sichuan peppercorns
2 tablespoons sea salt
2 teaspoons Chinese five-spice powder
2 teaspoons caster sugar
1 × 2–2.5 kg free-range chicken
4 spring onions, thinly sliced
1 cm piece ginger, grated
2 tablespoons light soy sauce
1 teaspoon vegetable or peanut oil

1   Place a frying pan over medium heat. When hot, add both types of peppercorns and cook for about 30 seconds, or until fragrant and slightly coloured. Grind them in a spice grinder or mortar and pestle until fine. Combine with the sea salt, five-spice powder and sugar.

2   Place the chicken in a clean sink. Boil a large kettle of water and pour it over the chicken. Pat completely dry with kitchen paper, then rub the breasts, thighs and legs well with the spice mixture. Place it, uncovered, in the fridge for at least 6 hours. Before roasting, brush off any excess spice mix.

3   Preheat the oven to 200°C (Gas Mark 6). Place the chicken, breast-side up, in a roasting tin and cook for 1–1¼ hours, or until cooked and golden. Check if the chicken is cooked by piercing the flesh between the thigh and leg – if the juices run clear, it's ready.

4   Combine the remaining ingredients in a small bowl to make a sauce. Serve the chicken immediately so the skin stays nice and crispy, with the sauce for dipping, and steamed Asian vegetables on the side.

Really Useful Stuff
Sichuan peppercorns add an interesting flavour to the spice mix, but if you can't find them, replace with a few extra black or white peppercorns. Any remaining spice mixture can be stored in an airtight container for future use.

Spatchcocked poussins

Poussins are small chickens, often confusingly called 'spatchcocks'. To spatchcock a bird means to remove the backbone and flatten the carcass.

Preparation time: 20 minutes, plus soaking and marinating time
Cooking time: 30 minutes
Serves 2

2 poussins
1 long red chilli, sliced
4–5 tablespoons olive oil
2 cloves garlic, crushed
2 sprigs rosemary, roughly chopped
juice of 1 lemon

You will also need
4 metal or wooden skewers

1   Put the poussins breast-side down on a chopping board. Using a pair of kitchen shears or strong scissors, cut down one side of the backbone, starting at the neck end of the bird, then cut down the other side of the backbone to completely remove it. Repeat with the second bird.

2   Open out the poussins, then turn them over so they are breast-side up and flatten them out using the heel of your hand.

3   Working with one bird at a time, turn it back over and skewer it diagonally, going from the top of one thigh across the bird and through the middle of the opposite wing. Repeat with the other thigh and wing.

4   Make the marinade by combining the chilli, oil, garlic, rosemary and lemon juice. Place the poussins in a shallow bowl and rub them all over with the marinade. Cover with plastic wrap and marinate in the fridge for at least 30 minutes, or up to 4 hours.

5   Preheat the oven to 200°C (Gas Mark 6). Heat an ovenproof ribbed grill pan until it is very hot. Place the flattened poussins, breast-side down, on the hot pan and cook for 4–5 minutes each side, or until golden. Transfer the pan to the oven and roast, breast-side up, for about 15–20 minutes or until cooked through. Check by piercing the thickest part of the thigh – the juices should run clear.

Really Useful Stuff
This is an excellent way of preparing poussins or small chickens for barbecuing as it ensures the birds are cooked evenly. If you are using wooden skewers, remember to soak them in warm water for 20 minutes before use to prevent them bursting into flames while the birds are cooking.

Roast poussin with spiced cabbage

This makes a great dish for a special occasion.

Preparation time: 30 minutes
Cooking time: 1 hour 20 minutes
Serves 6

6 poussins or small chickens
12 rashers streaky bacon
2 lemons, quartered

Stuffing
2 tablespoons vegetable oil
6 rashers streaky bacon, chopped
100 g pine nuts
1 large onion, finely chopped
250 g fresh breadcrumbs, made from day-old bread
1 large egg
150 g butter, melted
1 teaspoon Dijon mustard
2 tablespoons chopped flat-leaf parsley
1 tablespoon chopped sage
leaves of 8 sprigs thyme
grated zest and juice of 1 lemon
salt and freshly ground black pepper

Spiced cabbage
2 tablespoons olive oil, plus extra for drizzling
1 long red chilli, chopped
1 clove garlic, crushed
½ savoy cabbage, thinly sliced
salt and freshly ground black pepper

1 To make the stuffing, heat the oil in a large frying pan and sauté the bacon, pine nuts and onion for about 7 minutes. Transfer to a bowl and stir in the breadcrumbs. Place the egg, butter, mustard, herbs, lemon zest and juice in a blender and purée to a smooth paste. Add the paste to the breadcrumb mixture, season and mix well.

2 Preheat the oven to 180°C (Gas Mark 4). Rinse the poussins and dry well with kitchen paper. Stuff the cavity of each bird with 1–2 tablespoons stuffing (take care not to over-fill or the birds won't cook sufficiently). Roll any remaining stuffing into balls about the size of walnuts and set aside.

3 Cover each bird with two rashers of bacon. Place the birds in a large roasting tin (make sure they don't touch each other – use two roasting tins if necessary). Tuck the lemon quarters around the birds, then roast for about 1 hour, basting occasionally. Remove the bacon after about 20 minutes and set aside.

4 After 30 minutes, add the stuffing balls to the oven, either in a separate tray or sitting around the poussins. Once cooked, let the poussins rest for 20 minutes.

5 To make the cabbage, heat the oil in a large saucepan and sauté the chilli and garlic for 2 minutes. Add the cabbage and fry, stirring frequently, for about 5 minutes. Add 2 tablespoons water, reduce the heat a little and cook, covered, for 3–4 minutes until just tender. Season well and drizzle with a little extra oil.

6 Return the bacon to the oven for 5 minutes before serving.

7 Serve each poussin on a nest of cabbage, accompanied by the stuffing balls and topped with the crisp bacon rashers.

Ducks with marmalade

This is a very simple and delicious way to cook duck. I often do these for Christmas.

Preparation time: 15 minutes
Cooking time: 1 hour 20 minutes
Serves 4–6

2 × 2 kg ducks
450 g jar thick-cut marmalade
12 cumquats, halved lengthways
250 ml chicken stock (see page 229)
200 ml orange juice
½ teaspoon grated ginger
2 teaspoons brown sugar

1 Preheat the oven to 190°C (Gas Mark 5).

2 Wipe the ducks and prick all over with a sharp knife (just pierce the skin and not the flesh underneath). Place the ducks on a rack in a large roasting tin, breast down, making sure they don't touch each other, and roast for 40 minutes.

3 Remove the tray and ducks from the tin and pour off the fat into a bowl. Return the ducks to the rack, breast up, and spread each breast with a thick layer of the marmalade (you may need to warm it slightly to make it spreadable). Return to the oven and roast for a further 40 minutes, or until cooked through. Check by inserting a knife where the leg joins the body – the juices should run clear. Cover with foil if the marmalade is catching and burning – it should be a dark golden colour with the odd bit of slightly blackened peel.

4 Meanwhile, make the sauce by combining the cumquats, stock, orange juice, ginger, sugar and remaining marmalade in a small saucepan and bringing to the boil. Simmer for 10 minutes. Remove the ginger before serving.

Really Useful Stuff
The duck fat can be stored in a lidded container in the fridge for up to 2 months. Use it to roast potatoes.

Roast rib of beef

A roast rib of beef is a classic dish that I never mess about with. Serve with Yorkshire puddings and lashings of red wine gravy.

Preparation time: 10 minutes, plus resting time
Cooking time: varies according to weight
Serves 6–10

1 standing rib roast
olive oil
salt and freshly ground black pepper
mustard powder

1 Weigh the beef and calculate the cooking time (see page 178).

2 Preheat the oven to 220°C (Gas Mark 7). Rub the beef all over with oil, season well with salt and pepper and sprinkle with a little mustard powder. Place in a roasting tin and roast for 30 minutes.

3 Reduce the temperature to 170°C (Gas Mark 3) and open the door for a minute or two to cool the oven down. Continue to roast for the remainder of the calculated cooking time.

4 Remove the beef from the oven and transfer to a warm serving plate. Cover loosely with foil and leave to rest for 30 minutes. Serve with red wine gravy (see page 204), horseradish cream, roasted vegetables and Yorkshire puddings (see right).

Really Useful Stuff
Have all your vegetables partly cooked and ready to finish off in a hot oven while the beef is resting (see roast beetroot recipe below). If serving Yorkshire puddings, make the batter ahead of time and cook the puddings while the beef is resting.

Roast beetroot
Up to 24 hours ahead, rinse (but don't peel) 2 bunches of small beetroots and cook in a large saucepan of boiling water for about 15 minutes until tender. Drain. When the meat is just about ready to come out of the oven, slip off the skins and cut the beetroots in half. Drizzle with a little olive oil and roast on the lower shelf of a 200°C (Gas Mark 6) oven for 30 minutes while the meat is resting.

Yorkshire puddings

Start this recipe ahead of time as the batter needs to rest. When the meat is resting, increase the oven temperature and cook the puddings. This way, everything is ready to serve at the same time.

Preparation time: 10 minutes, plus standing time
Cooking time: 25 minutes
Makes 12

280 g plain flour
½ teaspoon salt
3 eggs, lightly beaten
500 ml milk
oil, dripping or lard

You will also need
individual Yorkshire pudding tins or a 12-hole muffin tin

1 Sift the flour and salt into a bowl and make a well in the centre. Combine the beaten eggs and milk, then gradually pour the mixture into the flour, beating with a wooden spoon until smooth. (Alternatively, you can place all the ingredients in a blender and whiz until smooth.) Leave the batter to rest for at least 1 hour.

2 Preheat the oven to 200°C (Gas Mark 6).

3 Put ½ teaspoon of oil, dripping or lard into each tin and place in the hot oven for 5 minutes, or until the fat is very hot and smoking.

4 Pour the batter evenly into the tins, return to the oven and cook on the top shelf for 15–20 minutes, or until risen and golden. Don't be tempted to open the oven before they're ready, otherwise they will collapse. Serve immediately.

Really Useful Stuff
Resting the batter is crucial. It allows the starch in the flour to swell, which bursts when it hits the hot oil, giving a light texture.

You can make one large Yorkshire pudding in a roasting tin, if you like. Use 2 tablespoons of oil, dripping or lard and heat the fat as above. Pour in the batter and cook for 35–40 minutes, or until risen and golden.

Roast lamb rack with a herb crust

A crisp, herby mustardy crust is perfect with a rack of lamb. If asparagus is out of season, leave it out of the recipe.

Preparation time: 15 minutes, plus resting time
Cooking time: 35 minutes
Serves 4

100 g day-old bread
2 tablespoons chopped flat-leaf parsley
1 teaspoon thyme leaves
1 clove garlic, chopped
finely grated zest of ½ lemon
1 tablespoon vegetable oil, plus extra for brushing
salt and freshly ground black pepper
2 racks of lamb (each with 8 chops)
Dijon mustard, for brushing
16 stems asparagus
200 g hummus

1 Preheat the oven to 220°C (Gas Mark 7).

2 Blend the bread, parsley, thyme, garlic and lemon zest in a food processor.

3 Heat the oil in a large frying pan. Season the lamb racks, add to the pan, flesh-side down, and cook for 2–3 minutes.

4 Brush the flesh side of the racks with Dijon mustard, then press the breadcrumb mixture onto the mustard. Season well, place in a roasting tin and roast for 10 minutes.

5 Brush the asparagus with oil, add to the roasting tin and cook for a further 15–20 minutes. By now the asparagus should be roasted, and the lamb should be medium (cover the bones with foil if they are browning too quickly). If needed, you can cook the asparagus for a little longer while the lamb rests.

6 Remove the lamb from the tin and rest in a warm place for 10 minutes. Slice the racks in half and serve with the hummus and asparagus.

Roast leg of lamb with lemony herb stuffing

This brilliant recipe comes from Jill Dupleix. The idea of slashing a leg of lamb, then stuffing the slashes, retying and roasting is inspired. It gives a wonderfully fragrant roast with lots of delicious breadcrumb stuffing.

Preparation time: 20 minutes, plus resting time
Cooking time: 1 hour 20 minutes
Serves 6

2 kg leg of lamb on the bone
3 tablespoons roughly chopped flat-leaf parsley
2 anchovies, chopped
3 garlic cloves, crushed
2 tablespoons small salted capers, rinsed
1 tablespoon finely grated lemon zest
8 tablespoons fresh breadcrumbs, made from day-old bread
3 tablespoons extra virgin olive oil, plus extra for drizzling
6 sprigs rosemary
6 sprigs thyme
baby rocket or English spinach leaves, to serve
1 lemon, cut into quarters

You will also need
kitchen string

1 Preheat the oven to 220°C (Gas Mark 7).

2 Holding the leg of lamb with its meatiest (thickest) side towards you, cut right through the meat almost to the bone, at finger-width intervals. The effect is almost like leaving steaks hanging on the bone.

3 Combine the parsley, anchovies, garlic, capers, lemon zest and breadcrumbs in a bowl. Add the olive oil and squish the mixture into a soft, mushy paste with your hands. Push the stuffing down between the lamb slices, and tie the whole leg back into shape with string.

4 Scatter the herbs over the lamb, drizzle with oil and roast in a roasting tin for 20 minutes. Reduce the heat to 170°C (Gas Mark 3) and cook for 1 hour. Transfer to a plate, cover loosely with foil and rest for 15 minutes.

5 Strain the lamb juices into a bowl and spoon off any surface fat. Remove the string and carve across the lamb, parallel to the bone, allowing the chunky fingers of lamb to fall onto warm dinner plates. Drizzle with the juices and scatter with baby rocket or English spinach. Serve with lemon wedges.

Really Useful Stuff
Make the fresh breadcrumbs by removing the crusts from day-old bread, breaking it into pieces and pulsing in a food processor.

Leg of lamb in the French style

The French make a great all-in-one dish where you layer potatoes in the bottom of the roasting tin and roast a leg of lamb on top. The recipe here is my version, giving you a lovely soft, garlicky gratin of potatoes and roast leg of lamb without too much washing up.

Preparation time: 25 minutes
Cooking time: 1½ hours
Serves 6

6–8 large potatoes, thinly sliced
1 onion, thinly sliced
2 cloves garlic, crushed
salt and freshly ground black pepper
30 g butter
1.6–2 kg leg of lamb
2 sprigs rosemary
2 cloves garlic, extra, thinly sliced
400 ml beef or chicken stock
olive oil, for brushing

1 Preheat the oven to 200°C (Gas Mark 6).

2 Layer the potato, onion and crushed garlic in a lightly oiled roasting tin just large enough to hold the leg of lamb, seasoning the layers as you go. The vegetables should come to a depth of about 3–4 cm (use extra potatoes, if needed). Add a couple of knobs of butter on the top.

3 With a sharp knife, poke 10 holes evenly around the lamb leg and push a few rosemary leaves and a thin slice of garlic in each slit. Place the lamb on top of the potatoes and pour the stock over the potatoes (there should be enough stock to come about three-quarters of the way up the potatoes – add more if needed). Season the lamb with a little salt and pepper and roast for 20 minutes. Reduce the heat to 170°C (Gas Mark 3) and roast for a further hour.

4 Transfer the lamb to a warm dish to rest for about 15 minutes. Increase the oven temperature to 200°C (Gas Mark 6). Brush the potatoes with a little olive oil and put them back in the oven for about 10 minutes to crisp up. Serve the lamb with the potatoes and a green salad.

Really Useful Stuff
Desiree potatoes work really well for this dish – they cook to a nice texture and you don't have to peel them.

Boned leg of lamb with mint & lemon

Get your butcher to bone a leg of lamb for you – this makes it easy to stuff and easy to carve.

Preparation time: 20 minutes, plus resting time
Cooking time: 1½ hours
Serves 6–8

1.5 kg boned leg of lamb
salt and freshly ground black pepper
1 preserved lemon
3–4 cloves garlic, chopped
3 tablespoons chopped mint
2–3 tablespoons olive oil
juice of 1 lemon
300 ml beef stock (see page 230)
2 tablespoons chopped mint, extra

You will also need
kitchen string

1 Preheat the oven to 200°C (Gas Mark 6).

2 Open out the leg of lamb and season well with salt and pepper. Remove the flesh from the preserved lemon and discard, then finely chop the skin. Sprinkle the inside of the lamb leg with the preserved lemon, garlic and mint.

3 Roll up the leg and tie firmly with string, then transfer to a deep roasting tin. Rub with olive oil and season with salt and pepper. Squeeze the lemon juice over the top and roast for about 25 minutes.

4 Reduce the heat to 170°C (Gas Mark 3). Add the stock to the tin and roast for a further 55–60 minutes (this will give you a nice medium-pink colour). Add a little water to the tray if the liquid is drying out too much.

5 Remove the lamb from the tin and rest in a warm place for 20 minutes. While it is resting, heat the pan juices to make a sauce. Add the extra mint and season to taste. Serve the lamb with the sauce.

Chinese-style roast spare ribs

These sticky pork ribs can be cooked in the oven, under a grill or on the barbecue. If eating them at the table, serve with plenty of finger bowls as things can get deliciously messy.

Preparation time: 20 minutes, plus marinating time
Cooking time: 35 minutes
Serves 6

1.5 kg pork spare ribs
3 cloves garlic, crushed
100 ml hoisin sauce
1½ tablespoons runny honey
2 tablespoons Chinese rice wine or dry sherry
1 tablespoon Chinese black vinegar or red wine vinegar
1 tablespoon Sichuan peppercorns

1   Cut the spare ribs into sections of about 3–4 ribs. Place them in a large saucepan of cold water and bring to the boil. Simmer gently for about 10 minutes, then drain well and dry with kitchen paper.

2   Meanwhile, make the marinade by combining the garlic, hoisin, honey, rice wine or sherry and vinegar. Heat a small frying pan over medium heat and toast the peppercorns for 2–3 minutes or until fragrant. Crush them in a mortar and pestle and add to the marinade.

3   Place the ribs in a ceramic dish and brush with the marinade, drizzling any remainder over them. Marinate in the fridge for about 3 hours (or up to 24 hours).

4   Preheat the oven to 220°C (Gas Mark 7). Place a rack in a large roasting tin and sit the ribs on the rack. Roast for about 20–25 minutes, or until starting to colour and look crisp.

Really Useful Stuff
These are great cooked on the barbecue. For best results, cook them over low–medium heat if possible.

Classic roast pork with crackling

The best crackling comes from the hindquarters, so choose either a pork leg or loin to roast. Ask your butcher to score the skin for you. Avoid buying pork from a supermarket or anything that is labelled 'lean' – a good piece of roast pork needs a little fat, both for flavour and texture (you don't have to eat the fat, but it needs to be there for the cooking). If you buy a piece of pork from the supermarket, you'll need to score it yourself using a very sharp knife or Stanley knife and cutting deep parallel lines into the skin about 5 mm apart. Cut through the skin and into the fat, but don't penetrate the flesh.

Preparation time: 15 minutes, plus resting time
Cooking time: 1½ hours
Serves 4–6

1.5 kg piece pork with scored skin
salt and freshly ground black pepper
3 sprigs rosemary
6 cloves garlic, unpeeled

1   Preheat the oven to 200°C (Gas Mark 6).

2   Pat the pork dry with kitchen paper and rub the scored skin well with salt. Season with pepper. Place the pork in a baking tin, skin-side up, and tuck the rosemary and garlic underneath. Roast for 20 minutes.

3   Reduce the temperature to 170°C (Gas Mark 3) and continue to cook for about 1–1¼ hours until cooked. Test by inserting a sharp knife or skewer into the centre of the thickest part – the juices should run clear.

4   Remove the pork from the oven. If the cracking isn't crisp, carefully remove it with a knife, then return it to a 200°C (Gas Mark 6) oven until crisp. For best results, put it on the top shelf. Cover the meat with foil and set aside to rest for 20–30 minutes.

5   Carve the pork into slices, and serve with crackling, apple sauce and gravy (see below). Delicious with roast potatoes.

Really Useful Stuff
To make gravy, refer to the recipe on page 204, replacing the red wine with apple cider or a combination of half apple juice and half chicken stock.

To make a simple apple sauce, peel, core and chop two apples and place in a small saucepan with 1–2 teaspoons of sugar, 20 g butter, a pinch of ground cinnamon and a little water. Cook, stirring occasionally, for 20 minutes or until soft.

If desired, you can add small apples (Cox or golden delicious) around the roast for the last hour of cooking. Don't peel them – simply score them around the middle to stop them bursting.

Pork roasted with milk

This may sound like an odd combination but the milk cooks down to give a wonderfully thick, full-flavoured sauce.

Preparation time: 15 minutes, plus resting time
Cooking time: 2 hours
Serves 6–8

1.5 kg loin pork, boned, tied and rolled with fat (rind removed)
salt and freshly ground black pepper
2 tablespoons olive oil
1 litre milk
50 g butter
4 cloves garlic, peeled and halved
2 unwaxed lemons, zest removed in strips

1   Preheat the oven to 180°C (Gas Mark 4).

2   Season the pork well with salt and pepper. Heat the oil in a large casserole or frying pan over medium heat, add the pork and sear on all sides until golden. Remove from the pan and wipe out the excess fat with kitchen paper.

3   Pour the milk into a large saucepan and bring to just under the boil.

4   Heat the butter in the casserole and cook the garlic for 1–2 minutes. Add the pork and pour in enough milk to come about halfway up the side of the pork. Drop the strips of lemon zest (minus any white pith) into the milk and bring to the boil.

5   Cover with foil or a lid and transfer to the oven. Cook for 1 hour, then remove the foil and cook for a further 45 minutes. The meat should have browned and the milk will have reduced into a golden curd. Rest the meat for 20–30 minutes, then cut into slices and serve with the curd.

Really Useful Stuff
Ask your butcher to remove the bones and rind from the pork loin, and then tie it with the layer of fat (from under the rind) covering the loin.

Italian-style pork fillets

I quite often use a spice paste or rub to add flavour to roasts and grills. This one is particularly good for pork as it borrows flavours from the classic Italian porchetta (roast pork with garlic and fennel). Here, I'm pairing it with pork fillets, which can be a bit light on flavour due to their lack of fat.

Preparation time: 15 minutes, plus resting time
Cooking time: 20 minutes
Serves 4

1 tablespoon dried fennel seeds
1 teaspoon sea salt flakes
2 teaspoons freshly ground black pepper
2 cloves garlic, finely chopped
1 teaspoon dried chilli flakes
½ teaspoon dried sage
1–2 tablespoons olive oil
2 × 500 g pork loin fillets (tenderloins)

1   Preheat the oven to 220°C (Gas Mark 7).

2   Grind the dried fennel seeds in a mortar and pestle, and combine with the sea salt, pepper, garlic, chilli flakes and dried sage. Mix with enough olive oil to make a thick but spreadable paste.

3   Slash each fillet a few times with a knife and place in a roasting tin. Spread a thin layer of paste over the fillets (you may not need all the spice paste) and drizzle with a little olive oil. Roast for about 20 minutes, or until just cooked. To test, insert a skewer into the thickest past of the meat – the juices should run clear. Rest in a warm place for 10–15 minutes before serving.

Really Useful Stuff
The spice mix is also great rubbed over a loin or leg of pork. I usually ask the butcher the score the skin of the loin and then remove it for me (but keep it). Then, I rub the pork with the paste, place the skin back over the spice mix and tie it in place. Roast, skin-side up, until cooked (see the classic roast pork method opposite for cooking times). The skin turns into magnificent crackling.

The spice mix makes enough for two or three large fillets or one large leg or loin. Any remaining paste can be stored in the fridge for up to 7 days, covered with a little oil.

Roast vegetables

Vegetables often play second fiddle to the meat when serving a roast, but not in my house. Roast vegetables are a real favourite – all the natural sugars (especially in carrots and parsnips) work their magic in the oven, resulting in golden, caramelised vegetables that are hard to resist. While potatoes are everybody's favourite, so many other vegetables roast well: butternut pumpkin, sweet potato, Jerusalem artichokes, cauliflower, fennel bulbs, celeriac, mushrooms, small whole red onions, zucchini, asparagus, beetroot and whole heads of garlic all make delicious combinations as an accompaniment or as a vegetarian course.

Hints & Tips

Vegetables such as potatoes, parsnips, beetroots, fennel are best par-boiled before roasting. For perfect roast potatoes, boil until just tender, then rough the potatoes up a bit with a fork and cook in very hot fat until tender and golden (heat the fat in a roasting tin before adding the potatoes).

Beetroot

Boil the beetroots in their skins for 10–15 minutes or until just tender, then slip off the skins and cut them into halves or quarters. Drizzle with a little olive oil, season with freshly ground black pepper and roast in a preheated 200°C (Gas Mark 6) oven for 20 minutes. Alternatively, brush whole beetroots with olive oil and wrap individually in foil. Roast at the same temperature for 1–2 hours until tender, depending on size, then slip off the skins to serve.

Carrots

Use small carrots or halve large ones lengthways. Scrub them clean and place in a large roasting tin. Drizzle with olive oil and roast in a preheated 180°C (Gas Mark 4) oven for about 50 minutes until tender, turning occasionally or shaking the pan. To speed things up a little you can boil them first until just tender, then drizzle with oil and roast in a preheated 200°C (Gas Mark 6) oven until golden – about 25 minutes.

Asparagus

Trim the stems, then brush them with a little olive oil and season with freshly ground black pepper. Place in a single layer in a roasting tray and cook in a preheated 200°C (Gas Mark 6) oven for 10–15 minutes, shaking the tray occasionally.

Zucchini (courgettes)

Halve the zucchini lengthways, then brush them with a little olive oil and season with freshly ground black pepper. Place in a single layer in a roasting tray and cook in a preheated 200°C (Gas Mark 6) oven for 10–15 minutes, turning them occasionally.

Roast spring vegetables

These are great served as an accompaniment to roasts or grills.

Preparation time: 15 minutes
Cooking time: 1 hour
Serves 6 as a side

6–8 small carrots, scrubbed
4 small beetroot, cut into quarters
2 red onions, cut into wedges
8 cloves garlic, unpeeled
4 tablespoons olive oil, plus extra to serve
   (optional)
salt and freshly ground black pepper
6 small zucchini (courgettes), halved
   lengthways
10 stems asparagus, trimmed
handful of chopped herbs (such as rosemary,
   flat-leaf parsley, chives or thyme)

1 Preheat the oven to 200°C (Gas Mark 6).

2 Place the carrots, beetroot, onion and garlic in a roasting tin, drizzle with half the oil and season with salt and pepper. Roast for 40–50 minutes.

3 About 20 minutes before the end of cooking, place the zucchini and asparagus in a separate tin, drizzle with the remaining oil and roast until the asparagus and zucchini are starting to colour.

4 Just before serving, combine all the vegetables, season with salt, toss through the chopped herbs and drizzle with a little extra olive oil, if desired.

Tuscan-style potatoes with rosemary & olives

This is my favourite potato dish – lovely crisp potatoes cooked in olive oil and flavoured with garlic and rosemary. You can leave out the olives, if you prefer.

Preparation time: 10 minutes
Cooking time: 1 hour
Serves 4–6 as a side

1 kg chat or waxy new potatoes or desiree
4 tablespoons olive oil
sea salt and freshly ground black pepper
1 head garlic, cloves separated
4 sprigs rosemary
100 g pitted black olives, roughly chopped
finely grated zest of 1 lemon

1   Preheat the oven to 200°C (Gas Mark 6). Halve the potatoes (or cut into chunks if large) and place in a roasting tin that is large enough to just hold them in a single layer. Pour on the olive oil and season generously with salt and pepper. Mix well. Roast for about 40 minutes, shaking the pan occasionally.

2   Stir the garlic and rosemary into the potatoes, then return to the oven and roast for a further 20 minutes, or until golden. Stir in the olives and lemon zest, mix well and adjust the seasoning if necessary. Remove the rosemary before serving if desired.

Really Useful Stuff

This dish is best made with new potatoes or the desiree variety. New potatoes are the first of the season and are generally small and waxy, often with a thin or flaky skin. They include most of the red- and purple-skin varieties as well as chats and the small finger-shaped potatoes. New potatoes keep their shaped when cooked and are good for boiling, steaming, in stews and in salads.

Sonia Stevenson's roast mushrooms with olive oil & pine nuts

Big, flat mushrooms are delicious roasted in the oven. So are the wild ones, especially with an added touch of hazelnut oil. Serve them as a first course, as part of an antipasti selection, or as an accompaniment to roast meats. This recipe is taken from Sonia Stevenson's book, *Roasts*.

Preparation time: 15 minutes
Cooking time: 20 minutes
Serves 4 as a side or 2 as a starter

1 tablespoon pine nuts
8 large mushrooms
4 tablespoons olive oil
2 cloves garlic, crushed
salt and freshly ground black pepper
1 tablespoon lemon juice, mixed with 3 tablespoons water
1 tablespoon chopped flat-leaf parsley

1   Preheat the oven to 220°C (Gas Mark 7).

2   Put the pine nuts in a dry frying pan and toast over low heat until golden. Shake from time to time and watch them closely because they burn easily. When aromatic, remove from the pan and set aside.

3   Wipe or gently brush the mushrooms with a pastry brush to remove any dirt and dust, but do not wash them unless absolutely necessary.

4   Combine the oil, garlic and a good seasoning of salt and pepper in a small jug or bowl. Pour half of it over the base of a large baking tray.

5   Arrange the mushrooms on the tray in one layer, open-side down, and brush the tops with the rest of the seasoned oil. Roast for 10 minutes, then turn them over with tongs. Brush the insides of the mushrooms with the diluted lemon juice, then return them to the oven for a further 5 minutes.

6   Sprinkle with the pine nuts and chopped parsley and serve immediately.

Slow-roast tomatoes

The best slow-roast tomatoes are made from roma or plum-shaped varieties. They are great in antipasti, salads, sandwiches or tossed through cooked pasta.

Preparation time: 15 minutes
Cooking time: 2 hours
Makes 24

12 roma (plum) tomatoes
olive oil, for drizzling
freshly ground black pepper

1 Preheat the oven to 120°C (Gas Mark 1) and lightly grease a large baking sheet.

2 Cut the tomatoes in half lengthways and place, cut-side up, on the prepared baking sheet. Drizzle with olive oil and season with pepper.

3 Roast for 1½–2 hours, or until the tomatoes are lightly dried and darkened, but still retain some moisture.

Really Useful Stuff
To store, pack the tomatoes in a lidded plastic container or glass jar and cover with olive oil. As long as the tomatoes are covered in oil (and are therefore airtight), they will keep for up to 3 months.

Baked soufflé potatoes

This recipe is so much more interesting than a regular baked potato. Here, the potato flesh is scooped out and the shell is filled with a delicious cheese and chive soufflé mixture.

Preparation time: 15 minutes
Cooking time: 1¼ hours
Serves 4

4 large floury potatoes
sea salt and freshly ground black pepper
30 g butter
100 ml milk
1 teaspoon Dijon mustard
2 tablespoons snipped chives
2 eggs, separated
150 g cheddar, grated

1 Preheat the oven to 200°C (Gas Mark 6).

2 Rinse the potatoes and place on a baking sheet. Sprinkle with sea salt and bake for about 50–60 minutes, or until tender and fluffy.

3 Cut a lid off each potato and spoon the flesh into a large bowl, leaving a 5 mm thick shell on the potato.

4 Mash the flesh with the butter, milk, mustard, chives and egg yolks until smooth. Stir in the cheese and season well with salt and pepper.

5 Whisk the egg whites until firm, then gently fold them into the potato mixture using a large metal spoon. Carefully spoon the mixture back into the potato shells. Return to the baking sheet and bake for 15–20 minutes or until risen and golden. Serve immediately.

Really Useful Stuff
Before cooking the potatoes, trim the base to help them stand level on the baking sheet.

You can cook the potatoes and prepare the filling up to the end of step 4 ahead of time. When ready to cook, whisk the egg whites and proceed with the recipe.

Roast butternut pumpkin with rocket

This is a delicious accompaniment to roast or grilled chicken, lamb or beef.

Preparation time: 15 minutes
Cooking time: 35 minutes
Serves 4 as a side

1 butternut pumpkin
2 tablespoons olive oil
1 clove garlic, crushed
1 teaspoon thyme leaves
salt and freshly ground black pepper
3 tablespoons extra virgin olive oil
1 tablespoon balsamic vinegar
50 g rocket
150 g feta, crumbled
freshly grated parmesan, to serve

1   Preheat the oven to 210°C (Gas Mark 6–7).

2   Cut the pumpkin into quarters and scoop out the seeds. Cut each quarter in half lengthways to give eight wedges.

3   Combine the olive oil, garlic and thyme and brush the wedges with the mixture. Season well.

4   Place the wedges, skin-side down, on a baking tray and drizzle with any remaining oil mixture. Roast for 35 minutes, or until tender and slightly caramelised.

5   Place the extra virgin olive oil and vinegar in a screw-top jar and shake until combined. Combine the rocket and feta in a bowl and drizzle with some of the dressing. Top with the warm pumpkin and sprinkle with parmesan.

Really Useful Stuff
Don't bother removing the skin from the pumpkin before roasting – it's easier to cut it away as you eat.

Any remaining dressing can be stored in the fridge for a few days and used to dress all sorts of salads.

Parmesan parsnips >

Boiling the parsnips before roasting helps them to become lovely and fluffy on the inside and crisp on the outside – perfect with roast chicken.

Preparation time: 15 minutes
Cooking time: 45 minutes
Serves 4–6 as a side

8–10 medium parsnips
140 g plain flour
3 tablespoons grated parmesan
salt and freshly ground black pepper
olive oil, for drizzling

1   Preheat the oven to 200°C (Gas Mark 6).

2   Scrub the parsnips and cut them into chunks (halve them lengthways if thick). Add to a saucepan of boiling salted water and boil for about 5 minutes.

3   Meanwhile, combine the flour, parmesan and some salt and pepper in a large bowl.

4. Drain the parsnips and drop them into the flour mixture, tossing to lightly coat. Transfer to a baking tray and drizzle with a little olive oil. Roast for 35–40 minutes or until golden.

Salads & dressings

The most successful salads have a variety of textures and flavours – think crispy salad leaves, smoky bacon, nutty parmesan slices and a thick creamy sauce flavoured with salty anchovies and you have a traditional Caesar salad. Or ripe cherry tomatoes, soft mozzarella and peppery basil leaves dressed with fruity olive oil and you have another classic combination. The dressing is almost as important as the ingredients of a good salad – it should complement the salad and boost the flavour.

Hints & Tips

* Use your imagination and try new varieties of salad leaves and vegetables. But don't forget to use old favourites like the humble iceberg, with its wonderfully crisp leaves – update it by cutting the lettuce into wedges rather than separating the leaves, and serve with classic mayonnaise or a creamy dressing. Whole iceberg leaves also make a great container for individual salads.

* Gently wash salad leaves in a clean sink full of cold water and then drain and spin in small portions in a salad spinner (a great investment) or dry with a clean tea towel. Loosely roll the leaves in damp kitchen paper or a damp tea towel and store in the fridge until ready to use.

* A small screw-top jar is the best tool when making vinaigrettes. Place the ingredients in the jar, screw the lid on tightly and shake until well combined. Store in the fridge for up to 5 days. Return to room temperature before use as the oil solidifies in the cold.

* Always remember to taste as you go, and that a dressing should not overpower the salad; it should simply complement the flavour and add some moisture.

* The flavour of olive oil can very enormously from very spicy and peppery to quite smooth and floral – take this into account when making a dressing and adjust the ingredients accordingly. I tend to use an extra virgin olive oil for most vinaigrette dressings. Nut oils like walnut or hazelnut oils also work well, as do newer varieties such as grapeseed or hempseed oil.

* There is a huge variety of vinegars on the market. Start with safe options like balsamic or white wine vinegar, and then try other flavours such as sherry, red wine or raspberry vinegar.

* Add a little crunch to your dressed salad by adding toasted pine nuts or hazelnuts, or seeds (try pumpkin or toasted sesame seeds). To make croutons, heat a 5 mm layer of oil in a frying pan over medium heat and fry small cubes of day-old bread until golden and crisp, stirring frequently. Drain well on kitchen paper.

My favourite dressings

Lemon and honey dressing

Put 3 tablespoons avocado, hempseed or extra virgin olive oil, 1 tablespoon lemon juice and 2 teaspoons runny honey in a screw-top jar and shake well to combine. Season to taste with sea salt and freshly ground black pepper. Store in the fridge for up to 5 days, and shake well before use.

Citrus, ginger and chilli dressing

Combine 1 tablespoon lemon juice, 3 tablespoons lime juice, 1 teaspoon grated ginger, 1 teaspoon finely sliced red chilli, 2 tablespoons finely chopped red onion and 150 ml olive oil in a screw-top jar and shake well. Season to taste with sea salt and freshly ground black pepper. Store in the fridge for up to 5 days, and shake well before use.

Tomato dressing

Place 150 g halved cherry tomatoes, 1 crushed clove garlic, 1 teaspoon balsamic vinegar, ½ teaspoon caster sugar and 100 ml olive oil in a blender or food processor and blend until smooth. Season to taste with salt and freshly ground black pepper. Store in the fridge for up to 5 days.

Blue cheese dressing

Place 150 g roughly chopped soft blue cheese, juice of 1 lemon, 1 tablespoon red wine vinegar, 1 crushed clove garlic, 125 g crème fraîche and 200 ml good-quality mayonnaise in a food processor and pulse until combined. Stir in 2 tablespoons chopped chives and 1 tablespoon chopped parsley. Season to taste with salt and freshly ground black pepper. Store in the fridge for up to 2 days.

Salad cream

Boil 4 eggs for 7 minutes. Cool, peel off the shells and remove the yolks. Using a fork, mash the yolks with 2 tablespoons white wine vinegar and ½ teaspoon English mustard until as smooth as possible, then mix in 4–5 tablespoons pouring cream to make a smooth sauce. If you want it super-smooth, whiz with a stick blender. Season with salt and white pepper. Store in the fridge for up to 3 days.

Really Useful Stuff

Classic vinaigrette

I usually use 3–4 parts oil to 1 part vinegar, but this can be varied according to the ingredients and personal taste.
Put 1 teaspoon Dijon mustard (smooth or seeded), 1 tablespoon white wine vinegar, 4 tablespoons extra virgin olive oil and 1 crushed clove garlic in a screw-top jar and shake well to combine. Season to taste with sea salt and freshly ground black pepper. Store in the fridge for up to 5 days, and shake well before use.

There are many ways to vary the basic recipe. Try using lemon juice instead of the white wine vinegar, or use a different flavoured vinegar such as balsamic, red wine, sherry or cider vinegar.

Remember that some vinegars are more intense than others, so taste as you go. Also, if you use citrus juice or verjuice in place of vinegar, you will probably need to add a little more to balance the flavour – make adjustments as needed

Boost a classic vinaigrette by adding a little lime juice, pomegranate molasses, grated ginger, chopped chilli, crushed garlic, mustard or even a little runny honey.

My Caesar salad

This is a classic – a well-loved and successful salad. I never tire of the combination of crisp cos lettuce and creamy anchovy dressing.

Preparation time: 20 minutes
Cooking time: 10 minutes
Serves 4

5 slices bacon or prosciutto, chopped
2 tablespoons vegetable oil
4 thick slices white bread, crusts removed and
   cut into 1.5 cm cubes
2 baby cos lettuce
40 g freshly shaved parmesan

Dressing
4 anchovy fillets
1 clove garlic, crushed
2 tablespoons lemon juice
1 egg yolk
½ teaspoon Dijon mustard
3 tablespoons olive oil
salt and freshly ground black pepper

1 Cook the bacon or prosciutto in a frying pan or under a hot grill until crisp (prosciutto should take 3–4 minutes, and bacon will take 5–7 minutes). Drain on kitchen paper.

2 Heat the oil in the frying pan over medium heat and fry the bread until golden, tossing constantly. Drain on kitchen paper.

3 To make the dressing, place the anchovies, garlic, lemon juice, egg yolk, mustard and olive oil in a blender and pulse until combined. Season to taste with salt and pepper.

4 Separate the lettuce leaves, rinse well and spin in a salad spinner or dry with a clean tea towel. Place the leaves in a serving bowl, sprinkle on the bacon and croutons, and drizzle with the dressing. To finish, scatter the shaved parmesan over the top.

Really Useful Stuff
You can make chicken Caesar salad simply by adding two cooked and sliced chicken breasts with the bacon and croutons.

Prawn fattouche ›

A fattouche is a wonderful crunchy, chopped Middle Eastern salad. I have added prawns to mine – I love the way they add a soft contrast to the crunchy leaves and bread.

Preparation time: 25 minutes, plus standing time
Cooking time: 5 minutes
Serves 4

2 pita or Lebanese breads
olive oil, for brushing
3 baby cos lettuce leaves, washed and dried
1 red onion, finely sliced
4 radishes, sliced
200 g cherry tomatoes, halved
1 cucumber, peeled and diced
1 red capsicum (pepper), finely diced
4 tablespoons roughly chopped flat-leaf parsley
4 tablespoons roughly chopped mint
salt and freshly ground black pepper
1 tablespoon ground or crushed sumac
¼ teaspoon ground allspice
extra virgin olive oil, for drizzling
500 g medium cooked prawns, peeled and deveined
juice of ½ lemon
1 teaspoon ras el hanout (optional)

Dressing
juice of ½ lemon
3 tablespoons extra virgin olive oil
1 clove garlic, crushed

1 Preheat the oven to 180°C (Gas Mark 4). Split the bread in half and brush each piece with olive oil. Bake for 4–5 minutes until crisp.

2 Slice the lettuce crossways into 1 cm strips and place in a large bowl with the onion, radish, tomatoes, cucumber, capsicum, parsley and mint. Season with a little salt and pepper. Sprinkle the sumac and allspice over the top, then drizzle with a little extra virgin olive oil. Toss well and set aside for 10 minutes for the flavours to infuse.

3 Place the prawns, lemon juice and ras el hanout in a bowl and mix together well.

4 Combine the dressing ingredients in a small screw-top jar and shake to combine.

5 Pour enough dressing over the salad to lightly dress it, and toss it through. Break the bread into pieces and mix through the salad. Divide the salad among four plates, top with the prawn mixture and serve immediately.

Really Useful Stuff
Ras el hanout is a Moroccan spice blend, made with up to 20 ingredients. Look for it in Middle Eastern shops, delis or spice suppliers.

Herby couscous salad

This salad is an exquisite balance of flavours – its spiciness is tempered by the occasional burst of sweetness when you bite into a sultana.

Preparation time: 20 minutes
Cooking time: 10 minutes
Serves 4

200 g couscous
50 g sultanas
3 tablespoons olive oil
75 g pine nuts
2 cloves garlic, crushed
2 zucchini (courgettes), thinly sliced
1 green capsicum (pepper), diced
6 spring onions, sliced diagonally
1 long red chilli, finely chopped
1 teaspoon ground cumin
2 tablespoons chopped flat-leaf parsley
1 tablespoon chopped basil
1 tablespoon chopped mint
salt and freshly ground black pepper
extra virgin olive oil, for drizzling

1 Place the couscous and sultanas in a large heatproof bowl. Pour on 400 ml boiling water, cover tightly with plastic wrap and set aside for 7–10 minutes.

2 Meanwhile, heat the oil in a large frying pan over medium heat and cook the pine nuts, stirring, until golden. Add the garlic, zucchini, capsicum, spring onion, chilli and cumin and cook, stirring, for about 5 minutes or until the vegetables are just tender.

3 Stir the mixture through the couscous, then add the herbs, tossing well to fluff up the couscous. Season to taste with salt and pepper, and set aside to cool. Just before serving, fluff up the couscous and drizzle with a little extra virgin olive oil. Serve warm or at room temperature.

Roast beetroot & feta salad

The sweetness of roast beetroot goes wonderfully with the salty flavour of the feta. The baby salad leaves add a good texture.

Preparation time: 15 minutes
Cooking time: 50 minutes
Serves 4–6

6–8 small beetroots
2 tablespoons olive oil
1 tablespoon balsamic vinegar
2 tablespoons extra virgin olive oil
50 g baby English spinach leaves or other baby salad leaves
1 tablespoon chopped chives
150 g feta or goat's cheese, crumbled or sliced
salt and freshly ground black pepper

1 Trim the tops off the beetroots, leaving about 2 cm of stem, but don't peel them. Simmer in a large saucepan of salted water for about 20 minutes, or until just tender (check by inserting a sharp knife). Drain and set aside.

2 Preheat the oven to 200°C (Gas Mark 6).

3 Slip the skins off the beetroots, then cut them in half (or into quarters if they are large). Place in a roasting tin, drizzle with olive oil and roast for 20–30 minutes, or until starting to caramelise.

4 Meanwhile, combine the balsamic vinegar and extra virgin olive oil to make a dressing.

5 Place the warm beetroot, spinach and chives in a bowl and toss gently to combine. Drizzle with the dressing and sprinkle the crumbled cheese over the top. Season with salt and pepper and serve warm or at room temperature.

Really Useful Stuff
A beetroot's colour is both its glory and its drawback: work surfaces, pans and your fingers can easily become stained with its juices. For this reason, never peel beetroot until after it is cooked (to prevent the juices leaching out) – I usually wear rubber gloves to be on the safe side. Don't buy beetroot if the stems have been cut level with the root, otherwise the colour will leach out as soon as you cook it. You can use the leaves as well – choose those that have bright tops, and are not drooping or yellowing.

Potato & asparagus salad

Potatoes have had all sorts of bad press of late, but that will never stop me enjoying an old-fashioned potato salad. The trick is to add the dressing while the potatoes are still warm as they act like a sponge, absorbing all the flavours.

Preparation time: 20 minutes
Cooking time: 20 minutes
Serves 4–6

750 g waxy new potatoes, scrubbed
1 bunch asparagus, trimmed
2–3 tablespoons chopped flat-leaf parsley, chives or mint
4 spring onions, finely sliced
½ small red onion, finely sliced
salt and freshly ground black pepper
5 thin slices bacon or prosciutto
12 mint leaves

Dressing
120 ml good fruity olive oil
1 tablespoon Dijon mustard
finely grated zest and juice of 1 lemon

1   Cook the potatoes in a large saucepan of gently boiling salted water for 12–15 minutes, or until just tender. Place a steamer over the pan of potatoes and steam the asparagus for about 3–5 minutes until tender (be careful not to overcook).

2   Drain the potatoes well. If they are large, cut them in half; if they're small, leave them whole. Place the hot potatoes and asparagus in a large bowl with the parsley, spring onion and red onion and season well with salt and pepper.

3   Place the dressing ingredients in a screw-top jar and shake well to combine. Pour half the dressing over the salad and toss gently to coat, being careful not to break up the potato. Allow to stand until most of the dressing has been absorbed.

4   Meanwhile, cook the bacon or prosciutto in a frying pan or under a hot grill until crisp (prosciutto should take around 3–4 minutes, and bacon will take 5–7 minutes). Allow to cool, then break into bite-sized pieces.

5   Gently stir half the bacon or prosciutto into the salad. Transfer to a serving dish, drizzle with the remaining dressing and sprinkle the mint leaves and remaining bacon or prosciutto over the top. Serve warm or at room temperature.

Really Useful Stuff
For best results, use waxy potatoes such as kipfler, desiree, pink eye, bintje or small new potatoes. There is no need to peel them, simply give them a good scrub.

The salad may also be made without the prosciutto or bacon. If you like a creamy potato salad, use half the amount of dressing. When the dressing has been absorbed, stir in some good-quality mayonnaise.

Prawns with cannellini beans

This is easy-assembly food – no cooking required. Serve as a starter or light lunch dish.

Preparation time: 20 minutes, plus marinating time
Serves 6

1 kg medium cooked prawns, peeled and deveined, tails intact
100 ml extra virgin olive oil
100 ml lemon juice
freshly ground black pepper
2 × 400 g tins cannellini beans, rinsed and drained
1 small red onion, finely sliced
2 preserved lemons, diced
1 avocado, peeled and diced
2 tablespoons roughly chopped flat-leaf parsley
150 g cherry tomatoes, halved
1 clove garlic, crushed
1 teaspoon Dijon mustard
2 tablespoons shredded basil

1   Place the prawns in a large ceramic bowl. Add half the olive oil, half the lemon juice and plenty of freshly ground black pepper and toss gently to combine. Cover and set aside for 20 minutes.

2   Combine the cannellini beans, red onion, preserved lemon, avocado, parsley and cherry tomatoes in a bowl.

3   Make a dressing by combining the remaining oil and lemon juice with the crushed garlic and mustard in a screw-top jar. Shake well.

4   Combine the prawns with the bean salad and stir in the basil. Pour enough dressing over the salad to dress it. Serve with crusty bread.

Halloumi, pea & asparagus salad

Fried halloumi cheese makes a delicious addition to just about everything – here it is combined in a fresh green salad with fennel, peas and asparagus.

Preparation time: 20 minutes
Cooking time: 10 minutes
Serves 4

4 tablespoons extra virgin olive oil
2 tablespoons lemon juice
1 teaspoon Dijon mustard
1 clove garlic, crushed
sea salt and freshly ground black pepper.
200 g shelled peas, fresh or frozen
2 bunches asparagus, trimmed
1 cucumber, peeled and sliced into rounds
1 fennel bulb, trimmed and very thinly sliced
2 baby cos lettuce, leaves washed and dried
10 basil leaves
500 g halloumi
plain flour, for dusting
olive oil, for pan-frying

1 Make a dressing by combining the oil, lemon juice, mustard and garlic in a screw-top jar. Shake well to combine. Taste, and season with a little salt and pepper.

2 Bring a large saucepan of salted water to the boil. Add the peas and asparagus and simmer for about 3 minutes or until just tender. Drain, rinse with cold water and dry the peas and asparagus well with a clean cloth or kitchen paper.

3 Combine the asparagus, peas, cucumber, fennel, lettuce and basil in a large bowl.

4 Shake the dressing and pour enough over the salad to lightly dress it. Season to taste and mix gently, then divide the salad among four large plates.

5 Cut the halloumi into 5 mm thick slices. Place the flour into a shallow dish and season with a little pepper. Dip each slice of halloumi into the flour to lightly dust and shake off any excess.

6 Heat 3–4 tablespoons olive oil in a large non-stick frying pan over medium heat. Cook the halloumi (in batches, if necessary) for about 1–2 minutes each side or until golden and heated through. Arrange over the salad plates and serve immediately.

Really Useful Stuff
Halloumi is a mild, salty Greek-style cheese that fries and grills well and keeps it shape while cooking.

Tomato & bread salad

This delicious Italian-inspired salad only works with really fresh, ripe tomatoes – beg, borrow or steal the best you can find.

Preparation time: 20 minutes
Serves 4

6 thick slices Italian bread (Pugliese or ciabatta), crusts on
1 clove garlic, flattened with a knife
750 g ripe tomatoes, halved or quartered
1 teaspoon capers (optional, but good)
100 ml extra virgin olive oil
2 tablespoons balsamic vinegar
salt and freshly ground black pepper
20 basil leaves

1 Toast the bread until golden. Rub each slice with the crushed garlic clove, then break into bite-sized pieces.

2 Combine the bread, tomatoes, capers (if using) and any remaining garlic in a bowl.

3 Mix together the olive oil and vinegar and pour enough over the salad to lightly dress it. Season well with salt and pepper. Stir well, then leave the salad for 10–15 minutes. Serve scattered with basil leaves.

Really Useful Stuff
For a bit of variety, use a mixture of cherry tomatoes and larger vine-ripened ones. Diced cucumber, sliced capsicum or olives also make good additions.

Sauces & gravy

Simple or sinful, sauces make the dish. If it's a really good one, you'll want to drench a hunk of bread in it or, when no one's looking, clean the plate with your finger to savour every last drop. Of course, a sauce is an accompaniment and not something that is consumed on its own – the secret is matching a good sauce to the food it's sharing a plate with.

Hints & Tips

* Many sauces can happily be made ahead of time, and some can even be frozen. Reduce your dinner-time stress by planning ahead and making the sauce in advance if possible.

* I love serving a sauce in a proper jug or sauce boat. I urge you to raid your cupboards for pretty jugs or look for them in junk markets. Warm the jug before adding the sauce by filling it with hot water. Small ladles are also useful serving tools.

* A water bath (or bain marie) is a useful way to keep sauces warm. The simplest way is to place a small, flat-bottomed roasting tin over low heat and add boiling water. Sauces in saucepans or metal bowls can be kept warm by sitting them in the water bath.

* Because lumpy sauce is not a good look, I always keep a good-quality fine-meshed sieve nearby. A chinoise (an upturned cone of fine mesh with a handle) is also useful as it allows liquid to drain in a steady stream from the cone.

Tapenade

Purée 180 g pitted black olives, 2 drained anchovies, 1 tablespoon drained capers and 2 crushed cloves garlic in a food processor. With the motor running, slowly add about 150 ml olive oil (in a thin stream) until thick. Season to taste. Store in the fridge for up to 5 days

Quick mint sauce

Heat 125 ml white wine vinegar, 3 tablespoons sugar and 2 tablespoons water in a small saucepan until the sugar dissolves and the liquid comes to the boil. Pour the hot liquid into a bowl containing 4 tablespoons chopped mint, stir and leave to cool. Good with roast lamb. Store in the fridge for up to 7 days.

Berry coulis

Place 125 ml water and 125 g caster sugar in a small saucepan and bring to the boil, stirring to dissolve the sugar. Add 300 g hulled and halved strawberries (or raspberries) and cook for 2–3 minutes, or until soft. Purée the mixture adding a squeeze of lemon juice and, if desired, stir in 1 tablespoon orange-flavoured liqueur. Serve with ice-cream, fresh fruit or pancakes. Store in the fridge for up to 2 days.

Béchamel or white sauce

The thing to remember when making a white sauce is to start with approximately equal quantities of flour and butter, and to make sure you cook the flour in the butter before adding the milk. It is easier if you remove the pan from the heat before you do this. Use a whisk as you add the milk to the flour and butter, then change to a wooden spoon as the mixture thickens.

Preparation time: 10 minutes,
  plus standing time
Cooking time: 15 minutes
Makes 600 ml

600 ml milk
1 small onion, halved
6 black peppercorns
1 bay leaf
40 g butter
40 g plain flour
salt and freshly ground black pepper
pinch of grated nutmeg

1 Place the milk, onion, peppercorns and bay leaf in a large saucepan and heat to just under boiling point. Remove the pan from the heat, cover and set aside for 20 minutes to allow the flavours to infuse.

2 Strain the mixture through a sieve. Discard the onion, peppercorns and bay leaf.

3 Using the same saucepan, melt the butter, then add the flour all in one go. Cook, stirring constantly, for 1–2 minutes. Remove from the heat, pour in a quarter of the milk and whisk until smooth. Gradually add the rest of the milk, whisking until smooth.

4 Return to the heat and bring to the boil, whisking constantly. As the sauce starts to boil, reduce the heat to low and simmer for 5 minutes, stirring frequently with a wooden spoon. Season with salt and pepper, and add the nutmeg. Serve with vegetables such as cauliflower or broccoli, or with fish or corned beef.

Really Useful Stuff
To make mornay sauce, add 50 g grated cheddar and ½ teaspoon of mustard powder to the white sauce. Stir over low heat until smooth and season to taste before serving. This is the sauce to use for cauliflower or macaroni cheese.

For parsley sauce, stir 2–3 tablespoons chopped parsley into the white sauce. You can also use other fresh herbs, such as chives or tarragon, or try a combination of your favourites.

Red wine gravy

No roast meat or chicken is complete without an old-fashioned gravy like this. You can change the red wine for white wine if serving with roast chicken. For this recipe, you need to keep the roasting tin in which you've roasted your meat and vegetables – fat, caramelised juices, browned bits and all.

Preparation time: 5 minutes
Cooking time: 15 minutes
Makes 500 ml

2–3 tablespoons plain flour
300 ml red wine (or white wine, if preferred)
300 ml stock or water
salt and freshly ground black pepper

1 Remove the meat and vegetables from the roasting tin. Pour off all but 2 tablespoons of the fat. Place the roasting tin over medium heat and sprinkle with the flour. Stir constantly with a wooden spoon for 1 minute, or until the flour has cooked and browned slightly.

2 Gradually add the wine and the stock or water, stirring constantly to loosen any browned bits stuck to the bottom of the tin. Heat, stirring well, until the sauce is thick and smooth. Simmer gently for 10 minutes, adding a little more stock or water if necessary to reach the desired consistency. Season to taste. Serve with roast beef, lamb, chicken or pork, or grilled sausages.

Really Useful Stuff
To accompany roast chicken or turkey, add a little redcurrant jelly or port to the gravy.

For onion gravy, melt 50 g butter in a large saucepan, add 3 onions, sliced, then cover and cook over low heat, stirring occasionally, for 30–40 minutes or until golden. Add flour, wine and stock or water, as above, and finish with a dash of Worcestershire sauce.

For pepper sauce, make the basic gravy, using 500 ml stock and omitting the red wine. Stir in 2 teaspoons of drained tinned pink peppercorns, 2 teaspoons of brandy and 100 ml double cream and simmer for 5 minutes.

Bread sauce

Bread sauce is the perfect accompaniment for roast chicken, turkey, guinea fowl or pheasant with gravy. I love this sauce and save it for special occasions.

Preparation time: 10 minutes, plus standing time
Cooking time: 15 minutes
Makes 1.5 litres

1 large onion, halved
2 bay leaves
6 cloves
8 black peppercorns
1 litre milk
250 g fresh white breadcrumbs
200 ml cream
good pinch of cayenne pepper
salt and freshly ground black pepper

1 Place the onion, bay leaves, cloves, peppercorns and milk in a saucepan and bring to the boil. Reduce the heat and simmer for 5 minutes. Remove from the heat, cover and leave to infuse for 1 hour.

2 Strain and return the milk to the saucepan. Bring it to the boil, then stir in the breadcrumbs and simmer, stirring frequently, for 5–7 minutes. Add the cream and cayenne pepper.

3 The sauce should be quite thick, but you can add a little extra milk or cream if you prefer it a little thinner. Season to taste with salt and pepper.

Really Useful Stuff
Get into the habit of making fresh breadcrumbs any time you have some leftover bread, then freeze until needed.

Bread sauce can be made up to 24 hours ahead of time. Store in the fridge, then heat gently and add extra milk, if needed.

For added flavour, stir in some of the roasting pan juices as a substitute for some of the cream or to thin the sauce.

Mayonnaise

Mayonnaise is simple to make at home. I mix it by hand with a wire whisk, rather than whizzing it in the food processor, because I prefer the silky texture of a handmade mayonnaise.

Preparation time: 15 minutes
Makes about 300 ml

2 egg yolks
1 teaspoon Dijon mustard
1 tablespoon lemon juice
pinch of salt
50 ml olive oil
200 ml vegetable oil
salt and freshly ground black pepper

1   Place the egg yolks, mustard, lemon juice and salt in a small bowl and whisk (using a balloon whisk) until frothy and combined.

2   Combine the olive oil and vegetable oil in a jug. Pour it very slowly, drop by drop, into the egg mixture, whisking constantly. As the mixture thickens, start adding the oil in a steady stream. Continue until all the oil has been incorporated and the mixture is thick. You can add more oil if desired, depending on how thick you like your mayonnaise.

3   Season with salt and pepper. Taste and add a little more lemon juice if desired. The mayonnaise can be thinned with a little boiling water, if necessary. Serve with seafood, salads, eggs and cold chicken.

Really Useful Stuff
It's a good idea to stand the mixing bowl on a folded damp tea towel while you're making mayonnaise. This prevents the bowl from moving as you whisk.

The mixture may separate if the oil is added too quickly. To remedy this, simply whisk up another egg yolk and gradually whisk it through the separated mixture in small amounts.

Mayonnaise can easily be flavoured. Chopped fresh herbs, garlic, anchovies, lemon zest, capers or chilli are just a few suggestions.

Tartare sauce
To make tartare sauce, combine 300 ml mayonnaise, 1 tablespoon chopped drained capers, 1 tablespoon finely chopped red onion, 3 chopped hard-boiled egg whites, 1 tablespoon chopped gherkins and 1 tablespoon chopped flat-leaf parsley. Season to taste. Great with fried or roasted fish and shellfish.

Easy no-chop tomato sauce

This incredibly simple tomato sauce requires only three ingredients, yet its clean, fresh flavour can enliven a whole host of dishes. Once you've tried it, you won't go back to the bottled variety.

Preparation time: 5 minutes
Cooking time: 25 minutes
Makes 500 ml

2 × 400 g tins chopped tomatoes
2 cloves garlic, peeled
2 sprigs thyme
salt and freshly ground black pepper

1   Put the tomatoes, garlic cloves and thyme in a large saucepan. Bring to the boil, then reduce the heat and simmer gently for about 25 minutes.

2   Remove the garlic and thyme, then purée the mixture in a blender or with a stick blender until smooth. Season well with salt and pepper. Serve with grilled steak, sausages, hamburgers or chicken, or over meatballs or pasta. You could also use it in a simple lasagne, or reduce the sauce a little by cooking for an extra 10 minutes and use it as a pizza topping.

Really Useful Stuff
To make chilli tomato sauce, add 1–2 long red chillies to the pan with the garlic and thyme. Remove before blending.

Salsa verde

I prefer to chop the herbs by hand as it gives the salsa verde an appealing rustic look. Pulse quickly in a food processor if rustic doesn't appeal, but be careful not to chop the herbs too finely or the mixture will get too mushy.

Preparation time: 10 minutes
Cooking time: nil
Makes about 150 ml

4 tablespoons roughly chopped flat-leaf parsley
1 tablespoon roughly chopped mint
2 tablespoons roughly chopped basil
2 tablespoons capers, drained
2 anchovy fillets in oil, drained
1 clove garlic
1 tablespoon Dijon mustard
juice of ½ lemon
125 ml extra virgin olive oil
sea salt

1   Finely chop the parsley, mint, basil, capers, anchovy fillets and garlic on a chopping board or whiz briefly in a food processor.

2   Scoop into a bowl and stir in the mustard, lemon juice and enough olive oil to make a paste-like consistency. Season well with sea salt. Serve with grilled fish, roasted or steamed chicken, roast lamb, boiled new potatoes, steamed beans or asparagus, or use as a dipping sauce.

Really Useful Stuff
You can make the salsa verde up to 6 hours ahead of time – just remember to stir well before serving.

Pesto
A classic pesto is made in a similar way. Wash and dry 2 bunches basil and place in a food processor with 25 g toasted pine nuts, 2 crushed cloves garlic and 50 g freshly grated parmesan. With the motor running, add 100–150 ml extra virgin olive oil in a thin stream until well combined.

Hollandaise sauce

Hollandaise is not a sauce I use every day – it's more for special occasions – but when I do make it, I wonder how I've managed to survive without it for so long.

Preparation time: 10 minutes
Cooking time: nil
Makes about 200 ml

1 tablespoon lemon juice
3 egg yolks
125 g butter
salt and freshly ground black pepper

1   Blend the lemon juice, egg yolks and 1 tablespoon water in a food processor for 10 seconds.

2   Melt the butter then, with the motor running, gradually add it to the egg mixture in a thin stream until the sauce is smooth and thick. Season to taste. Keep warm in a heatproof bowl set over a saucepan of hot water, whisking occasionally. Serve with poached chicken, salmon or eggs, steamed asparagus or eggs Benedict.

Really Useful Stuff
For fluffy hollandaise, whisk 2 egg whites to soft peaks and gently fold through the finished sauce. You can make fluffy hollandaise up to 12 hours ahead of time, then reheat by lightly whisking in a heatproof bowl set over a saucepan of simmering water. Delicious with poached fish or steamed vegetables, such as asparagus.

For orange hollandaise, replace the lemon juice with 2 tablespoons strained freshly squeezed orange juice.

For Béarnaise sauce, combine 4 tablespoons white wine vinegar, ½ golden shallot, sliced, and 6 black peppercorns in a small saucepan and simmer over medium heat until reduced by half. Strain into a small food processor or blender. Add 2 egg yolks and whiz using the pulse action. Slowly add 125 g melted butter in a thin stream and whiz until the sauce becomes thick and creamy. Stir in 2 teaspoons chopped tarragon, season to taste and serve immediately.

Skewers

Food on sticks is perfect fare for both indoor and outdoor entertaining. The skewers can be cooked indoors in a grill pan or under a hot grill, or outdoors on the barbecue. Cooking out of doors is a fun, relaxed way to entertain: most of the food can be prepared ahead of time and then cooked quickly when you're ready to eat. And to simplify matters even further, using skewers means you can pretty much abandon cutlery.

Hints & Tips

* If using wooden skewers, soak them in warm water for about 20 minutes. This prevents them from bursting into flames when placed on the barbecue or grill. Use metal skewers if you can find them – they can withstand the heat, and are easily washed and reused.

* Cut the vegetables or meat into similar-sized pieces to help them cook evenly.

* Remember to leave a little space between each vegetable or piece of meat on the skewer (for even cooking) and brush with a little olive oil or marinade before grilling.

* Lots of vegetables grill well on skewers – try slices of capsicum (pepper), red onion or zucchini (courgette). Feta and halloumi also make a great addition, particularly on vegetable skewers.

* Most skewers can be assembled ahead of time and refrigerated for up to 8 hours before cooking.

Chicken & bacon skewers

The bacon wrapped around the chicken adds both flavour and a little fat, which is good when grilling or frying.

Preparation time: 15 minutes, plus soaking and marinating time
Cooking time: 10 minutes
Makes 6

3 skinless chicken breasts
6 rashers streaky bacon
3 tablespoons olive oil
2 cloves garlic, crushed
juice of ½ lemon
½ teaspoon thyme leaves
salt and freshly ground black pepper
1 lemon, quartered

You will also need
6 metal or wooden skewers

1   If using wooden skewers, soak them in warm water for 20 minutes.

2   Cut each chicken breast into six equal-sized pieces. Place three pieces of chicken in a line and interweave a rasher of bacon between them. Push a skewer through the chicken and bacon to secure. Separate the chicken pieces a little on the skewer so there is a small space between them. Repeat with the remaining chicken and bacon to make six skewers.

3   Combine the oil, garlic, lemon juice and thyme and brush over the chicken and bacon. Marinate in the refrigerator for up to 4 hours.

4   Season each skewer with salt and pepper and cook on a barbecue plate or on a ribbed grill pan over medium–high heat for about 8 minutes or until cooked through, turning every 2 minutes. Serve with the lemon quarters.

Really Useful Stuff
You can always use pieces of chicken thigh meat for these skewers, if preferred.

Green chilli fish kebabs

Rather than threading meat onto skewers, many southeast Asian recipes mould minced meat on the skewers. This technique works particularly well with fish.

Preparation time: 25 minutes, plus soaking and refrigeration time
Cooking time: 10 minutes
Makes 12

350 g firm white fish fillets, skin removed
250 g salmon fillet, skin removed
3 long green chillies, seeded and finely chopped
4 spring onions, finely sliced
2 tablespoons finely chopped coriander leaves
1 tablespoon chopped mint
2 teaspoons finely grated ginger
2 cloves garlic, crushed
finely grated zest and juice of 1 lime
1 tablespoon fennel seeds
1 tablespoon coriander seeds
1 teaspoon white peppercorns
sea salt
250 g plain yoghurt
1 small cucumber, grated or finely chopped
2–3 tablespoons roughly chopped mint, extra

You will also need
12 metal or wooden skewers

1   If using wooden skewers, soak them in warm water for 20 minutes.

2   Remove any bones from the fish, roughly chop and place in a food processor. Process until minced. Transfer to a bowl and stir in the chilli, spring onion, coriander, mint, ginger, garlic, lime zest and juice.

3   Heat the fennel seeds, coriander seeds and peppercorns in a frying pan over medium heat for 2–3 minutes until fragrant. Grind in a spice mill or with a mortar and pestle, then stir into the fish mixture and season with sea salt.

4   Mould handfuls of the mixture (about the size of a small egg) onto the skewers and chill for at least 30 minutes.

5   Just before cooking, combine the yoghurt, cucumber and extra mint. Season to taste with a little sea salt.

6   Cook the kebabs on a barbecue plate or on a ribbed grill pan over medium heat for 5–7 minutes until golden on both sides. Serve with the cucumber sauce.

Really Useful Stuff
Use less expensive varieties of white fish for this recipe (check what's available at your local fishmonger's). The mixture also makes really good pan-fried fish cakes.

Five-spice duck kebabs ›

Five-spice powder and Sichuan pepper are perfect flavours with duck.

Preparation time: 15 minutes, plus soaking time
Cooking time: 15 minutes
Makes 8

4 duck breasts, with skin on
1 tablespoon Chinese five-spice powder
1 teaspoon Sichuan peppercorns, crushed
2 teaspoons crushed sea salt
1 red onion, peeled and quartered

You will also need
8 metal or wooden skewers

1   If using wooden skewers, soak them in warm water for 20 minutes.

2   Preheat the oven to 180°C (Gas Mark 4). Cut each duck breast into eight even cubes.

3   Combine the five-spice powder, Sichuan peppercorns and salt and lightly sprinkle over the duck. Separate the onion quarters into individual slices.

4   Thread the ingredients onto the skewers, starting with a piece of duck, followed by a slice of onion. Continue to thread the duck and onion until you have four pieces of duck on each skewer.

5   Heat a large non-stick frying pan over high heat and sear the skewers for about 1 minute on each side. Transfer to the oven and cook for a further 8–10 minutes, or until cooked through and nicely coloured. Serve with steamed Chinese vegetables.

Really Useful Stuff
The five-spice mixture also works well with chicken breasts or thighs. After searing, cook them in the oven for about 10–12 minutes.

Balinese chicken skewers

This is another recipe where the meat is minced, then moulded onto the skewer.

Preparation time: 25 minutes, plus soaking time
Cooking time: 10 minutes
Makes 12

500 g minced chicken
3 spring onions, thinly sliced
4 tablespoons coconut milk
1 tablespoon palm sugar or soft brown sugar
juice of 1 lime
salt
lime wedges, to serve

Spice paste
3–4 small red chillies
2 cloves garlic, chopped
3 cm piece turmeric, chopped
2 cm piece ginger, chopped

You will also need
12 metal or wooden skewers

1 If using wooden skewers, soak them in warm water for 20 minutes.

2 Make the spice paste by pounding the chilli, garlic, turmeric and ginger in a mortar and pestle.

3 Place the chicken in a bowl, add the spice paste, spring onion and coconut milk and mix to combine. Dissolve the sugar in the lime juice and add to the chicken mixture. Season well with salt.

4 Shape heaped tablespoons of the mixture into balls and mould onto the skewers. Chill for at least 30 minutes.

5 Cook on a ribbed grill pan over high heat or under a hot grill for 6–7 minutes until nicely golden and cooked through. Serve with lime wedges and steamed rice.

Beef satays

This satay sauce is lightly spiced and full of peanuts, and the recipe is well worth adding to your repertoire. The secret is to use crunchy peanut butter.

Preparation time: 25 minutes, plus marinating time
Cooking time: 15 minutes
Makes 12

500 g beef steak (fillet, sirloin or rib eye), cut into 5 mm strips
3 tablespoons vegetable oil
1 long red chilli, finely chopped
1 clove garlic, crushed
juice of 1 lime
1 teaspon sugar
2 teaspoons fish sauce
2–3 tablespoons coriander leaves

Satay sauce
2 tablespoons vegetable oil
2 large golden shallots, peeled and finely chopped
2 cloves garlic, crushed
2 cm piece ginger, grated
1 long red chilli, finely chopped
1½ tablespoons light soy sauce
250 ml coconut milk
1 tablespoon caster sugar
125 g crunchy peanut butter

You will also need
12 metal or wooden skewers

1 Place the beef strips in a ceramic dish. Mix together the vegetable oil, chilli, garlic, lime juice, sugar and fish sauce and brush over the beef. Cover and leave to marinate in the fridge for a few hours or overnight.

2 If using wooden skewers, soak them in warm water for 20 minutes.

3 To make the peanut sauce, heat the oil in a saucepan over medium heat, add the shallots and cook for about 5 minutes or until softened. Add the garlic, ginger and chilli and cook for a few more minutes. Add the soy sauce, coconut milk and sugar, stirring to dissolve the sugar. Bring to the boil, then immediately remove from the heat and stir in the peanut butter. Mix well until combined.

4 Thread the beef, zig-zag fashion, onto the skewers and cook on a ribbed grillpan over high hot or under a hot grill for about 2 minutes each side or until browned and cooked. Serve with the peanut sauce. Garnish with coriander leaves.

Skewered prawns

Large king prawns respond really well to the classic combination of lemon, chilli and garlic. Cooking these skewers on a barbecue grill plate seems to bring out the flavours.

Preparation time: 15 minutes, plus marinating time
Cooking time: 6 minutes
Makes 16

2 cloves garlic, finely chopped
grated zest of 1 lemon
1 long red chilli, finely sliced
2 tablespoons chopped flat-leaf parsley
100 ml olive oil
16 large uncooked king prawns
salt and freshly ground black pepper
2 lemons, cut into thin wedges

You will also need
16 metal skewers

1   Combine the garlic, lemon zest, chilli, parsley and olive oil in a bowl. Add the prawns and toss well. Season with freshly ground black pepper. Cover with plastic wrap and marinate in the fridge for about 2 hours. Remove from the fridge about 10 minutes before cooking so they lose their chill.

2   Insert a skewer into the tail of each prawn, then thread the skewer through the centre of the prawn to keep it straight. Thread a lemon wedge onto each skewer.

3   Cook the prawns on a hot barbecue plate, ribbed grill pan or frying pan for about 1–2 minutes each side or until cooked. They will continue to cook for a minute after being removed from the heat – take care not to overcook them or they will be dry. To eat them, peel the prawns and squeeze some of the grilled lemon over the top.

Really Useful Stuff
I prefer to use metal skewers for the prawns, but you can use wooden skewers, if preferred. Just remember to soak them in warm water for about 20 minutes before use.

Grilled pineapple skewers

Pineapple is the perfect fruit to barbecue – especially when marinated in a little rum – because the sweet juices caramelise so beautifully.

Preparation time: 15 minutes minutes,
    plus soaking and refrigeration time
Cooking time: 5 minutes
Makes about 20

1 ripe pineapple
90 ml white rum
3 tablespoons maple syrup
1 tablespoon brown sugar
double cream, to serve (optional)

You will also need
20 metal or wooden skewers

1   Slice the bottom and the leafy top off the pineapple. Stand it on a board and, using a large sharp knife, slice downwards, cutting off the tough skin in long strips. Cut away any eyes that remain. Cut the pineapple into quarters through the core, then cut away the core and slice the pieces into 2 cm chunks.

2   Place the pineapple in a bowl and add the rum, maple syrup and brown sugar. Mix well and refrigerate for at least 1 hour.

3   If using wooden skewers, soak them in warm water for 20 minutes.

4   Just before cooking, thread two or three chunks of pineapple onto the skewers, reserving the marinade. Cook on a ribbed grill pan over high heat or under a hot grill for 1–2 minutes each side, or until golden and starting to char. Brush with the marinade as they cook. Serve warm with cream, if desired.

Really Useful Stuff
Lots of other fruits grill well – try ripe figs, apples, pears or stone fruit such as nectarines, peaches or plums, when in season.

Soufflés

A proper homemade soufflé is a rare treat these days. Despite their reputation, they really are simple to make – the only slightly tricky bit is whisking the egg whites (and an electric beater makes easy work of that). If you are nervous about attempting your first soufflé, try out the impressive double-baked cheese version first – they are virtually foolproof and most of the work is done well ahead of time.

Hints & Tips

* A soufflé is basically a flavoured base into which beaten egg whites are folded. The heat of the oven expands the air in the beaten egg white and stiffens the proteins to create the soufflé – an extraordinary dish that is firm and risen on the outside, but soft and creamy within.
* Some soufflés are based on a fruit purée. These are fairly light and low in calories – they also tend to sink quickly when removed from the oven so must be served immediately. Soufflés made with an egg and flour or custard base (see passionfruit soufflé, page 216) will be more stable, giving you a little more time before they sink.

* I place a heavy baking tray in the oven while it's preheating. The filled soufflé dishes are then placed on the hot tray, and immediately put back in the oven. This heated base helps the soufflés start to rise. Using a tray also makes it easy to retrieve them when cooked, and catches any mess in case they overflow.
* To get a good rise it is important to grease the dishes well. Rub the inside of the dish thickly with softened butter. If you're making a sweet soufflé, follow this with a dusting of caster sugar and then shake out any excess. For savoury soufflés, such as cheese, grease the dish with butter and then dust with

a little finely grated parmesan, if desired.
* Whisking and folding the egg whites is a crucial step in the method. Make sure the egg whites are at room temperature and free of any specks of egg yolk. When whisking egg whites, the bowl and beaters you are using must be spotlessly clean and free of grease. To be sure, I often rub the inside of the bowl with a cut lemon.
* I always add a pinch of cream of tartar to the egg whites before whisking – it seems to stabilise the whites and makes it easier to mix them into the flavoured base. It is not essential though, and you can go ahead with the recipe without it.
* To ensure an even rise, once the dishes are filled with the mixture, run a knife or your finger around the inside edge of the dish (making a groove in the mixture).
* To check if a soufflé is cooked lightly touch the top – it should feel firm to the touch. Another way is to give the tray a little shake – the soufflé should only wobble slightly.

* If you are dusting a soufflé with icing sugar before serving, make sure you have the sieve and sugar ready the second it comes out of the oven. A baked soufflé will remain risen for just a minute or two, so it is important to get it to the table with a minimum of delay.
* The batter for most soufflés can be made and spooned into the dish a few hours before cooking. Keep chilled in the fridge until ready to bake. If you do this, increase the oven temperature slightly before placing the dish in the oven, then reduce to the correct temperature when you put it in.
* I often make soufflés ahead of time, then freeze them (uncooked) in their dishes. To cook, place them on a baking tray and bake from frozen, allowing an extra 5 minutes.

Simple chocolate soufflés

This is my slightly simplified version of the classic chocolate soufflé – it gives a really good result without being too temperamental.

Preparation time: 20 minutes
Cooking time: 15 minutes
Serves 6

softened butter, for greasing
caster sugar, for dusting
200 g good-quality dark chocolate
120 ml cream
6 free-range eggs at room temperature, separated
pinch of cream of tartar
1 teaspoon vanilla extract
80 g caster sugar, extra
icing sugar, to serve

You will also need
six 150 ml ramekins

1　Preheat the oven to 200°C (Gas Mark 6). Grease the ramekins with a little butter and dust them with caster sugar. Shake out any excess.

2　Melt the chocolate and cream in a small bowl set over a saucepan of hot water, stirring occasionally until smooth.

3　Whisk the egg yolks until they just start to thicken, then lightly whisk in the melted chocolate and vanilla.

4　Place the egg whites and cream of tartar in a clean bowl and whisk with clean beaters until soft peaks form. Continue to beat, gradually adding the extra caster sugar, until stiff and glossy. Using a large metal spoon, gently fold a spoonful of the egg whites into the chocolate mixture (this helps to loosen the mixture), then gently fold in the remaining egg whites until just combined.

5　Place the ramekins on a baking tray. Spoon the mixture into the ramekins to just below the rim. Transfer the tray to the oven and bake for 10–15 minutes, or until risen and firm on the top. Use a pair of tongs to transfer each soufflé dish to a plate, then dust with icing sugar. Serve immediately with a jug of cream or custard.

Really Useful Stuff

The soufflé can also be made in one large dish (1 litre would be about right). Bake for about 40 minutes.

Make a simple jug of chocolate sauce to pour into the centre of the soufflés when served. To do this, break up 200 g good-quality dark chocolate and place in a heatproof bowl. Heat 125 ml pouring cream to just under boiling point and then pour over the chocolate. Let the chocolate melt, stirring occasionally. Transfer to a jug and serve with the soufflés.

Passionfruit soufflé

It doesn't get much better than this. Passionfruit soufflé is a classic dish (and the secret is it's not that difficult to achieve brilliant results).

Preparation time: 20 minutes
Cooking time: 45 minutes
Serves 4–6

softened butter, for greasing
caster sugar, for dusting
25 g unsalted butter
2 tablespoons plain flour
150 ml milk
8 passionfruit
4 large free-range eggs at room temperature, separated
1 teaspoon vanilla essence
pinch of cream of tartar
75 g caster sugar, extra
icing sugar, to serve

You will also need
a 1.25 litre soufflé dish

1 Preheat the oven to 190°C (Gas Mark 5) Grease a 1.25 litre soufflé dish with a little butter and dust with caster sugar. Shake out any excess.

2 Melt the butter in a large saucepan, add the flour and stir over low heat for 1–2 minutes or until golden. Gradually add the milk, whisking with a metal whisk until smooth and combined. Stir over medium heat until the mixture boils and thickens, then set aside to cool.

3 Cut the passionfruit in half, spoon out the pulp and push through a small sieve to remove the seeds.

4 One by one, beat the egg yolks into the milk mixture. Beat in the vanilla and passionfruit pulp.

5 Place the egg whites and cream of tartar in a clean bowl and whisk with clean beaters until soft peaks form. Continue to beat, gradually adding the extra caster sugar, until stiff and glossy. Using a large metal spoon, gently fold a spoonful of the egg whites into the passionfruit mixture (this helps to loosen the mixture), then gently fold in the remaining egg whites until just combined.

6 Spoon the mixture into the prepared soufflé dish, filling almost to the top. Bake for 35–45 minutes or until nicely risen and golden. Dust with icing sugar and serve immediately.

Really Useful Stuff
If you like passionfruit seeds (as I do), add some to the mixture, discarding any surplus.

Double-baked cheese soufflés ›

Making a twice-baked soufflé is the way to gain confidence if you feel unsure about the process. They are made in advance and then reheated, so everything can be done ahead of time. This cheese version offers a winning combination: it's very easy to make, but incredibly impressive to serve.

Preparation time: 20 minutes
Cooking time: 45 minutes
Serves 4

softened butter, for greasing
40 g unsalted butter
40 g plain flour
250 ml milk
pinch of grated nutmeg
pinch of cayenne pepper
225 g gruyère, grated
salt and freshly ground black pepper
3 large free-range eggs, at room temperature, separated
400 ml cream

You will also need
4 ramekins and 4 shallow gratin dishes

1 Preheat the oven to 190°C (Gas Mark 5). Grease the ramekins with a little butter.

2 Melt the butter in a small saucepan over low heat, add the flour and cook, stirring, for 1 minute. Gradually add the milk and whisk over medium heat until it comes to the boil. Cook for 2 minutes. Stir in the nutmeg, cayenne and 160 g of the cheese and season to taste with salt and pepper. Remove from the heat and allow to cool for 5 minutes, then transfer to a bowl.

3 Lightly beat the egg yolks and whisk into the cheese mixture.

4 Place the egg whites in a clean bowl and whisk with clean beaters until soft peaks form. Using a large metal spoon, gently fold a spoonful of the egg whites into the cheese mixture (this helps to loosen the mixture), then gently fold in the remaining egg whites until just combined.

5 Place the ramekins in a roasting tin. Spoon the mixture into the ramekins to just below the rim. Transfer the tin to the oven and pour in enough boiling water to come a third of the way up the dishes. Bake for 20–25 minutes or until risen and golden. Allow to cool. They can now be refrigerated for up to 24 hours if you are preparing these in advance.

6 To serve, preheat the oven to 200°C (Gas Mark 6). Run a knife around the edges of the cooled soufflés and turn them out. Place each soufflé in a gratin dish and pour about 100 ml of the cream over each one. Sprinkle the remaining gruyère over the top and bake for 10–15 minutes or until bubbling and golden. Serve immediately.

Really Useful Stuff
You can use a mixture of gruyère and goat's cheese as a variation; 1–2 tablespoons fresh thyme leaves or snipped chives also make a lovely addition.

Soups

I am such a fan of soup that if left to my own devices, I would eat it every other day. I love the versatility and the endless possibilities it presents for the home cook, regardless of what time of year it is. Whether you're making hot or cold soup, look for fabulous, seasonal ingredients and put them to good use.

Hints & Tips

✳ True, nothing beats the homemade stuff, but stocks are available in all shapes and sizes, including stock cubes, powders, concentrates, tins, commercial ready-made or fresh ready-made. If I don't have any fresh stock I usually use an organic stock cube.

✳ When making a puréed-style soup, I usually use a stick blender. These are great as you can purée the soup in the saucepan you made it in (think of the washing-up benefits). You can easily vary the smoothness of the soup to suit your taste. For a really velvety-smooth texture, push the soup through a sieve.

✳ Be careful when seasoning soup, especially if using commercial stocks, which can be salty. It is best not to season until just before serving.

✳ Most soups will freeze well. Let the soup come to room temperature and then freeze it in small containers that hold just one or two servings. Defrost the soup in the fridge before reheating. It is a good idea to add a handful of chopped fresh herbs just before serving to perk up the flavour.

✳ For best results, serve chilled soups really cold – make them well ahead of time and chill in the fridge for at least 6 hours.

✳ Chilled soups need to have lots of flavour and seasoning, as the cold slightly dulls the taste buds.

✳ Chilled soups such as gazpacho travel really well – pour into a wide-mouthed thermos and add to your picnic hamper.

A few garnishes

✳ Chopped fresh herbs make a good garnish, as does a dollop of double cream, crème fraîche or sour cream added just before serving. Asian supermarkets sell tubs of crispy fried shallots which make a good garnish for Asian soups such as laksa.

✳ Croutons are a classic garnish and add a nice crunch (they're especially good for puréed vegetable soups). To make croutons, remove the crusts from 4 thick slices of white bread, then cut the bread into 1 cm cubes. Heat 2 tablespoons olive oil in a frying pan until hot (you can also add a whole peeled garlic clove to the oil to flavour it). Add the bread cubes and fry until golden, stirring and turning them frequently. Drain on kitchen paper (discard the garlic, if using).

Gazpacho

On a hot summer day, few dishes taste as refreshing as this simple, no-cook, chilled soup.

Preparation time: 20 minutes,
    plus refrigeration time
Cooking time: nil
Serves 4

1 kg ripe tomatoes, peeled and chopped (see
    note below)
1 small cucumber, roughly chopped
1 red capsicum (pepper), seeded and chopped
2 cloves garlic, chopped
½ red onion, chopped
2 thick slices good Italian white bread
3 tablespoons sherry vinegar or
    red wine vinegar
salt and freshly ground black pepper
extra virgin olive oil, for drizzling
diced avocado or capsicum (pepper),
    to garnish (optional)

1 Place the tomato, cucumber, capsicum, garlic and onion in a large mixing bowl. Remove the crusts from the bread, then chop the bread and add it to the bowl. Stir in 375 ml cold water.

2 Transfer the mixture to a food processor or blender and pulse until the mixture is roughly combined and still slightly chunky (you may need to do this in batches). Add a little extra water if the soup needs thinning.

3 Chill for at least 6 hours, or preferably overnight, to allow the flavours to develop.

4 Just before serving, stir in the vinegar and season to taste with salt and pepper. Serve with a good drizzle of extra virgin olive oil, and bowls of diced avocado or capsicum, to garnish, if desired.

Really Useful Stuff

Decent tomatoes are essential for a good gazpacho – if possible, beg, borrow or steal home-grown ones. To peel them, use a sharp knife to cut a cross in the base of each tomato. Place in a heatproof bowl and cover with boiling water. Leave for 45 seconds, then transfer to cold water and peel the skin away, beginning at the cross.

Don't overblend the soup – it is much better with a little texture. And serve it very chilled; add an ice cube to each serving, if necessary.

Chilled pea & mint soup

This delicious soup is also good served hot.

Preparation time: 15 minutes, plus cooling and refrigeration time
Cooking time: 20 minutes
Serves 4

1 tablespoon olive oil
1 onion, chopped
1 stick celery, chopped
1 leek, washed and sliced into rings
1 litre chicken or vegetable stock (see pages 229 and 231)
600 g fresh or frozen peas
1 tablespoon chopped mint, plus extra to serve
salt and freshly ground black pepper

1   Heat the oil in a large saucepan over medium heat, add the onion, celery and leek and cook, stirring, for 5–7 minutes until the vegetables are soft, but not coloured.

2   Add the stock, peas and mint and simmer for 15 minutes. Remove from the heat and allow to cool a little.

3   Purée the soup in batches in a blender or with a stick blender until smooth. Season with salt and pepper. Let the soup cool at room temperature, then place in the fridge for at least 6 hours – you want the soup to be nice and cold before serving. Garnish with a little extra mint.

Really Useful Stuff
If serving hot, I sometimes chop a few rashers of bacon and cook them with the onions, then follow the recipe as above.

This soup also freezes well, so make a large batch and freeze individual portions in small containers. Perk it up by serving with lots of fresh herbs.

Prawn & coriander laksa ›

Spiced Asian-style soups work best in a hot climate – after the initial kick of the chilli, the spice works to cool the body down. Packed with prawns and noodles, this laksa is certainly a meal on its own.

Preparation time: 15 minutes
Cooking time: 25 minutes
Serves 4

1 kg uncooked medium prawns
1 litre fish or chicken stock (see pages 229 and 230)
100 g rice vermicelli noodles
1 tablespoon vegetable oil
4 tablespoons laksa paste, or more to taste
1 teaspoon palm sugar or soft brown sugar
375 ml coconut milk
2–3 teaspoons Thai fish sauce
2–3 tablespoons lime juice
160 g bean sprouts
½ small cucumber, seeded and finely sliced
6 spring onions, sliced diagonally
handful of coriander leaves
2 tablespoons mint leaves
lime wedges, to serve

1   Peel and devein the prawns, leaving the tails intact. Place the prawn heads and shells in a large saucepan, add the stock and bring to the boil. Reduce the heat and simmer for 15 minutes. Strain and discard the solids.

2   Meanwhile, place the noodles in a large heatproof bowl and cover with boiling water. Set aside for 5–8 minutes, or until tender. Drain.

3   Heat the oil in a large saucepan, add the laksa paste and sugar and stir over medium heat for 2 minutes. Add the stock and coconut milk. Bring to the boil, then reduce the heat and simmer for 5 minutes.

4   Add the prawns and simmer for about 3 minutes until the prawns are pink and just cooked. Add the fish sauce and lime juice, to taste.

5   Divide the noodles among four deep soup bowls and top with the bean sprouts and cucumber. Ladle the soup over the noodles, and garnish with the spring onion, coriander and mint leaves. Serve with lime wedges.

Really Useful Stuff
Laksa pastes are available in Asian food stores or in larger supermarkets. Add a little more or less than the quantity stated in the recipe, depending on your taste.

You can also turn this into a simple prawn broth by leaving out the coconut milk. Taste as you go: the flavour should be a balance of sweet (coconut milk and sugar), sour (lime juice), salty (fish sauce) and hot (chilli).

Greek-style fish & lemon soup

This soup is thickened with a mixture of egg and lemon, the latter adding a wonderful freshness – perfect for a hot day.

Preparation time: 10 minutes
Cooking time: 20 minutes
Serves 4–6

1.5 litres fish, vegetable or chicken stock (see pages 229–231)
pinch of sumac
handful of small pasta shapes (such as risoni or orzo)
850 g white fish fillets, skin removed
2 eggs
1 egg yolk
juice of 1 large lemon
salt and freshly ground black pepper
2 teaspoons chopped chives or flat-leaf parsley

1 Bring the stock and sumac to the boil in a large saucepan. When boiling, add the pasta and cook for 7–10 minutes or until just tender.

2 Cut the fish fillets into large bite-sized pieces and add to the stock. Bring back to the boil, then remove from the heat.

3 In a bowl whisk together the eggs, yolk and lemon juice until combined. Add a ladle of the hot soup to the egg mixture and whisk well, then pour the mixture back into the saucepan. Place the pan over low heat and stir gently for about 5 minutes until heated through and the soup has thickened slightly (don't let it come to the boil or it will curdle). Season with salt and pepper, then taste and add a little extra lemon juice, if desired. Stir in the chives or parsley, and serve immediately.

Really Useful Stuff
To make a quick fish stock, place fish bones (ask your local fishmonger), an onion, a carrot, 2 sticks of celery and a bay leaf in a large saucepan and cover with water. Bring to the boil, then reduce the heat and simmer gently for about 30 minutes, then strain.

You can also add cooked prawns or mussels as a variation.

Spring minestrone

Minestrone is such an adaptable soup I make it at all times of the year, working with whatever vegetables are in season.

Preparation time: 15 minutes
Cooking time: 30 minutes
Serves 4–6

2 tablespoons olive oil
2 leeks, washed and sliced into rounds
1 onion, chopped
1 carrot, chopped
1 clove garlic, crushed
1.5 litres chicken or vegetable stock (see pages 229 and 231)
350 g frozen peas
120 g small pasta shapes
50 g English spinach leaves, shredded
salt and freshly ground black pepper
2 tablespoons roughly chopped flat-leaf parsley
2 tablespoons pesto (see page 206)
freshly grated parmesan, to serve

1 Heat the oil in a large saucepan over low heat, add the leek, onion, carrot and garlic and cook, stirring, for 5 minutes or until soft.

2 Stir in the stock, peas and pasta and bring to the boil. Skim off any froth, then reduce the heat and simmer gently for 20 minutes.

3 Add the spinach and cook until wilted, then season to taste with salt and pepper. Ladle into bowls, sprinkle with parsley and add a dollop of pesto. Serve with freshly grated parmesan.

Really Useful Stuff
This is a really versatile recipe and works well with other seasonal vegetables – asparagus or diced zucchini (courgettes) make great additions.

Terry Durack's Sichuan hot & sour soup

This is adapted from a recipe in Terry Durack's book *Yum*, now sadly out of print.

Preparation time: 15 minutes, plus soaking time
Cooking time: 10 minutes
Serves 4

1.5 litres chicken stock (see page 229)
200 g pork fillet, cut into thin strips
4 cm piece ginger, cut into matchsticks
1 tablespoon soy sauce
4 dried Chinese mushrooms, soaked in warm water
   for 15 minutes and cut into thin strips
handful of bean sprouts
250 g firm bean curd, cut into 1 cm cubes
¼ teaspoon freshly ground white pepper
1 teaspoon sugar
2 tablespoons white vinegar
1½ tablespoons cornflour, mixed with water to a wet paste
2 eggs, beaten
salt
1 teaspoon sesame oil
1 teaspoon freshly ground Sichuan pepper
1–2 tablespoons chopped coriander

1 Bring the stock to the boil in a large saucepan, add the pork, ginger, soy sauce and mushrooms and simmer for 5 minutes. Add the bean sprouts, bean curd, white pepper, sugar and vinegar and return to the boil. Stir the cornflour mixture well and slowly pour it into the simmering soup, stirring constantly. Return to a gentle simmer for 2–3 minutes, or until the soup has thickened slightly.

2 Place the beaten egg in a jug and pour in a thin steady stream into the simmering soup, stirring as you go so it forms strands. Season to taste with salt (you may need up to 1 teaspoon), add the sesame oil and Sichuan pepper and serve immediately. Garnish with coriander.

Really Useful Stuff
The secret to this peppery soup is the addictive Sichuan pepper, which you can find in Asian food stores.

Spiced roast butternut soup

Roasting the butternut pumpkin gives the soup a good rich colour and a lovely depth of flavour

Preparation time: 20 minutes
Cooking time: 50 minutes
Serves 4

1 small butternut pumpkin, peeled and cut into 2 cm chunks
2 carrots, sliced
4 roma (plum) tomatoes, quartered
1 onion, peeled and cut into 6 wedges
3 cloves garlic, skins removed
2–3 tablespoons olive oil
1 teaspoon ground coriander seeds
1 teaspoon ground cumin
½ teaspoon ground turmeric
½ teaspoon dried chilli flakes
1 litre chicken or vegetable stock (see pages 229 and 231)
1 tablespoon chopped flat-leaf parsley
salt
1 lemon, quartered

1 Preheat the oven to 190°C (Gas Mark 5) and grease a large roasting tray.

2 Place the pumpkin, carrot, tomato, onion and garlic in a large bowl. Add the oil, sprinkle on the spices and mix until well coated. Transfer to the prepared tray and roast in the oven for about 30–35 minutes, or until the vegetables have softened and coloured.

3 Transfer the vegetables to a large saucepan, add enough stock to cover and bring to the boil. Simmer gently for 15 minutes, or until the vegetables are tender.

4 Remove the pan from the heat and allow the soup to cool a little. Purée in batches in a food processor or with a stick blender. Stir in the parsley and season to taste with a little salt. Serve with lemon wedges.

Really Useful Stuff
This recipe can easily be doubled. It also freezes well – freeze in small portions for up to 2 months.

Sardinian lamb soup

This recipe took its inspiration from a soup made by my Sardinian friend Francesca Zedda. She's an instinctive cook who never writes anything down, but she did give this version the thumbs up!

Preparation time: 15 minutes
Cooking time: 1 hour
Serves 4

3 tablespoons olive oil, plus extra for drizzling
2 cloves garlic, crushed
2 sticks celery, chopped
2 spring onions, sliced
1 fennel bulb, cut into 5 mm slices
750 g lamb leg or shoulder, cut into 2 cm pieces
2 litres vegetable stock (see page 231)
1 bay leaf
2 tablespoons chopped mint
1 tablespoon chopped rosemary
salt and freshly ground black pepper
4 thick slices Italian bread
150 g pecorino, coarsely grated

1　Heat half the oil in a large frying pan over medium heat and cook the garlic, celery, spring onion and fennel for about 5 minutes. Transfer to a large saucepan.

2　Heat the remaining oil in the frying pan and cook the lamb for about 5–7 minutes or until browned – you may need to do this in two batches. Add to the vegetables in the saucepan.

3　Add the stock and bay leaf and bring to the boil, then reduce the heat and simmer, partially covered, for about 30 minutes, or until the lamb is tender. Stir in the herbs and season well with salt and pepper.

4　Preheat the oven to 180°C (Gas Mark 4).

5　Toast the bread until golden and drizzle with a little olive oil. Cut the bread slices in half.

6　Place four ovenproof bowls on a sturdy roasting tray. Divide the lamb, fennel slices and half the cheese among the bowls, top with the toasted bread and ladle on the broth. Sprinkle with the remaining cheese and bake in the oven for about 15 minutes or until golden. Serve immediately.

Really Useful Stuff
You can make the soup up to the end of step 3 at least two days ahead of time. To serve, continue from step 4.

Mushroom minestrone

Use a variety of mushrooms to make this hearty soup – look for wild mushrooms, which usually appear at markets in autumn.

Preparation time: 15 minutes
Cooking time: 40 minutes
Serves 4

4 tablespoons olive oil
500 g mixed mushrooms, roughly chopped
2 leeks, washed and sliced into rounds
1 onion, chopped
1 carrot, chopped
1 clove garlic, crushed
2 litres chicken or vegetable stock (see pages 229 and 231)
50 g dried porcini mushrooms, soaked in 250 ml warm water for 15 minutes then chopped
1 bay leaf
120 g small pasta shapes
salt and freshly ground black pepper
2 tablespoons roughly chopped flat-leaf parsley
freshly grated parmesan, to serve

1　Heat half the olive oil in a large frying pan over low heat. Add the fresh mushrooms and sauté for about 7 minutes, or until softened and any liquid has evaporated. Transfer to a large saucepan.

2　Heat the remaining oil in the frying pan, add the leek, onion, carrot, and garlic and cook, stirring, for 5 minutes or until softened. Transfer to the saucepan.

3　Add the stock, porcini (and their soaking liquid) and the bay leaf to the saucepan and bring to the boil. Skim off any scum, then reduce the heat and simmer gently for 10 minutes. Add the pasta and cook for a further 15 minutes. Season to taste with salt and pepper.

4　Ladle the soup into bowls and sprinkle the parsley over the top. Serve with freshly grated parmesan.

Really Useful Stuff
You can cheat a little bit here and buy ready-made stock or use organic powdered vegetable stock (made according to the packet instructions). If you're really pushed, use water.

Cauliflower & stilton soup

The stilton adds quite a discreet cheesy flavour to this soup. Any mild soft cheese can be used in its place, if preferred.

Preparation time: 20 minutes
Cooking time: 50 minutes
Serves 4

30 g butter
1 tablespoon olive oil, plus extra for brushing
1 leek, washed and sliced into thin rounds
1 small onion, finely chopped
2 cloves garlic, crushed
1.25 kg cauliflower, cut into bite-sized florets
1 litre chicken or vegetable stock (see pages 229 and 231)
4 sprigs thyme, leaves only
200 g stilton, crumbled
250 ml milk
salt and freshly ground white pepper
1 baguette
2 tablespoons chopped chives
crème fraîche, to serve

1 Melt the butter with the oil in a large saucepan over medium heat. Add the leek, onion and garlic and cook, stirring, for about 5 minutes. Add the cauliflower and cook, stirring occasionally, for about 10 minutes or until softened.

2 Add the stock and thyme and simmer, partially covered, for about 30 minutes.

3 Preheat the oven to 160°C (Gas Mark 2–3).

4 Add the crumbled stilton to the soup and stir over low heat until it starts to soften. Pour in the milk and cook until heated through – do not let it boil. Remove from the heat and season to taste with salt and white pepper.

5 Slice the baguette into diagonal slices and brush with a little olive oil. Arrange in a single layer on a baking tray and bake until crisp, turning once.

6 Spoon the soup into bowls and top with a sprinkling of chives and a dollop of crème fraiche. Serve with the crisp bread slices.

Really Useful Stuff
You can start making this soup ahead of time, but stop at the end of step 2. Add the stilton and milk and reheat when ready to serve.

Spiced lentil soup ›

Red lentils are a great ingredient for an easy soup as they don't need soaking and cook very quickly.

Preparation time: 15 minutes
Cooking time: 30 minutes
Serves 4

2 tablespoons olive oil
2 leeks, washed and sliced into thin rounds
2 carrots, thinly sliced
2 sticks celery, thinly sliced
2 cloves garlic, crushed
1 bay leaf
175 g red lentils, rinsed
1–2 teaspoons harissa paste
1.25 litres chicken or vegetable stock (see pages 229 and 231)
salt and freshly ground black pepper
juice of ½ lemon
2 tablespoons chopped coriander or flat-leaf parsley
pita or Lebanese bread, to serve

1 Heat the olive oil in a large saucepan over medium heat and cook the leek, carrot, celery, garlic and bay leaf for 5 minutes. Stir in the lentils and harissa paste. Add the stock and bring to the boil, then reduce the heat and simmer, partially covered, for 25 minutes or until the lentils are tender. Taste and add extra harissa, if desired.

2 Season with salt and pepper, and add the lemon juice. Stir in the chopped herbs and serve with pita or Lebanese bread.

Really Useful Stuff
Harissa paste is a spicy Middle Eastern condiment made from chillies – use with discretion!

Stocks

Having so many fresh ingredients available to us makes food preparation very easy, and we can often assemble a great dish with very little cooking. This is fantastic, but it is also good to balance this with some of the lovely soups, braises and slow-cooked dishes that we enjoy in the cooler weather. This is where making your own stock comes in. They are really easy to pull together, fill your kitchen with all sorts of delicious aromas as they tick away, freeze beautifully and vastly improve the flavour of so many recipes.

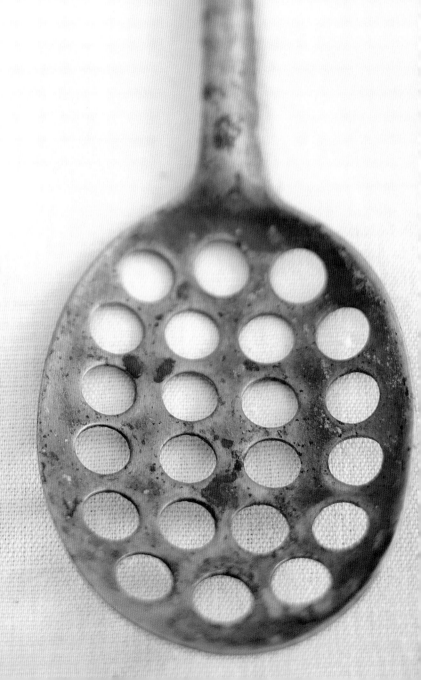

Hints & Tips

✱ Leaving the onion skins on gives the stock good colour, but if you want a paler broth, peel the onions.

✱ I never season stock; I usually just season the food that is made from the stock. This is because the saltiness of stock can vary according to what ingredients are used and how much the stock has been reduced (which intensifies the flavour).

✱ Do not let the stock continue to boil once it has come to its initial boil; it must simmer very gently. Cooking it fast will not speed thing up – rather, it will emulsify the fat and leave you with a cloudy stock.

✱ Froth (or scum) will form as the stock comes to the boil. When this happens, add some cold water – this helps to bring it to the surface, making it easier to skim it off with a spoon. Skim frequently.

✱ Personally, I love the smell of stock cooking, but if you want to stop the smell from filling the house, cover the stockpot with a lid.

✱ All stocks must be skimmed of fat before use. Chilling overnight brings the fat to the surface where it will solidify, making it easy to lift off.

✱ Stocks freeze really well. I usually make it in big batches, then freeze it in smaller containers. Because I use regularly small quantities of beef stock in sauces, I also freeze it in ice-cube trays. This has a dual effect: when you add frozen stock cubes to a pan while making gravy, the sudden cold addition makes any fat solidify, making it easier to scoop out with a spoon. Using these cubes also means you don't waste any valuable stock if only a small amount is required.

✱ The bones for a beef, veal or lamb stock should be roasted to a golden brown rather than charred. Always remove as much fat as possible from the bones – this will save you having to skim it off later.

Chicken stock

This is the most useful of all stocks, a real building block that's great for soups, sauces, risottos, pies and many other dishes. It releases the most wonderful, comforting aroma when you are making it.

Preparation time: 10 minutes
Cooking time: 2 hours
Makes 2 litres

- 1.5 kg chicken bones (wings, necks and giblets are good)
- 2 unpeeled onions, quartered, or 2 large spring onions, trimmed
- 2 carrots, chopped
- 2 sticks celery, roughly chopped
- 1 leek, washed and sliced
- 1 teaspoon black peppercorns
- 1 bay leaf
- 6–8 stalks parsley
- 4 sprigs thyme

1 Place the chicken bones in a large stockpot. Add the remaining ingredients and enough cold water to cover by 5 cm. Bring to the boil, then reduce the heat and simmer gently for 2 hours. Be careful not to let the mixture boil, otherwise the stock will become cloudy. Skim the surface regularly with a spoon to remove any froth.

2 Strain the stock and discard the solids. Allow the liquid to cool, then refrigerate overnight.

3 Skim off any fat that has solidified on the top. Refrigerate for 2–3 days, or freeze for up to 3 months.

Really Useful Stuff

Save the bones from your next roast chicken – boosted by a few extra wings or giblets, they will make a perfectly good stock. If you have just one chicken carcass, freeze it until you have enough to make stock. Chicken carcasses can usually be bought from a good butcher.

Play around with the flavours by using other vegetables in the stock – mushroom trimmings add a lovely depth of flavour.

Make a game stock by replacing some of the chicken bones with the carcass of a pheasant, quail or pigeon.

For a delicious Chinese-style chicken stock, add a 5 cm piece of ginger, chopped, some chopped spring onions and a star anise to the pan. This is a great base for soups, and is also excellent for poaching.

Beef stock

This basic stock makes a real difference to gravy or sauces.

Preparation time: 10 minutes
Cooking time: 6 hours
Makes about 4 litres

1.5 kg beef bones (see note below)
1 veal knuckle or pig's trotter
2 unpeeled onions, quartered
2 carrots, chopped
2 sticks celery, roughly chopped
1 teaspoon black peppercorns
2 cloves
1 bay leaf
1 clove garlic
2 cm strip orange zest
6–8 stalks parsley

1 Preheat the oven to 200°C (Gas Mark 6). Place the bones in a large roasting tin and roast for about 30 minutes, or until starting to colour. Add the onion and carrot and return to the oven for a further 30 minutes, or until golden.

2 Transfer the roasted bones and vegetables to a large stockpot. Add the celery, peppercorns, cloves, bay leaf, garlic, orange zest and parsley stalks. Pour about 1 litre boiling water into the roasting tin and use a wooden spoon to lift any bits stuck to the tin. Pour into the stockpot, then add about 4 litres of water – there needs to be enough to cover all the bones and vegetables.

3 Bring to the boil, then reduce the heat and simmer gently for 4–5 hours. Be careful not to let the mixture boil, otherwise the stock will become cloudy. Skim the surface regularly with a spoon to remove any froth.

4 Strain the stock and discard the solids. Allow the liquid to cool, then refrigerate overnight.

5 Skim off any fat that has solidified on the top. Refrigerate for 2–3 days, or freeze for up to 3 months.

Really Useful Stuff
The best stock is made from a selection of bones. Look for some marrow bones as well as bones with scraps of meat, such as shin.

You can make a quicker (but less rich) stock by not roasting the bones first – simply place all the ingredients in the stockpot and bring to the boil.

To make veal stock, replace the beef bones with veal bones and proceed with the recipe.

To make lamb stock, replace the beef bones with lamb bones and proceed with the recipe.

Fish stock

I eat a lot of fish, so I always have a supply of bones and heads for making this lovely light stock

Preparation time: 10 minutes
Cooking time: 35 minutes
Makes about 2 litres

1 kg fish bones, heads or tails (from non-oily fish)
1 onion, peeled and quartered
200 ml white wine
1 stick celery, roughly chopped
6 peppercorns
6–8 stalks parsley

1 Rinse the fish bones in cold water and roughly chop them.

2 Place all the ingredients in a large saucepan, add 2.5 litres cold water and bring to the boil. There needs to be enough water to cover all the bones, so add more if necessary. Skim the surface with a spoon to remove the froth, then reduce the heat to low and simmer gently for about 30 minutes, skimming occasionally. Be careful not to let the mixture boil, otherwise the stock will become cloudy.

3 Strain the stock and discard the solids. Allow the liquid to cool, then refrigerate overnight. Skim off any fat that has solidified on the top. Refrigerate for up to 5 days or freeze for up to 3 months.

Really Useful Stuff
Avoid strong aromatics such as garlic or woody herbs like rosemary or sage when making fish stock as they will overpower the delicate flavour of the fish.

Make a shellfish stock by replacing some of the fish with prawn, crab or yabby shells and proceeding with the recipe.

Quick vegetable stock

This really useful stock can be made in just half an hour. It gives a delicious base for vegetable soups.

Preparation time: 10 minutes
Cooking time: 30 minutes
Makes about 2 litres

2 tablespoons vegetable oil
2 onions, peeled and roughly chopped
2 carrots, chopped
1 leek, washed and sliced
2 sticks celery, roughly chopped
1 small fennel bulb, chopped (optional)
1 teaspoon black peppercorns
1 bay leaf
6–8 stalks parsley
4 sprigs thyme

1 Place all the ingredients and 2.5 litres water in a large saucepan and bring to the boil. Skim the surface with a spoon to remove the froth that forms when it comes to the boil. Reduce the heat to low, half-cover with a lid and simmer gently for about 30 minutes, skimming occasionally. Be careful not to let the mixture boil, otherwise the stock will become cloudy.

2 Strain the stock and discard the solids. Allow the liquid to cool, then refrigerate overnight. Skim off any fat that has solidified on the top. Refrigerate for up to 5 days or freeze for up to 3 months.

Really Useful Stuff
Vary the flavour by adding vegetable scraps or trimmings from mushrooms, beans, asparagus and so on. Avoid starchy vegetables like potatoes as they add little flavour and tend to make the stock cloudy.

Chinese-style duck stock

This lovely stock, infused with ginger and star anise, is perfect for making Asian-style soups, especially those with noodles or dumplings.

Preparation time: 10 minutes
Cooking time: 2 hours
Makes about 2 litres

1 kg duck bones
1 golden shallot
6 spring onions
2 sticks celery
5 cm piece ginger, chopped
1 star anise
1 teaspoon black or Sichuan peppercorns
2 tablespoons dry sherry

1 Place the ingredients in a large saucepan, add 2.5 litres cold water and bring to the boil. Skim the surface with a spoon to remove the froth, then reduce the heat to low and simmer gently for about 2 hours, skimming regularly. Be careful not to let the mixture boil, otherwise the stock will become cloudy.

2 Strain the stock and discard the solids. Allow the liquid to cool, then refrigerate overnight. Skim off any fat that has solidified on the top. Refrigerate for up to 5 days or freeze for up to 3 months.

Really Useful Stuff
The easiest way to remove the fat is to chill the stock overnight – the fat will rise to the surface and solidify. Duck fat can be saved in the fridge for up to 2 months – it's great for cooking roast potatoes.

Stuffed vegetables

I have never thought that life is too short to stuff a mushroom, as Shirley Conran once famously remarked. In fact, I am a big fan of stuffed vegetables of all sorts, and really enjoy spending the time in the kitchen preparing these comforting dishes, then leaving them to cook slowly in the oven.

Hints & Tips

* Stuffed vegetables work well as a delicious lunch dish, vegetarian starter or as an accompaniment to a main course.

* Fresh breadcrumbs are often used as a stuffing ingredient. They are easily made by pulsing day-old slices of crustless bread in a food processor until fine. They can be made whenever you have some leftover bread, and then frozen until needed.

* Rice also makes a great filling for stuffing vegetables. Make a classic risotto flavoured with lemon, saffron or herbs and use it to stuff capsicums (peppers) or hollowed-out tomatoes, or fill the seed cavity of a halved butternut pumpkin and then bake until the pumpkin is tender.

* You can generally make the stuffing and assemble the vegetables ready for baking up to 12 hours ahead of time. Store in the refrigerator, then cook in a preheated oven when ready to serve.

* Seeds add a crunchy texture to the topping – try sunflower or sesame seeds.

Stuffed onions

These onions are always a huge hit. I often serve them with roast chicken or turkey, rather than stuffing the bird. This recipe serves 10, and I usually freeze any leftover stuffing to have some on hand for another day. You can always halve the quantities below if it's too much.

Preparation time: 25 minutes
Cooking time: 1 hour
Makes 10

10 medium red onions
2 tablespoons olive oil, plus extra for brushing
8 rashers bacon, chopped
100 g pine nuts
450 g fresh breadcrumbs, made from
   day-old bread
2 large eggs
250 g butter, melted
1 teaspoon Dijon mustard
3 tablespoons chopped flat-leaf parsley
10–12 sprigs thyme, leaves only
finely grated zest and juice of 1 lemon
finely grated zest and juice of 1 orange

1 Peel any dry skin from the onions, then place in a large saucepan of boiling water and simmer for 12 minutes to soften. Drain and cool.

2 Cut a 1 cm slice off the top of each onion, reserving these 'lids' for later. Using a teaspoon, remove the inner core of each onion, keeping the three outer layers intact. Finely chop the inner cores of four of the onions.

3 Heat the oil in a large frying pan and cook the bacon, pine nuts and chopped onion for 7–10 minutes, or until softened. Transfer to a bowl and stir in the breadcrumbs.

4 Preheat the oven to 180°C (Gas Mark 4).

5 Place the eggs, butter, mustard, herbs and lemon and orange zest and juice in a blender and purée to a paste. Add the paste to the breadcrumb mixture and mix well.

6 Spoon the filling into the onion cases and replace the lids. Brush each onion with a little extra olive oil and place in a roasting tin – if the onions will not stand up, slice a small sliver off the bottom. Cover the tin with foil and bake for 20 minutes. Remove the foil and bake for a further 10–20 minutes or until the onions are golden and beginning to soften.

Really Useful Stuff
Any leftover stuffing can be rolled into a log, then wrapped in foil and baked for about 20 minutes until cooked through.

For a different stuffing, mix goat's cheese or feta with the chopped onion centres, olives and chopped herbs (such as thyme or parsley). Both red and brown onions are great for stuffing.

Stuffed capsicums

This is the simplest recipe for stuffed vegetables I know. What could be easier than filling half a capsicum with cherry tomatoes and feta then baking it?

Preparation time: 20 minutes
Cooking time: 40 minutes
Makes 4

2 large red capsicums (peppers)
200 g cherry tomatoes, halved
125 g feta, crumbled
2 anchovies, chopped (optional)
1 clove garlic, chopped
10 basil leaves, roughly chopped
2 tablespoons olive oil
2 teaspoons balsamic vinegar
salt and freshly ground black pepper
3–4 tablespoons fresh breadcrumbs,
　　made from day-old bread

1　Preheat the oven to 200°C (Gas Mark 6).

2　Cut the capsicums in half lengthways and remove the seeds and pith.

3　Put the tomatoes, feta, anchovies (if using), garlic, basil, oil and vinegar in a bowl and mix gently to combine. Season with salt and plenty of pepper.

4　Spoon the mixture into the capsicum halves and sprinkle the breadcrumbs on top. Place in a roasting tin and bake for about 35–40 minutes, or until the capsicums have softened and the tops are golden.

Really Useful Stuff
You can slice capsicums in one of two ways: either halved lengthways as above (giving you two shells), or by cutting off the top (like a lid), scooping out the centres and then filling. Replace the lids for serving. The cooking times will vary according to the size of the capsicums, but it usually takes at least 30 minutes for the capsicums to become tender enough.

Stuffed zucchini›

I used to have a zucchini plant in my garden and it thrived in the sunshine. This was one of my favourite ways to prepare my freshly picked crop.

Preparation time: 20 minutes
Cooking time: 30 minutes
Makes 8

4 large zucchini (courgettes)
1 tablespoon olive oil
1 onion, finely chopped
1 clove garlic, crushed
50 g breadcrumbs, made from day-old bread
2 tablespoons roughly chopped flat-leaf parsley
1 tablespoon chopped mint
125 g goat's cheese or feta, crumbled
50 g freshly grated parmesan
1 small egg, beaten
salt and freshly ground black pepper
extra virgin olive oil, for drizzling
1–2 tablespoons pine nuts

1　Preheat the oven to 200°C (Gas Mark 6) and lightly oil a baking dish.

2　Cook the zucchini in a large saucepan of boiling salted water for 4 minutes, then drain. Cut each zucchini in half lengthways and, using a spoon, scoop out some of the flesh to leave a shell. Roughly chop the flesh.

3　Heat the oil in a frying pan, add the chopped zucchini, onion and garlic and cook, stirring, for 7 minutes or until the onion is soft. Remove from the heat and stir in half the breadcrumbs, the parsley, mint, goat's cheese or feta, parmesan and egg. Season well.

4　Spoon the mixture into the zucchini shells and place in the prepared baking dish.

5　Sprinkle the remaining breadcrumbs over the zucchini, drizzle lightly with extra virgin olive oil and bake for 15–20 minutes. Sprinkle the pine nuts over the top about 5 minutes before the end of the cooking time.

Stuffed tomatoes

Tomatoes stuffed with mushrooms and spinach is a delicious combination – perfect as a light vegetarian lunch or side dish.

Preparation time: 20 minutes
Cooking time: 25 minutes
Makes 12

6 ripe tomatoes
1 tablespoon olive oil
20 g butter
1 clove garlic, crushed
6 medium mushrooms, thinly sliced
large handful of baby English spinach leaves
1 tablespoon chopped flat-leaf parsley
salt and freshly ground black pepper
4–5 tablespoons freshly grated parmesan

1 Preheat the oven to 180°C (Gas Mark 4) and lightly grease a large baking tray.

2 Cut the tomatoes in half horizontally and scoop out the flesh, leaving a thick shell. Reserve the flesh, but discard the seeds.

3 Heat the oil and butter in a large frying pan over medium heat and cook the garlic for about 1 minute. Add the mushrooms and reserved tomato flesh and cook until tender and most of the liquid has evaporated. Stir in the spinach and cook just until the leaves have softened. Add the parsley and season well with salt and pepper.

4 Fill each tomato half with the mushroom filling, then sprinkle the parmesan over the top. Place on the prepared baking tray then bake for 20 minutes, or until the tomatoes have coloured and the cheese is golden.

Really Useful Stuff
If you have the time, sprinkle the inside of the tomato shells with salt and turn them upside-down to drain for about an hour – the shells will be firmer and dryer.

Fondue-filled butternut pumpkin

I first had this inspired concoction when English food writer Annie Bell cooked it for a photo shoot to celebrate British Bonfire Night. It works so well as an autumn dish when butternuts are plentiful.

Preparation time: 20 minutes
Cooking time: 40 minutes
Serves 4

2 small butternut pumpkins
olive oil, for brushing
1 clove garlic, crushed
1 tablespoon kirsch or white wine
1 tablespoon cornflour
150 g gruyère, grated
3 tablespoons crème fraîche
salt and freshly ground black pepper
thyme leaves, to serve
freshly grated nutmeg, to serve

1 Preheat the oven to 200°C (Gas Mark 6).

2 Cut the pumpkins in half lengthways and scoop out the seeds and any fibrous bits. Using a sharp knife, score the flesh in a criss-cross fashion at 1 cm intervals. Brush with a little olive oil, then rub the crushed garlic clove over the surface.

3 Mix together the wine and cornflour in a small bowl. Add the gruyère and crème fraîche and stir until combined.

4 Spoon the cheese mixture into the pumpkin cavities, then transfer to a baking tray. It is important that the pumpkins lie level in the pan; bunch up pieces of foil into flattened balls and place under the thinner ends of the pumpkins to help keep them level, if necessary. Season with salt and pepper and sprinkle with the thyme leaves and a little nutmeg.

5 Bake for about 40 minutes or until the filling is golden and the pumpkin flesh is tender when pierced with a sharp knife. Serve immediately.

Really Useful Stuff
For added texture, serve the pumpkins with croutons. Remove the crusts from 2–3 thick slices of day-old bread and cut into 1 cm dice. Heat a layer of vegetable oil in a large frying pan – it needs to be hot enough to brown a cube of bread in about 20 seconds. Add the bread cubes and cook, tossing occasionally, until golden. Drain on kitchen paper.

To avoid spilling the fondue filling, serve the pumpkins with their steadying pieces of foil in place to keep them level when eating.

Index

almonds
  Almond bread 107
  Coffee almond cake 17
Angela Boggiano's scallop & crab pies 144
apples
  Apple & blueberry crumble 35
  Apple & cinnamon pizzas 160
  Apple & pear pie 148
  Apple sauce 186
  Blackberry & apple pie 148
  Chilli jelly 97
  Peach & blackberry pie 148
Arancini 176
artichokes
  Artichoke pizza 156
  Deep-fried artichokes 61
  Four seasons pizza 156
asparagus
  Farfalle with spring vegetables 128
  Halloumi, pea & asparagus salad 201
  Potato & asparagus salad 200
  Roast asparagus 188

bacon
  Chicken & bacon pie 147
  Chicken & bacon skewers 209
  My Caesar salad 196
Baked penne with capsicums 134
Baked soufflé potatoes 191
Balinese chicken skewers 212
bananas
  Banana bread 14
  Banana & caramel crumble 36
  Banana caramel sauce 169
  Banana pancakes 122
  Banana tarte tatin 152
  Sticky banana pudding 169
Basic butter icing 16
Basic chicken curry 42
Basic crêpes 121
Basic risotto 174
Basic waffles 124
basil
  Calzone 160
  Margherita pizza 156
  Pesto 206
  Spaghettini with crab & basil 128
  Tomato & bread salad 201
batters
  Beer batter 58
  Tempura batter 58

Yorkshire puddings 183
beans
  Prawns with cannellini beans 200
Béarnaise sauce 206
Béchamel (white) sauce 203
beef
  for casseroles & braises 22
  for roasting 178
  Beef goulash 26
  Beef satays 212
  Beef stock 230
  Hamburgers 103
  Roast rib of beef 183
  Simple beef casserole 23
Beer batter 58
  Beer-battered fish 62
beetroot
  Roast beetroot 183, 188
  Roast beetroot & feta salad 199
berries
  Berry coulis 202
  Berry jam with liqueur 95
  Mixed berry jam 95
  see also blackberries; blueberries; raspberries;
    strawberries
biscuits
  hints & tips 2
  Cheese straws 65
  Chocolate fudge cookies 30
  Chocolate spiral cookies 4
  Coconut thins 3
  Fruit mince spirals 4
  Orange & pecan thins 3
  Very easy cheddar biscuits 4
blackberries
  Blackberry & apple pie 148
  Blackberry & peach ripple terrine 92
  Fruity bread & butter pudding 168
  Peach & blackberry pie 148
  Pear & blackberry crumble 35
  Quince & blackberry crumble 35
  Steamed blackberry jam pudding 168
blind baking 136
Blinis 124
Blue cheese dressing 195
blueberries
  Apple & blueberry crumble 35
  Blueberry jam 95
  Blueberry meringue pie 152
  Blueberry pancakes 122
  Classic blueberry muffins 111
  Fruity bread & butter pudding 168
Bomb Alaska mince pies 108
Boned leg of lamb with mint & lemon 185
Boodles orange cream 55
braises *see* casseroles & braises
brandy, flaming 169
breads
  hints & tips 6
  Bread rolls 7
  Bread sauce 204
  Bread sticks (grissini) 8
  Brown bread 7
  Chilli Pita Triangles 65
  Croutons 194, 218
  Fig, sultana & rosemary bread 10
  Fruity bread & butter pudding 168
  Fruit loaf 8
  Linseed & sunflower bread 8

  Olive oil toasts 65
  Roast cob loaf 65
  Simple white loaf 7
  Tomato & bread salad 201
  Turkish-style pide 10
  see also toasts
breads, quick
  hints & tips 12
  Banana bread 14
  Cheese & walnut damper 13
  Coconut bread 14
breadcrumbs 70
  Chilli breadcrumbs 83
Broccoli gratin 83
broths *see* soups & broths
Brown bread 7
Brown sugar crumble topping 34
buckwheat flour 124
buffalo mozzarella 159
burgers
  Hamburgers 103
  Vegetarian burgers 103
buttermilk 12, 110
butternut pumpkin
  Fondue-filled butternut pumpkin 236
  Risotto with roast butternut pumpkin 174
  Roast butternut & feta pizza 159
  Roast butternut pumpkin with rocket 192
  Spiced roast butternut soup 223

cabbage
  Spiced cabbage 182
cakes
  hints & tips 16
  Caramel upside-down pear cake 19
  Chocolate madeleines 113
  Claudia Roden's Middle Eastern orange
    & almond cake 19
  Coffee almond cake 17
  Katie Stewart's Victoria sponge 17
  Lemon sandwich 17
  Lemon syrup cake 20
  Marble loaf cake 17
  Nigel Slater's plum cake 20
  Orange cupcakes 113
  Orange madeleines 113
  Peach & raspberry crumble cake 38
  Pecan & coffee cake 18
  Pistachio & white chocolate friands 112
  Rich chocolate cake 18
  Rock cakes 114
  Simple lemon cupcakes 113
  Sunken chocolate soufflé cake 32
  see also icing
calamari
  Fried calamari 59
Calzone 160
capsicums
  Baked penne with capsicums 134
  Capsicum & cumin pilaf 172

capsicums (*continued*)
  Gazpacho 219
  Stuffed capsicums 234
caramel
  Banana & caramel crumble 36
  Banana caramel sauce 169
  Caramel sauce 36
  Caramel upside-down pear cake 19
  Vanilla caramel sauce 86
carrots
  Roast carrots 188
  Spiced carrot purée with feta 67
casseroles & braises
  as pie filling 23
  beef cuts for 22
  hints & tips 22
  Beef goulash 26
  Braised pork chops with cider & fennel 25
  Chinese-style red pork 26
  Cobbler topping 24
  Guinea fowl with peas & pancetta 25
  Lamb shanks – Italian style 24
  Simple beef casserole 23
Cauliflower with chilli breadcrumbs 82
Cauliflower & stilton soup 226
Celeriac & feta gratin 84
Cheat's flaky pastry 140
cheese
  Arancini 176
  Blue cheese dressing 195
  Calzone 160
  Cauliflower & stilton soup 226
  Celeriac & feta gratin 84
  Cheese croquetas 60
  Cheese & chive muffins 114
  Cheese straws 65
  Cheese & walnut damper 13
  Cherry tomato & mozzarella calzone 160
  Double-baked cheese soufflé 216
  Goat's cheese & herb calzone 160
  Gougères 138
  Halloumi, pea & asparagus salad 201
  Italian baked rice with fontina
      & parmesan 172
  Leek gratin with gruyère 82
  Macaroni cheese 133
  Margherita pizza 156
  Mascarpone, zucchini & parmesan
      frittata 118
  Mushroom & goat's cheese crumble 38
  Nigel Slater's chicken & gruyère
      rissoles 102
  Parmesan parsnips 192
  Pizza bianca 156
  Roast beetroot & feta salad 199
  Roast butternut & feta pizza 159
  Simple mozzarella & tomato pizza 159
  Spiced carrot purée with feta 67
  Spinach, feta & mint pie 148
  Spinach & ricotta cannelloni 134
  Sweet potato purée with feta 67
  Vegetarian burgers 103
  Very easy cheddar biscuits 4
chicken
  for roasting 178
  Balinese chicken skewers 212
  Basic chicken curry 42
  Chicken & bacon pie 147
  Chicken & bacon skewers 209

Chicken Caesar salad 196
Chicken saag 43
Chicken stock 229
Chinese-style chicken stock 229
Five-spice roast chicken 180
Herb & nut stuffing 179
Nigel Slater's chicken & gruyère
    rissoles 102
Pappardelle with chicken ragu 133
Pot-roast chicken 16
Red chicken curry 44
Roast chicken 179
Roast poussin with spiced cabbage 182
Spatchcocked poussins 180
Thai-style chicken meatballs in
    lemongrass broth 100
chickpeas
  Spiced hummus 66
Chilled pea & mint soup 220
chilli
  handling chillies 40
  Chilli breadcrumbs 83
  Chilli dipping sauce 68
  Chilli jelly 97
  Chilli pita triangles 65
  Chilli tomato sauce 205
  Citrus, ginger & chilli dressing 195
  Green chilli fish kebabs 210
Chinese-style chicken stock 229
Chinese-style duck stock 231
Chinese-style red pork 26
Chinese-style roast spare ribs 186
Chips 62
chocolate
  hints & tips 28
  how to melt 28
  types of chocolate 28
  Chocolate & cherry strudel 31
  Chocolate chip muffins 112
  Chocolate crumble topping 34
  Chocolate custard 48
  Chocolate fingers 105
  Chocolate fudge cookies 30
  Chocolate fudge sauce 86
  Chocolate & hazelnut semifreddo 91
  Chocolate madeleines 113
  Chocolate meringues 105
  Chocolate sauce 215
  Chocolate spiral cookies 4
  Chocolate truffles 29
  Ganache 28
  Hot chocolate mousse 30
  Hot chocolate sauce 28, 32
  Marbled chocolate pudding with
      hot chocolate sauce 32
  No-cook chocolate & hazelnut torte 31
  Orange & chocolate iced pops 91
  Pear & chocolate crumbles 36
  Pistachio & white chocolate friands 112
  Rich chocolate cake 18
  Rich chocolate truffle ice-cream 92
  Simple chocolate ice-cream 88
  Simple chocolate soufflés 215
  Sunken chocolate soufflé cake 32
Choux pastry 138
Citrus, ginger & chilli dressing 195
Classic American-style pancakes 122
Classic blueberry muffins 111
Classic Christmas pudding 169

Classic custard 47
Classic herb omelette 117
Classic roast pork with crackling 186
Classic trifle 48
Classic vinaigrette 195
Claudia Roden's Middle Eastern orange
    & almond cake 19
Cobbler topping 24
cocoa powder 28
coconut
  Coconut crumble topping 34
  Coconut thins 3
  Coconut bread 14
  Macadamia & coconut tart 151
coffee
  Coffee almond cake 17
  Coffee fudge frosting 18
  Coffee & hazelnut kisses 108
  Pecan & coffee cake 18
courgettes *see* zucchini
couscous
  Fish baked with couscous 71
  Herby couscous salad 199
couverture chocolate 28
crab
  Angela Boggiano's scallop & crab pies 144
  Crab cakes 77
  Spaghettini with crab & basil 128
cream, whipping 46
cream-based desserts
  Boodles orange cream 55
  Crème brûlée 52
  Eton mess 56
  Ginger syllabub 52
  Lemon syllabub 52
  Mango fool 56
  Panna cotta 55
  Passionfruit fool 56
  Passionfruit syllabub 52
  Strawberry fool 56
Crème brûlée 52
crêpes
  hints & tips 120
  Basic crêpes 121
  Crêpes with ham & pesto 122
  Savoury crêpes 121
  Sweet crêpes 121
Croutons 194, 218
crumbles
  hints & tips 34
  Apple & blueberry crumble 35
  Banana & caramel crumble 36
  Mushroom & goat's cheese crumble 38
  Peach & raspberry crumble cake 38
  Pear & blackberry crumble 35
  Pear & chocolate crumbles 36
  Plum crumble 37
  Quince & blackberry crumble 35
  Roast pears with muesli topping 37
crumble toppings 34, 110
  Basic 35
  Brown sugar 34
  Chocolate 34
  Coconut 34
  Gluten-free 34
  Nutty 34
  Oatmeal 34
  Savoury 34
  Spiced 34

cucumber
    Gazpacho 219
    Tzatziki 66
cupcakes
    Orange cupcakes 113
    Simple lemon cupcakes 113
curries
    hints & tips 40
    Basic chicken curry 42
    Chicken saag 43
    Goan prawn curry 42
    Indian-style curry powder 43
    Lamb curry 42
    Red chicken curry 44
    Red duck curry 44
    Salmon curry 42
    Simple sweet potato & pea curry 44
    Thai red curry paste 41
custard
    baking 46
    hints & tips 46
    pouring 48
    Chocolate custard 48
    Classic custard 47
    Classic trifle 48
    Crème Anglaise 48
    Custard tarts 51
    Liqueur custard 48
    Orange custard 48
    Orange & cardamom custards 51

D

dark chocolate 28
deep-frying
    batters 58
    hints & tips 58
    Beer-battered fish 62
    Cheese croquetas 60
    Chips 62
    Deep-fried artichokes 61
    Fried calamari 59
    Prawn toasts 60
    Stuffed zucchini flowers 61
dips
    Chilli dipping sauce 68
    Quail eggs with dipping spice 67
    Spiced carrot purée with feta 67
    Spiced hummus 66
    Spiced prawn dip 68
    Sweet potato purée with feta 67
    Tzatziki 66
    Za'atar 67
Double-baked cheese soufflé 216
dressings
    hints & tips 194
    Blue cheese dressing 195
    Citrus, ginger & chilli dressing 195
    Classic vinaigrette 195
    Lemon & honey dressing 195
    Mayonnaise 205
    Salad cream 195

    Tomato dressing 195
dried fruit
    Classic Christmas pudding 169
    Fig, sultana & rosemary bread 10
    Fruit loaf 8
drinking chocolate 28
duck
    Chinese-style duck stock 231
    Ducks with marmalade 182
    Five-spice duck kebabs 210
    Red duck curry 44
duck fat 182, 231

E

Easy homemade tomato sauce for pizza 156
Easy no-chop tomato sauce 205
eggs
    separating 104
    testing freshness 116
    Greek-style fish & lemon soup 222
    Quail eggs with dipping spice 67
    see also frittatas; omelettes
Eton mess 56

F

Farfalle with spring vegetables 128
fennel
    Braised pork chops with cider &
       fennel 25
Fig, sultana & rosemary bread 10
Fig & honey pizzas 160
fish
    hints & tips 70, 73
    Beer-battered fish 62
    Fish baked with couscous 71
    Fish stock 222, 230
    Greek-style fish & lemon soup 222
    Green chilli fish kebabs 210
    Italian-style stuffed sardines 72
    Lyn Hall's fish baked with potatoes, olives,
       tomato & Mediterranean herbs 73
    Malaysian-style baked snapper 72
    Monkfish wrapped in prosciutto 74
    Oven-roasted salmon with lemon butter
       sauce 74
    Salmon curry 42
    Salt-baked fish 73
    Smoked fish gratin 83
fish cakes
    hints & tips 70
    Crab cakes 77
    Prawn & chive cakes 78
    Salmon fish cakes 77

    Thai fish cakes 78
Five-spice duck kebabs 210
Five-spice roast chicken 180
Fluffy hollandaise sauce 206
Fondue-filled butternut pumpkin 236
fools
    Mango fool 56
    Passionfruit fool 56
    Strawberry fool 56
Four seasons pizza 156
Fresh strawberry icing 113
friands
    Pistachio & white chocolate
       friands 112
Fried calamari 59
Fried rice 173
frittatas 118
    Mascarpone, zucchini & parmesan
       frittata 118
frozen yoghurt
    Raspberry ripple frozen yoghurt 87
    Strawberry frozen yoghurt 87
Fruit loaf 8
fruit mince
    Bomb Alaska mince pies 108
    Fruit mince spirals 4
Fruity bread & butter pudding 168

G

Ganache 28
Garlic pizza 156
Gazpacho 219
ginger
    Citrus, ginger & chilli dressing 195
    Ginger syllabub 52
Gluten-free crumble topping 34
Goan prawn curry 42
Goat's cheese & herb calzone 160
Golden syrup pudding 167
Gougères 138
goulash
    Beef goulash 26
gratins
    hints & tips 80
    Broccoli gratin 83
    Cauliflower with chilli breadcrumbs 82
    Celeriac & feta gratin 84
    Leek gratin with gruyère 82
    Potato gratin 81
    Smoked fish gratin 83
    Zucchini & tomato gratin 84
gravy
    for roast chicken 179
    for roast pork 186
    Onion gravy 204
    Red wine gravy 204
Greek-style fish & lemon soup 222
Green chilli fish kebabs 210
Green pizza 159
Gremolata 22, 164
Grilled pineapple skewers 213

Grissini (bread sticks) 8
Guinea fowl with peas & pancetta 25

Halloumi, pea & asparagus salad 201
ham
  Crêpes with ham & pesto 122
  Four seasons pizza 156
  Linguine with mascarpone & ham 132
  Prosciutto or parma ham pizza 159
Hamburgers 103
herbs
  Classic herb omelette 117
  Fig, sultana & rosemary bread 10
  Goat's cheese & herb calzone 160
  Herb & nut stuffing 179
  Herby couscous salad 199
  Lemony herb stuffing 184
  Persian rice with pistachio & dill 173
  Pilaf with herbs 172
  Prawn & chive cakes 78
  Prawn & coriander laksa 220
  Salsa verde 206
  Tuscan-style potatoes with rosemary &
    olives 190
  see also basil; mint; parsley
Hollandaise sauce 206
honey
  Fig & honey pizzas 160
  Lemon & honey dressing 195
Hot chocolate mousse 30
Hot chocolate sauce 28, 32
hummus
  Spiced hummus 66

ice-cream
  hints & tips 86
  Blackberry & peach ripple terrine 92
  Chocolate & hazelnut semifreddo 91
  Orange & chocolate iced pops 91
  Passionfruit parfait 88
  Rich chocolate truffle ice-cream 92
  Simple chocolate ice-cream 88
  Strawberry ice-cream 88
  Vanilla bean ice-cream 88
  see also frozen yoghurt
icing
  Basic butter icing 16
  Coffee fudge frosting 18
  Fresh strawberry icing 113
  Lemon icing 20
Indian-style curry powder 43

Individual meringues 105
Individual pizzettes 159
Italian baked rice with fontina
  & parmesan 172
Italian-style pork fillets 187
Italian-style stuffed sardines 72

jams & preserves
  hints & tips 94
  Berry jam with liqueur 95
  Blueberry jam 95
  Chilli jelly 97
  Lime marmalade 96
  Mixed berry jam 95
  Peach jam 96
  Simple raspberry jam 97
  Steamed blackberry jam pudding 168
  Three-fruit marmalade 96
  Whole strawberry conserve 95

Katie Stewart's Victoria sponge 17
kebabs
  Five-spice duck kebabs 210
  Green chilli fish kebabs 210
  see also skewers

laksa
  Prawn & coriander laksa 220
lamb
  roasting times 178
  Boned leg of lamb with mint & lemon 185
  Lamb curry 42
  Lamb shanks – Italian style 24
  Lamb shank pie 147
  Lamb stock 230
  Leg of lamb in the French style 185
  Pot-roast lamb with gremolata 164
  Roast lamb rack with herb crust 184
  Roast leg of lamb with lemony herb
    stuffing 184

Sardinian lamb soup 225
  Spiced Turkish lamb & mint meatballs 102
Lasagne with mushrooms 131
Leek & saffron pilaf 172
Leek gratin with gruyère 82
Leg of lamb in the French style 185
lemon
  Citrus, ginger & chilli dressing 195
  Greek-style fish & lemon soup 222
  Lemon & honey dressing 195
  Lemon butter sauce 74
  Lemon icing 20
  Lemon sandwich 17
  Lemon syllabub 52
  Lemon syrup cake 20
  Lemony herb stuffing 184
  Pea & lemon risotto 174
  Simple lemon cupcakes 113
Lemongrass broth 100
lentils
  Spiced lentil soup 226
Lime marmalade 96
Linguine with mascarpone & ham 132
Linseed & sunflower bread 8
Liqueur custard 48
Little prawn & pea pasties 144
Lyn Hall's fish baked with potatoes, olives,
  tomato & Mediterranean herbs 73

Macadamia & coconut tart 151
Macaroni cheese 133
madeleines
  Chocolate madeleines 113
  Orange madeleines 113
Malaysian-style baked snapper 72
Mango fool 56
Mango tarte tatin 152
Marble loaf cake 17
Marbled chocolate pudding with hot
  chocolate sauce 32
Marbled meringues 105
Margherita pizza 156
marmalade
  Lime marmalade 96
  Three-fruit marmalade 96
Mascarpone, zucchini & parmesan
  frittata 118
Mayonnaise 205
meatballs
  hints & tips 98
  Nigel Slater's chicken & gruyère
    rissoles 102
  Polpette 99
  Sicilian meatballs 100
  Spiced Turkish lamb & mint meatballs 102
  Thai-style chicken meatballs in lemongrass
    broth 100
meringues
  hints & tips 104
  Almond bread 107

Blueberry meringue pie 152
Bomb Alaska mince pies 108
Chocolate fingers 105
Chocolate meringues 105
Coffee & hazelnut kisses 108
Eton mess 56
Individual meringues 105
Marbled meringues 105
Pavlova 107
milk chocolate 28
mint
Chilled pea & mint soup 220
Quick mint sauce 202
Spiced Turkish lamb & mint meatballs 102
Spinach, feta & mint pie 148
Mixed berry jam 95
Monkfish wrapped in prosciutto 74
Mornay sauce 203
mousse
Hot chocolate mousse 30
Mrs Maietta's tomato lasagne 131
Muesli topping 37
muffins
hints & tips 110
Cheese & chive muffins 114
Chocolate chip muffins 112
Classic blueberry muffins 111
Crumble topping 110
mushrooms
Lasagne with mushrooms 131
Mushroom & goat's cheese crumble 38
Mushroom minestrone 225
Mushroom risotto 174
Pizza bianca 156
Sonia Stevenson's roast mushrooms with
    olive oil & pine nuts 190
My Caesar salad 196
My favourite dressings 195

N

Nigel Slater's chicken & gruyère rissoles 102
Nigel Slater's plum cake 20
No-cook chocolate & hazelnut torte 31
noodles 26, 100
Prawn & coriander laksa 220
see also pasta
nuts
Almond bread 107
Cheese & walnut damper 13
Chocolate & hazelnut semifreddo 91
Claudia Roden's Middle Eastern orange &
    almond cake 19
Coffee almond cake 17
Coffee & hazelnut kisses 108
Herb & nut stuffing 179
Macadamia & coconut tart 151
No-cook chocolate & hazelnut torte 31
Nutty crumble topping 34
Orange & pecan thins 3
Pecan & coffee cake 18
Persian rice with pistachio & dill 173

Pistachio & white chocolate friands 112
Satay sauce 212

O

Oatmeal crumble topping 34
oil
for deep-frying 58
re-using 58
olives
Spinach & olives pizza 159
Tapenade 202
Tuscan-style potatoes with rosemary &
    olives 190
olive oil 194
Olive oil toasts 65
omelettes
fillings 117
hints & tips 116
Classic herb omelette 117
Prawn tortilla 118
Tortilla Española 118
onions
Onion gravy 204
Stuffed onions 233
orange
Boodles orange cream 55
Claudia Roden's Middle Eastern orange &
    almond cake 19
Orange & chocolate iced pops 91
Orange cupcakes 113
Orange custard 48
Orange & cardamom custards 51
Orange hollandaise sauce 206
Orange madeleines 113
Orange & pecan thins 3
Oven-roasted salmon with lemon butter
    sauce 74

P

pancakes
hints & tips 120
Banana pancakes 122
Blinis 124
Blueberry pancakes 122
Classic American-style pancakes 122
Savoury pancakes 122
see also crêpes
Panna cotta 55
Pappardelle with chicken ragu 133
Parmesan parsnips 192
parsley
Gremolata 164
Parsley sauce 203

parsnips
Parmesan parsnips 192
passionfruit
Passionfruit fool 56
Passionfruit parfait 88
Passionfruit soufflé 216
Passionfruit syllabub 52
pasta
hints & tips 126
Baked penne with capsicums 134
Farfalle with spring vegetables 128
Lasagne with mushrooms 131
Linguine with mascarpone & ham 132
Macaroni cheese 133
Mrs Maietta's tomato lasagne 131
Pappardelle with chicken ragu 133
Penne with spicy tomato & sausage
    sauce 132
Spaghetti with garlic, chilli & olive oil 127
Spaghettini with crab & basil 128
Spinach & ricotta cannelloni 134
pasties
Little prawn & pea pasties 144
pastry
hints & tips 136
Cheat's flaky pastry 140
Choux pastry 138
Puff pastry 140
Rough puff pastry 138
The simplest shortcrust pastry 137
Sweet shortcrust pastry 137
pastries *see* pies & pasties; tarts
Pavlova 107
peaches
Blackberry & peach ripple terrine 92
Peach & blackberry pie 148
Peach jam 96
Peach & raspberry crumble cake 38
pears
Apple & pear pie 148
Caramel upside-down pear cake 19
Pear & blackberry crumble 35
Pear & chocolate crumbles 36
Pear tarte tatin 152
Roast pears with muesli topping 37
Stuffed pears wrapped in pastry 151
peas
Chilled pea & mint soup 220
Guinea fowl with peas & pancetta 25
Halloumi, pea & asparagus salad 201
Little prawn & pea pasties 144
Pea & lemon risotto 174
Simple sweet potato & pea curry 44
Pecan & coffee cake 18
pectin 94
Penne with spicy tomato & sausage sauce 132
Pepper sauce 204
peppers *see* capsicums
Perfect steamed rice 171
Persian rice with pistachio & dill 173
Pesto 206
Crêpes with ham & pesto 122
pies
casseroles as a filling 23
hints & tips 142
Angela Boggiano's scallop & crab pies 144
Apple & pear pie 148
Blackberry & apple pie 148
Blueberry meringue pie 152

pies (*continued*)
Bomb Alaska mince pies 108
Chicken & bacon pie 147
Lamb shank pie 147
Peach & blackberry pie 148
Spinach, feta & mint pie 148
Vegetable pot pies 143
pilaf 170
Capsicum & cumin pilaf 172
Leek & saffron pilaf 172
Pilaf with herbs 172
Simple rice pilaf 172
pineapple
Grilled pineapple skewers 213
Pistachio & white chocolate friands 112
pizza
hints & tips 154
Apple & cinnamon pizzas 160
Artichoke pizza 156
Calzone 160
Cherry tomato & mozzarella calzone 160
Easy homemade tomato sauce for pizza 156
Fig & honey pizzas 160
Four seasons pizza 156
Garlic pizza 156
Goat's cheese & herb calzone 160
Green pizza 159
Individual pizzettes 159
Margherita pizza 156
Pizza bianca 156
Pizza dough 155
Potato pizza 159
Prosciutto or parma ham pizza 159
Roast butternut & feta pizza 159
Salad pizza 159
Simple mozzarella & tomato pizza 159
Spicy sausage pizza 156
Spinach & olives pizza 159
Turkish-style pizza base 10
plums
Nigel Slater's plum cake 20
Plum crumble 37
Polpette 99
pork
roasting times 178
Braised pork chops with cider
   & fennel 25
Chinese-style red pork 26
Chinese-style roast spare ribs 186
Classic roast pork with crackling 186
Italian-style pork fillets 187
Pork roasted with milk 187
Sicilian meatballs 100
Slow-roast pork 164
pot-roasts
hints & tips 162
Pot-roast chicken 163
Pot-roast lamb with gremolata 164
Slow-roast pork 164
potatoes
Baked soufflé potatoes 191
Chips 62
Leg of lamb in the French style 185
Potato & asparagus salad 200
Potato gratin 81
Potato pizza 159
Tortilla Española 118
Tuscan-style potatoes with rosemary
   & olives 190

prawns
Goan prawn curry 42
Little prawn & pea pasties 144
Prawns with cannellini beans 200
Prawn & chive cakes 78
Prawn & coriander laksa 220
Prawn fattouche 196
Prawn toasts 60
Prawn tortilla 118
Prawn & zucchini risotto 176
Shellfish stock 230
Skewered prawns 213
Spiced prawn dip 68
prosciutto
Monkfish wrapped in prosciutto 74
Prosciutto or parma ham pizza 159
puddings
hints & tips 166
Classic Christmas pudding 169
Fruity bread & butter pudding 168
Golden syrup pudding 167
Marbled chocolate pudding with
   hot chocolate sauce 32
Steamed blackberry jam pudding 168
Sticky banana pudding 169
Puff pastry 140
pumpkin *see* butternut pumpkin

Q

Quail eggs with dipping spice 67
quick breads *see* breads, quick
Quick mint sauce 202
Quick vegetable stock 231
Quince & blackberry crumble 35

R

raspberries
Berry coulis 202
Peach & raspberry crumble cake 38
Raspberry ripple frozen yoghurt 87
Raspberry sauce 86
Simple raspberry jam 97
Red chicken curry 44
Red duck curry 44
Red wine gravy 204
rice
Basmati rice 170
Fried rice 173
Italian baked rice with fontina
   & parmesan 172
Jasmine rice 170

Perfect steamed rice 171
Persian rice with pistachio & dill 173
see also pilaf; risotto
Rich chocolate cake 18
Rich chocolate truffle ice-cream 92
risotto
hints & tips 170, 171
rice for 170
stuffing for vegetables 23
Arancini 176
Basic risotto 174
Mushroom risotto 174
Pea & lemon risotto 174
Prawn & zucchini risotto 176
Risotto alla Milanese 174
Risotto with roast butternut pumpkin 174
Roast cob loaf 65
roast dinners
hints & tips 178
Boned leg of lamb with mint & lemon 185
Chinese-style roast spare ribs 186
Classic roast pork with crackling 186
Ducks with marmalade 182
Five-spice roast chicken 180
Italian-style pork fillets 187
Leg of lamb in the French style 185
Pork roasted with milk 187
Roast chicken 179
Roast lamb rack with herb crust 184
Roast leg of lamb with lemony herb
   stuffing 184
Roast poussin with spiced cabbage 182
Roast rib of beef 183
Spatchcocked poussins 180
Yorkshire puddings 183
see also gravy
Roast pears with muesli topping 37
roast vegetables
parboiling 188
Baked soufflé potatoes 191
Parmesan parsnips 192
Roast asparagus 188
Roast beetroot 183, 188
Roast beetroot & feta salad 199
Roast butternut & feta pizza 159
Roast butternut pumpkin with rocket 192
Roast carrots 188
Roast spring vegetables 189
Roast zucchini 188
Slow-roast tomatoes 191
Sonia Stevenson's roast mushrooms with
   olive oil & pine nuts 190
Tuscan-style potatoes with rosemary
   & olives 190
Vegetable pot pies 143
Rock cakes 114
Rough puff pastry 138

S

salads
hints & tips 194

Chicken Caesar salad 196
Halloumi, pea & asparagus salad 201
Herby couscous salad 199
My Caesar salad 196
Potato & asparagus salad 200
Prawns with cannellini beans 200
Prawn fattouche 196
Roast beetroot & feta salad 199
Tomato & bread salad 201
see also dressings
Salad cream 195
Salad pizza 159
salmon
Oven-roasted salmon with lemon butter
    sauce 74
Salmon curry 42
Salmon fish cakes 77
Salsa verde 206
Salt-baked fish 73
Sardinian lamb soup 225
Satay sauce 212
sauces (savoury)
hints & tips 202
keeping warm 202
Béarnaise sauce 206
Béchamel or white sauce 203
Bread sauce 204
Chicken ragu 133
Chilli dipping sauce 68
Chilli tomato sauce 205
Dipping sauce 78
Easy homemade tomato sauce for pizza 156
Easy no-chop tomato sauce 205
Fluffy hollandaise sauce 206
Hollandaise sauce 206
Lemon butter sauce 74
Mornay sauce 203
Orange hollandaise sauce 206
Parsley sauce 203
Pepper sauce 204
Quick mint sauce 202
Salsa verde 206
Satay sauce 212
Spicy tomato & sausage sauce 132
Tapenade 202
Tartare sauce 205
Tzatziki 66
see also gravy
sauces (sweet)
hints & tips 202
keeping warm 202
Apple sauce 186
Banana caramel sauce 169
Berry coulis 202
Caramel sauce 36
Chocolate fudge sauce 86
Chocolate sauce 215
Hot chocolate sauce 32
Raspberry sauce 86
Vanilla caramel sauce 86
sausages
Calzone 160
Penne with spicy tomato & sausage
    sauce 132
Spicy sausage pizza 156
Savoury crêpes 121
Savoury crumble topping 34
Savoury pancakes 122
seafood *see* calamari; crab; prawns

setting point (jams & preserves) 94
Shellfish stock 230
Sichuan peppercorns 180
Sicilian meatballs 100
Simple beef casserole 23
Simple chocolate ice-cream 88
Simple chocolate soufflés 215
Simple lemon cupcakes 113
Simple mozzarella & tomato pizza 159
Simple raspberry jam 97
Simple rice pilaf 172
Simple sweet potato & pea curry 44
Simple white loaf 7
The simplest shortcrust pastry 137
skewers
hints & tips 208
Balinese chicken skewers 212
Beef satays 212
Chicken & bacon skewers 209
Five-spice duck kebabs 210
Green chilli fish kebabs 210
Grilled pineapple skewers 213
Skewered prawns 213
Slow-roast pork 164
Slow-roast tomatoes 191
Smoked fish gratin 83
Sonia Stevenson's roast mushrooms with olive
    oil & pine nuts 190
soufflés
Double-baked cheese soufflé 216
hints & tips 214
Passionfruit soufflé 216
Simple chocolate soufflés 215
soups & broths
garnishes 218
hints & tips 218
Cauliflower & stilton soup 226
Chilled pea & mint soup 220
Gazpacho 219
Greek-style fish & lemon soup 222
Lemongrass broth 100
Mushroom minestrone 225
Prawn broth 220
Prawn & coriander laksa 220
Sardinian lamb soup 225
Spiced lentil soup 226
Spiced roast butternut soup 223
Spring minestrone 222
Terry Durack's Sichuan hot & sour
    soup 223
see also stock
Spaghetti with garlic, chilli & olive
    oil 127
Spaghettini with crab & basil 128
Spatchcocked poussins 180
Spiced cabbage 182
Spiced carrot purée with feta 67
Spiced crumble topping 34
Spiced hummus 66
Spiced lentil soup 226
Spiced prawn dip 68
Spiced roast butternut soup 223
Spiced Turkish lamb & mint meatballs 102
Spinach, feta & mint pie 148
Spinach & olives pizza 159
Spinach & ricotta cannelloni 134
Spring minestrone 222
Steamed blackberry jam pudding 168
Sticky banana pudding 169

stock
hints & tips 228
Beef stock 230
Chicken stock 229
Chinese-style chicken stock 229
Chinese-style duck stock 231
Fish stock 222, 230
Lamb stock 230
Quick vegetable stock 231
Shellfish stock 230
Veal stock 230
strawberries
Berry coulis 202
Eton mess 56
Fresh strawberry icing 113
Strawberry fool 56
Strawberry frozen yoghurt 87
Strawberry ice-cream 88
Whole strawberry conserve 95
strudel
Chocolate & cherry strudel 31
Stuffed pears wrapped in pastry 151
stuffed vegetables
hints & tips 232
Fondue-filled butternut pumpkin 236
Stuffed capsicums 234
Stuffed onions 233
Stuffed tomatoes 236
Stuffed zucchini 234
Stuffed zucchini flowers 61
sugar
for jams & preserves 94
Brown sugar crumble topping 34
Sunken chocolate soufflé cake 32
Sweet crêpes 121
sweet potato
Simple sweet potato & pea curry 44
Sweet potato purée with feta 67
Sweet shortcrust pastry 137
syllabubs
Ginger syllabub 52
Lemon syllabub 52
Passionfruit syllabub 52

T

Tapenade 202
Tartare sauce 205
tarts
Banana tarte tatin 152
Custard tarts 51
Macadamia & coconut tart 151
Mango tarte tatin 152
Pear tarte tatin 152
Stuffed pears wrapped in pastry 151
Tempura batter 58
Terry Durack's Sichuan hot & sour soup 223
Thai fish cakes 78
Thai red curry paste 41
Thai-style chicken meatballs in lemongrass
    broth 100
Three-fruit marmalade 96

toasts
    Olive oil toasts 65
    Prawn toasts 60
tomatoes
    skinning 43
    Calzone 160
    Cherry tomato & mozzarella calzone 160
    Chilli tomato sauce 205
    Easy homemade tomato sauce for pizza 156
    Easy no-chop tomato sauce 205
    Four seasons pizza 156
    Gazpacho 219
    Individual pizzettes 159
    Margherita pizza 156
    Mrs Maietta's tomato lasagne 131
    Penne with spicy tomato & sausage sauce 132
    Simple mozzarella & tomato pizza 159
    Slow-roast tomatoes 191
    Stuffed tomatoes 236
    Tomato & bread salad 201
    Tomato dressing 195
    Zucchini & tomato gratin 84
tortilla
    Prawn tortilla 118
    Tortilla Española 118
trifle
    Classic trifle 48
Turkish-style pide 10
Turkish-style pizza base 10
Tuscan-style potatoes with rosemary & olives 190
Tzatziki 66

Vanilla bean ice-cream 88
Vanilla caramel sauce 86
veal
    Polpette 99
    Veal stock 230
Vegetarian burgers 103
Very easy cheddar biscuits 4
vinegars 194, 195

waffles
    Basic waffles 124
white chocolate 28
White sauce (béchamel) 203
Whole strawberry conserve 95

yeast 6
yoghurt
    Raspberry ripple frozen yoghurt 87
    Strawberry frozen yoghurt 87
    Tzatziki 66
Yorkshire puddings 183

Za'atar 67
zucchini
    Mascarpone, zucchini & parmesan frittata 118
    Prawn & zucchini risotto 176
    Roast zucchini 188
    Stuffed zucchini 234
    Stuffed zucchini flowers 61
    Zucchini & tomato gratin 84

Conversions

All cup and spoon measurements are level.

I use 60 g eggs.

All recipes were tested using a regular convection oven. If you are using a fan-forced oven, set your oven temperature approximately 20°C lower than is recommended in the recipe.

Cup conversions

1 cup uncooked arborio rice = 220 g (7 oz)
1 cup uncooked basmati/long-grain rice = 200 g (6½ oz)
1 cup sugar = 250 g (8 oz)
1 cup raw sugar = 220 g (7 oz)
1 cup brown sugar = 185 g (6 oz)
1 cup caster (superfine) sugar = 250 g (8 oz)
1 cup icing (confectioner's) sugar = 150 g (5 oz)
1 cup fresh breadcrumbs = 80 g (2½ oz)
1 cup plain (all-purpose) or self-raising (self-rising) flour = 140 g (4½ oz)
1 cup cornflour (cornstarch) = 125 g (4 oz)
1 cup couscous = 185 g (6 oz)
1 cup rolled (porridge) oats = 100 g (3½ oz)
1 cup yoghurt = 250 g (8 oz)
1 cup grated cheddar = 125 g (4 oz)
1 cup grated mozzarella = 150 g (5 oz)
1 cup grated parmesan = 100 g (3½ oz)
1 cup frozen peas = 150 g (5 oz)

Liquid measurements

metric	imperial	tablespoons/cups
30 ml	1 fl oz	2 tablespoons
60 ml	2 fl oz	¼ cup
80 ml	2¾ fl oz	⅓ cup
125 ml	4 fl oz	½ cup
185 ml	6 fl oz	¾ cup
250 ml	8 fl oz	1 cup

Dry measurements

metric	imperial
15 g	½ oz
30 g	1 oz
45 g	1½ oz
55 g	2 oz
125 g	4 oz
150 g	5 oz
185 g	6 oz
200 g	6½ oz
225 g	7 oz
250 g	8 oz
500 g	1 lb
1 kg	2 lb

Oven temperatures

	Celsius	Fahrenheit	Gas Mark
very slow	120°C	250°F	1
slow	150°C	300°F	2
warm	160°C	315°F	2–3
moderate	180°C	350°F	4
moderately hot	190°C	375°F	5
moderately hot	200°C	400°F	6
hot	220°C	425°F	7
very hot	230°C	450°F	8
very hot	240°C	475°F	9

Acknowledgements

Without my friends and family, this book would not have been possible. Thanks especially to Francis, for happily taste-testing most of my culinary creations (both good and bad).

Many 'foodie' friends and writers have rallied around, encouraged me, and shared their wisdom and recipes; a special thanks to Katie Stewart, Nigel Slater, Jill Dupleix, Terry Durack, Anna del Conte, Angela Boggiano, Michele Cranston and Lyn Hall.

A cookbook is rarely the work of a single person – I want to thank all the friendly Penguins (past and present), both in Australia and the UK, for their help and encouragement. In Australia, I would especially like to thank my wonderful editors Alison Cowan and Rachel Carter. You guys have turned my scribbles and rough old notes into something that makes sense and I am incredibly grateful to you both. What a treat and a lovely surprise it was to find myself working with Rachel again. Also many thanks to Daniel New and his design team. In the UK, thanks to Camilla Stoddart and Lindsey Evans for their friendship, support and guidance.

Thank you to the bright shining star who is Julie Gibbs; without your kindness, encouragement, support and numerous cups of tea at the Wolseley, this would never have been possible.

Also thanks to Rosie Scott and Jules Berner for their help with the props and the cooking on the shoot, and to David Loftus for his friendship and photos.

Bibliography

Bell, Annie, *In My Kitchen*, Conran Octopus, London, 2007.
Boggiano, Angela, *Pie*, Cassell, London, 2006.
del Conte, Anna, *The Gastronomy of Italy*, Pavilion, London, 2004.
Dupleix, Jill, *Very Simple Food*, Hardie Grant, Melbourne, 2003.
Durack, Terry, *Yum*, William Heinemann, Melbourne, 1996.
Hall, Lyn, *Lyn Hall's Cookery Course*, Conran Octopus, London, 2004.
Moran, Sean, *Let It Simmer*, Lantern Penguin, Melbourne, 2006.
Roden, Claudia, *A New Book of Middle Eastern Food*, Penguin, London, 1986.
Slater, Nigel, *Kitchen Diaries*, Fourth Estate, London, 2005.
Smith, Delia, *Delia Smith's Winter Collection*, BBC Books, London, 2004.
Stevenson, Sonia, *Roasts*, Ryland Peters & Small, London, 2007.
Stewart, Katie, *The Times Cookery Book*, Pan, London, 1979.
Werle, Loukie, *Splendido*, Hardie Grant, Melbourne, 2001.

MICHAEL JOSEPH

Published by the Penguin Group
Penguin Group (Australia)
250 Camberwell Road, Camberwell, Victoria 3124, Australia
(a division of Pearson Australia Group Pty Ltd)
Penguin Group (USA) Inc.
375 Hudson Street, New York, New York 10014, USA
Penguin Group (Canada)
90 Eglinton Avenue East, Suite 700, Toronto, Canada ON M4P 2Y3
(a division of Pearson Penguin Canada Inc.)
Penguin Books Ltd
80 Strand, London WC2R 0RL England
Penguin Ireland
25 St Stephen's Green, Dublin 2, Ireland
(a division of Penguin Books Ltd)
Penguin Books India Pvt Ltd
11 Community Centre, Panchsheel Park, New Delhi – 110 017, India
Penguin Group (NZ)
67 Apollo Drive, Rosedale, North Shore 0632, New Zealand
(a division of Pearson New Zealand Ltd)
Penguin Books (South Africa) (Pty) Ltd
24 Sturdee Avenue, Rosebank, Johannesburg 2196, South Africa

Penguin Books Ltd, Registered Offices: 80 Strand, London, WC2R 0RL, England

First published by Penguin Group (Australia), 2009
First published in the UK by Michael Joseph, 2009

10 9 8 7 6 5 4 3 2 1

Text copyright © David Herbert 2009
Photographs copyright © David Loftus 2009

Design by Daniel New © Penguin Group (Australia)
Cover photographs by David Loftus
Typeset in Goudy Old Style and Meta by Post Pre-press Group, Brisbane, Queensland
Colour reproduction by Splitting Image, Clayton, Victoria
Printed and bound in China by South China Printing Company Limited

A CIP catalogue record for this book is available from the British Library

ISBN: 978–0–718–15311–3